Commissioners Massachusetts. Bank

Nineteenth Annual Report of the Board of Commissioners of

Savings Banks, 1894

Part 2

Commissioners Massachusetts. Bank

Nineteenth Annual Report of the Board of Commissioners of Savings Banks, 1894
Part 2

ISBN/EAN: 9783337120894

Printed in Europe, USA, Canada, Australia, Japan

Cover: Foto ©Suzi / pixelio.de

More available books at **www.hansebooks.com**

NINETEENTH ANNUAL REPORT

OF THE

BOARD OF COMMISSIONERS

SA

CO-OPERATIVE BAN
MORTGAGE LOAN

BOSTON:
WRIGHT & POTTER PRINTING CO., STA
18 POST OFFICE SQUARE.
1895.

Commonwealth of Massachusetts.

OFFICE OF THE BOARD OF COMMISSIONERS OF SAVINGS BANKS,
STATE HOUSE, BOSTON, Feb. 1, 1895.

*To the Honorable the Senate and House of Representatives in General Court
assembled.*

The Board of Commissioners of Savings Banks, in accordance with the provisions of statute, presents Part II. of its nineteenth annual report, showing the condition of the following institutions at close of business Oct. 31, 1894, viz. : —

117 co-operative banks with assets of	$18,584,671 13
2 collateral loan companies with assets of . . .	1,932,349 34
2 mortgage loan companies with assets of . , .	408,421 76
	$20,925,442 23

CO-OPERATIVE BANKS.

Permission has been given during the year to organize the following banks, viz. : —

The Lafayette Co-operative Bank, located at Fall River; commenced business July 12, 1894.

The Winchester Co-operative Bank, located at Winchester; commenced business Nov. 13, 1893.

The Roger-Conant Co-operative Bank, located at Salem. This bank did not commence business until November, consequently no return is included in this report.

The Spencer Co-operative Bank at Spencer has discontinued business and distributed its assets without loss to the shareholders; its books and papers have been deposited with this Board, and it is recommended that the corporation be now dissolved.

During the year fourteen banks have each had two series and nine banks have each had one series of shares mature; the number of months between the dates of issue and the date of maturity in the several banks was as follows : —.

1 bank, {	1 series, ...	143 months.	
	1 "	142 "	
1 "	1 " . . .	132 "	
1 "	1 "	143 "	
1 "	2 " . . .	139 "	each series.
1 "	2 "	136 "	each series.
1 "	2 "	140 "	each series.
1 "	2 " . .	138 "	each series.
1 "	1 "	134 "	
1 "	1 "	137 "	
1 " {	1 "	134 "	
	1 "	133 "	
1 " {	1 "	139 "	
	1 " . . . ;	138 "	
1 " {	1 "	140 "	
	1 " . .	142 "	
1 "	2 . " . .	138 "	each series.
1 "	2 "	138 "	each series.
1 "	1 "	138 "	
1 "	2 "	138 "	each series.
1 "	1 "	141 "	
1 "	2 " . . .	139 "	each series.
1 "	1 "	134 "	
1 "	1 " . . .	144 "	
1 "	2 " . .	140 "	each series.
1 "	1 " . . .	133 "	
1 "	2 "	134 "	each series.

The average time of maturity, as shown by the table, is $138\frac{6}{37}$ months.

The total number of shares matured was 1,869, of the aggregate value of $378,282.66, equivalent to $202.40 per share; of the aggregate value, the amount paid in as dues was $257,487; the balance of $120,795.66 was the amount of profits credited to the shares, an average of $64.63 to each.

Of the above-mentioned 1,869 shares, 293 were pledged for real estate loans and 306 for share loans, 1,270 being free or unpledged.

The shares which matured were held by 457 members, an average of $4\frac{9}{100}$ to each; of these, 123 were borrowers.

The number of loans cancelled by the maturity of shares was 62 real estate loans, amounting to $55,875; and 84 share loans, amounting to $38,525.

The following table gives particulars of all shares matured during the year : —

Statement of Shares Matured since Last Report.

NAME OF BANK.	Number of Series.	Date of Issue.	Date of Maturity.	Amount paid in per Share.	Maturing Value per Share.	Number of Shares Matured: Pledged for R. E. Loans	Pledged for Share Loans	Unpledged.	Total.	Number of Holders.	Number of Borrowers.	Real Estate Loans Cancelled by Maturity of Shares: Number.	Amount.	Share Loans Cancelled by Maturity of Shares: Number.	Amount.	Total Value of Shares Matured.
Cambridge Co-operative Bank,	17	Sept., 1881,	Nov., 1893,	$143	$200 58	-	5	-	5	1	1	-	-	2	$100 00	$1,002 90
" "	18	March, 1882,	Dec., 1893,	142	202 19	-	5	-	5	1	1	-	-	2	950 00	1,010 95
Campello "	7	Oct., 1883,	Oct., 1894,	132	206 58	38	-	-	38	9	9	9	$7,600	-	-	7,850 04
Equitable "	9	April, 1882,	March, 1894,	143	203 76	7	10	18	28	5	1	-	-	1	725 00	5,705 28
Fitchburg "	10	May, 1882,	Dec., 1893,	139	201 44	7	14	65	86	34	6	2	1,300 00	11	1,660 00	17,323 84
" "	11	Nov., 1882,	June, 1894,	139	201 37	18	2	28	48	21	6	6	3,475 00	3	250 00	9,665 76
Haverhill "	9	Jan., 1883,	April, 1894,	136	201 78	17	1	78	96	20	4	3	3,400 00	1	100 00	19,370 88
" "	10	July, 1883,	Oct., 1894,	136	200 94	8	1	94	103	19	3	2	1,600 00	1	150 00	20,696 82
Holyoke "	5	May, 1882,	Dec., 1893,	140	202 37	17	52	12	81	11	8	3	3,400 00	5	7,350 00	16,391 97
" "	6	Nov., 1882,	June, 1894,	140	202 27	1	46	15	62	13	11	1	200 00	10	4,550 00	12,540 74
Home "	1	June, 1882,	Dec., 1893,	138	204 63	4	14	61	79	26	5	1	760 00	7	1,620 00	16,165 77
" "	2	Dec., 1882,	June, 1894,	138	204 69	-	22	43	65	11	4	-	-	5	2,090 00	13,304 85
Homestead "	12	March, 1883,	April, 1894,	134	200 08	13	-	10	23	3	2	2	2,500 00	-	-	4,601 84
Mechanics "	7	Jan., 1883,	June, 1894,	137	200 00	-	-	89	89	26	1	-	-	-	-	17,800 00
Merchants "	3	Dec., 1883,	Jan., 1894,	134	201 48	-	5	56	61	16	1	-	-	1	660 00	12,290 23
" "	4	June, 1884,	June, 1894,	133	200 46	-	18	59	77	19	4	-	-	4	1,750 00	15,435 42

Bank	No.															
New Bedford "	3	Aug., 1882	March, 1894,	139	203 93	11	-	30	41	15	2	2	2,200 00	-	-	8,361 13
"	4	Feb., 1883	Aug., 1894,	138	201 53	3	6	16	25	12	4	1	600 00	3	950 00	5,038 25
People's "	1	March, 1882	Nov., 1893,	140	205 69	14	5	57	76	18	3	3	2,700 00	1	450 00	15,632 44
"	2	July, 1882	May, 1894,	142	209 47	5	-	30	35	5	1	1	1,000 00	-	-	7,331 45
Pioneer "	9	Oct., 1882	April, 1894,	138	204 78	6	-	8	14	4	1	1	1,200 00	-	-	2,860 92
"	10	April, 1883	Oct., 1894,	138	204 64	12	-	15	27	7	3	4	2,400 00	-	-	5,525 28
Plymouth "	1	June, 1882	Dec., 1893,	138	200 06	4	2	11	17	8	3	1	800 00	2	200 00	3,401 02
"	2	Dec., 1882	June, 1894,	138	200 12	-	-	7	7	2	-	-	-	-	-	1,400 84
Security "	6	Dec., 1882	May, 1894,	138	200 27	16	20	61	97	18	5	2	1,200 00	3	4,200 00	19,426 19
Somerville "	6	Oct., 1882	March, 1894,	138	202 90	-	-	22	22	8	-	-	-	-	-	4,463 80
"	7	April, 1883	Sept., 1894,	138	202 59	7	18	72	97	14	4	1	1,400 00	3	2,100 00	19,651 23
Springfield "	1	May, 1882	Feb., 1894,	141	202 52	-	-	33	33	13	-	-	-	-	-	6,683 16
Troy "	5	April, 1882	Oct., 1893,	139	203 28	2	-	41	43	9	1	1	350 00	1	50 00	8,741 04
"	6	Oct., 1882	April, 1894,	139	202 59	-	-	37	37	7	-	-	-	-	-	7,495 83
Waltham "	5	Oct., 1882	Nov., 1893,	134	200 08	22	7	85	114	25	6	4	4,250 00	2	1,100 00	22,809 12
Westfield "	1	Dec., 1881	Dec., 1893,	144	204 26	-	23	55	78	18	4	-	-	4	3,470 00	15,332 28
West Roxbury "	3	March, 1882	Nov., 1893,	140	203 57	-	13	15	28	8	5	-	-	5	1,800 00	5,699 96
"	4	Sept., 1882	May, 1894,	140	203 66	3	-	1	4	2	1	1	600 00	-	-	814 64
Worcester "	6	Oct., 1882	April, 1894,	138	292 97	17	17	46	80	22	7	4	3,400 00	7	2,250 00	16,237 60
Workingmen's "	6	Dec., 1882	Jan., 1891,	134	200 55	14	-	-	14	2	2	2	2,800 00	-	-	2,807 70
"	7	June, 1883	July, 1894,	134	200 16	34	-	-	34	5	5	5	6,800 00	-	-	6,805 44
						293	306	1,270	1,869	457	123	62	$55,875 00	84	$38,525 00	$378,282 66

Business of the Year.

During the year the sum of $5,132,330.68 has been paid into the banks as dues.

During the same period there has been paid back to members $2,727,641.47 for dues on shares withdrawn ; $44,414 for dues on shares forfeited ; $975,864 for dues on shares retired ; and $257,445 for dues on shares matured, — a total of $4,005,364.47.

During the same time there has been paid into the banks for interest $1,044,737.65 ; for premiums, $69,095.43 ; and for fines, $39,769.77.

The number of shares issued during the year was 117,210, the number cancelled being 110,277, viz. : —

Shares withdrawn,	94,243
Shares forfeited,	1,952
Shares retired,	12,213
Shares matured,	1,869

Several of the banks, in consequence of not being able to loan their accumulations, have availed themselves of the provisions of law and retired shares in addition to the number required by statute.

It would be well if the banks generally should limit the issue of shares to a smaller number than has been usual heretofore, and take their choice of loans offering rather than continue to issue a large number and then have to seek borrowers, in some instances at a distance from the bank, thereby taking greater risks.

The following table gives a consolidated statement in detail of the receipts and disbursements of all the banks during the year : —

Detailed Statement of Receipts and Disbursements for the Year ending Oct. 31, 1894.

RECEIPTS.		DISBURSEMENTS.	
From dues capital, . . .	$5,132,330 68	For real estate loans, . ·	$4,774,168 79
From interest, ...	1,044,737 65	For share loans, . . .	714,650 17
From premiums, . . .	69,095 43	For dues capital (withdrawn),	2,727,641 47
From fines, ...	39,769 77	For dues capital (forfeited),	44,414 00
From transfer fees, . . .	358 86	For dues capital (retired), .	975,864 00
From real estate loans repaid,	3,750,897 61	For dues capital (matured),	257,445 00
From share loans repaid, .	744,164 22	For profits capital (withdrawn), ...	379,740 84
From withdrawal profits, .	48,342 36		
From forfeiture profits, . .	2,039 83	For profits capital (forfeited), ·	8,115 05
From forfeited shares, . .	25,480 61	For profits capital (retired),	251,377 15
From expense, ...	1,686 00	For profits capital (matured),	120,142 16
From real estate, . . .	112,781 54	For temporary expenses, .	90,728 70
From bonds and notes, . .	86,275 00	For permanent expenses, .	3,827 08
From retired shares, . .	250,449 04	For forfeited shares, . .	20,269 05
From matured shares, . .	78,785 01	For bonds and notes, . .	65,774 98
From sundries, . . .	62,051 06	For real estate, . . .	166,619 02
Cash on hand Oct. 31, 1893, .	352,886 40	For interest, ...	12,626 03
		For retired shares, . .	247,665 78
		For matured shares, . .	58,662 14
		For sundries, ...	53,133 06
		Cash on hand Oct. 31, 1894, .	829,266 60
	$11,802,131 07		$11,802,131 07

A comparison of the consolidated balance sheet on page 236 with that for the year ending Oct. 31, 1893, shows an increase in total assets of $1,498,749.20. Loans on real estate have increased $1,012,671.18, while loans on shares have decreased $31,039.05, a net increase of $981,632.13 in loan account.

The amount of cash on hand is $829,266.60, as against $352,886.40 in October, 1893, and $685,046.68 in October, 1892. Of the cash on hand the sum of $270,186.69 is reported as having been sold, leaving an accumulation of about $500,000 not required to meet the direct liabilities of the banks for shares matured, retired and forfeited.

This large accumulation of unemployed money, if long continued, is liable to prove an element of danger to the banks;

for, as it is with the individual so is it with corporations, when money comes freely and in large amounts, it frequently happens that less care is given to its disposition than when it is harder to obtain or comes in smaller sums.

Some of the banks appear to have realized this condition of affairs, and have recently limited their issues of new shares to actual borrowers and those whose holdings had been retired or matured, and in some cases to borrowers only. Such a course is to be commended, and the good results thereof will be manifest when later in the history of those banks the question of retiring shares is reached.

City and town bonds and notes have decreased $21,863.27.

Mortgages (usually taken in part payment upon sale of real estate taken under foreclosure) have increased $20,659.59.

The unpaid interest, premiums and fines amount to $86,-383.26, as against $66,461.73 in 1893. This would appear to indicate that the depression in business had seriously affected the ability of the borrowers to keep good their agreements, as the increase of $19,921.53 is out of proportion to the increase in business.

The item of real estate held by foreclosure has changed during the year from $105,197.75 to $139,136.92, — an increase of nearly $34,000, or about $32\frac{1}{2}$ per cent., notwithstanding the banks advise sales of real estate during the same period of $112,781.54.

This increase is also very largely out of proportion to the general increase in business. The aggregate amount of the holdings is also out of proportion to the amount held by the savings banks, which institutions have less than one-third of one per cent. of their assets in real estate held under foreclosure, while the co-operative banks have three-quarters of one per cent. of their assets so held.

This large holding leads one to infer that in some of the banks there may have been a want of proper care in granting applications for loans. While the question of loss on the property now held cannot be determined until sales have been made, it would seem that if closer attention had been given by the security committees to the value and location of the estates, and a sufficient margin had been required in the same over the sum loaned, so large an amount, even in the present disturbed state of business affairs, would not have been found on the books of the banks.

The fact of such holdings would seem to add emphasis to what is said elsewhere regarding the danger of banks issuing shares in excess of what are required to meet the demands of borrowers of the best class.

A bank which shows the largest number of shares issued and the greatest receipts of money is not by any means the most successful if it has to foreclose some of its loans and be at the trouble and expense of carrying for a longer or shorter time the real estate so acquired, with possibility of loss when the property is disposed of.

A more pleasing exhibit in the consolidated balance sheet is the items of guaranty fund and surplus; these show an aggregate increase for the year of $48,470.38, and now amount to $199,636.48; the undivided earnings also show an increase of $9,368.53.

FINES.

The law regulating the business of the co-operative banks is generally admirable in its provisions, but in that part which relates to the charging of fines it is ambiguous in its meaning, and would be improved by proper amendment.

Under the law as it now stands it is possible and in fact it is frequently the case, that a member who subscribes for shares, after making a few payments, is unable or unwilling to continue his monthly dues, and, omitting to give notice of intended withdrawal, becomes delinquent; he is then fined to such an extent that a large portion of his investment is absorbed by such fines, and he is able to recover only a portion of his actual payments.

While we are not willing to coincide with a technical journal published in another State, which characterizes such transactions as " robbery," we do feel that a law which permits such a practice is out of place on the statute books of this Commonwealth, is unjust to the members and against the best interests of the bank, and should be amended.

Whatever may be the opinions of those interested in the management of the banks as regards the matter of fines generally, they will, we think, agree with this Board that as a rule

a member should at all times be able upon leaving the bank
to receive back all he has paid into it; and such a provision
exists in the laws of at least one State.

DISTRIBUTION OF PROFITS.

In view of the diversity of methods in use by the banks in
making up their division of profits, especially upon the dues
paid in during the term for which the dividend is computed,
the commissioners, in October last, acting under the provisions
of statute, directed that in all divisions of profits made thereafter, the rate having been determined, the calculations should
be made in a uniform manner, as prescribed in the following
rules : —

Rule for Banks issuing Shares Annually.

	1st Year.	2d Year.	3d Year.	4th Year.	5th Year.	6th Year.
Value at beginning of term,	–	$12 39	$25 52	$39 44	$54 20	$69 84
Interest for 12 months at 6 per cent.,	–	74	1 53	2 37	3 25	4 19
Dues paid during term,	$12 00	12 00	12 00	12 00	12 00	12 00
Interest on same,	39	39	39	39	39	39
Total value per share,	$12 39	$25 52	$39 44	$54 20	$69 84	$86 42
Dividend per share, at the rate of 6 per cent.,	$0 39	$1 13	$1 92	$2 76	$3 64	$4 58

	7th Year.	8th Year.	9th Year.	10th Year.	11th Year.	12th Year.
Value at beginning of term,	$86 42	$104 00	$122 63	$142 38	$163 31	$185 50
Interest for 12 months at 6 per cent.,	5 19	6 24	7 36	8 54	9 80	11 13
Dues paid during term,	12 00	12 00	12 00	12 00	12 00	12 00
Interest on same,	39	39	39	39	39	39
Total value per share,	$104 00	$122 63	$142 38	$163 31	$185 50	$209 02*
Dividend per share, at the rate of 6 per cent.,	$5 58	$6 63	$7 75	$8 93	$10 19	$11 52

* Shares mature at this point.

Rule for Banks issuing Shares Semi-annually.

	1st 6 Mos.	2d 6 Mos.	3d 6 Mos.	4th 6 Mos.	5th 6 Mos.	6th 6 Mos.
Value at beginning of term, .	–	$6 10	$12 38	$18 85	$25 52	$32 39
Interest for 6 months at 6 per cent.,	–	18	37	57	77	97
Dues paid during term, . .	$6 00	6 00	6 00	6 00	6 00	6 00
Interest on same, ...	10	10	10	10	10	10
Total value per share, . .	$6 10	$12 38	$18 85	$25 52	$32 39	$39 46
Dividend per share, at the rate of 6 per cent. per annum, . .	$0 10	$0 28	$0 47	$0 67	$0 87	$1 07

	7th 6 Mos.	8th 6 Mos.	9th 6 Mos.	10th 6 Mos.	11th 6 Mos.	12th 6 Mos.
Value at beginning of term, .	$39 46	$46 74	$54 24	$61 97	$69 93	$78 13
Interest for 6 months at 6 per cent.,	1 18	1 40	1 63	1 86	2 10	2 34
Dues paid during term, . .	6 00	6 00	6 00	6 00	6 00	6 00
Interest on same, ...	10	10	10	10	10	10
Total value per share, . .	$46 74	$54 24	$61 97	$69 93	$78 13	$86 57
Dividend per share, at the rate of 6 per cent. per annum, . .	$1 28	$1 50	$1 73	$1 96	$2 20	$2 44

	13th 6 Months.	14th 6 Months.	15th 6 Months.	16th 6 Months.	17th 6 Months.	18th 6 Months.
Value at beginning of term,	$86 57	$95 27	$104 23	$113 46	$122 96	$132 75
Interest for 6 months at 6 per cent., ...	2 60	2 86	3 13	3 40	3 69	3 98
Dues paid during term, .	6 00	6 00	6 00	6 00	6 00	6 00
Interest on same at 6 per cent., ...	10	10	10	10	10	10
Total value per share, .	$95 27	$104 23	$113 46	$122 96	$132 75	$142 83
Dividend per share, at the rate of 6 per cent. per annum, ...	$2 70	$2 96	$3 23	$3 50	$3 79	$4 08

Rule for Banks issuing Shares Semi-annually — Concluded.

	19th 6 Months.	20th 6 Months.	21st 6 Months.	22d 6 Months.	23d 6 Months.
Value at beginning of term,	$142 83	$153 22	$163 92	$174 94	$186 29
Interest for 6 months at 6 per cent.,	4 29	4 60	4 92	5 25	5 59
Dues paid during term,	6 00	6 00	6 00	6 00	6 00
Interest on same at 6 per cent.,	10	10	10	10	10
Total value per share,	$153 22	$163 92	$174 94	$186 29	$197 98
Dividend per share, at the rate of 6 per cent. per annum,	$4 39	$4 70	$5 02	$5 35	$5 69

Value per share at end of 23d term, ... $197 98
Three months' dues, ...   3 00

Making the shares reach the value of $200 98
when payments of dues thereon shall cease, and the holder be entitled to receive said value with interest at the rate of 6 per cent. per annum for all full months from the last adjustment of profits to the date of payment, as provided by the statutes relating to co-operative banks.

Formula for computing Interest on Dues paid in during a Term of either Three, Six or Twelve Months.

	Quarterly Division of Profits.	Semi-annual Division of Profits.	Annual Division of Profits.
$1 paid the first month is entitled to interest for	3 months.	6 months.	12 months.
" " second " " "	2 "	5 "	11 "
" " third " " "	1 month.	4 "	10 "
" " fourth " " "	. . .	3 "	9 "
" " fifth " " "	. . .	2 "	8 "
" " sixth " " "	. . .	1 month.	7 "
" " seventh " " "	. . .	. . .	6 "
" " eighth " " "	. . .	. . .	5 "
" " ninth " " "	. . .	. . .	4 "
" " tenth " " "	. . .	. . .	3 "
" " eleventh " " "	. . .	. . .	2 "
" " twelfth " " "	. . .	. . .	1 month.
Equivalent to the interest on $1 for . . .	6 months.	21 months.	78 months.
Which at the rate of 6 per cent. per annum would be	3 cents.	10 cents.	39 cents.
Which at the rate of 6½ per cent. per annum would be	3 "	11 "	42 "
Which at the rate of 7 per cent. per annum would be	4 "	12 "	45 "

Banks issuing shares quarterly, as also those distributing profits at rates other than six per cent., to conform to same rules, modified to meet difference in rates and dividend terms.

Rates of Interest paid by Borrowers.

The question whether loans obtained through co-operative banks are more or less economical to the borrower than those secured from savings banks has recently received considerable attention and been discussed in the public prints and elsewhere. Figures can be assumed to prove either phase of the question; the methods of business in the two classes of institutions are, however, so dissimilar that, unless actual simultaneous transactions in one of each class can be quoted, and all the lapses in payments and ramifications of book-keeping in both cases be taken into account, such figures are of comparatively little importance.

The person who comes into possession at some time of a small sum of money, and who is not sure as to when in the future he may have any more which he may desire to invest, naturally seeks the savings bank in which to deposit his accumulations; such a person, when he desires to borrow money on a mortgage of real estate, as naturally applies to the savings bank therefor, knowing, if the loan be so obtained, that so long as he keeps his interest paid promptly he can usually pay upon account of the principal at such irregular intervals as may best suit his convenience. On the other hand, the one who can every month reserve out of his or her income the sum of one dollar or more, joins some one of the co-operative banks, which institutions are especially designed for the accommodation of such persons; and when the time arrives that he desires a loan he naturally turns to the co-operative bank therefor, knowing that his monthly payments of dues (which must be met) are continually reducing the sum due from him to the bank.

It is these compulsory monthly payments of dues and interest which makes a loan from a co-operative bank the best for a person of small means and income, whether the cost of interest be a trifle more or less than on a loan from a savings bank.

The person who might without special effort be able to pay into the co-operative bank $10 each month (the sum required

to be paid on a loan of $1,000), would oftentimes — the tempta-
tions to spend money are so numerous — find it extremely
difficult to put aside each month the same sum, and to deposit
in a savings bank $60 at the end of six months, when only half
the sum would be required at that time to pay his interest due
to the savings bank.

The discussion of the question referred to, even should it be
made to appear that a loan from a savings bank is more economical to the borrower than is a loan from a co-operative bank,
which is very questionable, does the latter institutions far less
injury than do the statements put forth by some of the co-
operative banks that loans in these banks cost the borrower
only $3\frac{1}{6}$, $3\frac{1}{2}$ or 4 per cent. per annum interest, notwithstanding
the rate at which the money was hired may have been as high
as 6 to $7\frac{1}{2}$ per cent. To the man of business, judging quickly,
without time to analyze the operations and methods of co-
operative banking, such a statement seems incredible; and he
is led to at once, and very properly, doubt its accuracy, and is
inclined to condemn the whole system as misleading and unworthy of confidence and support.

There is an old adage, as true now as when first uttered, that
" one man can't loan money at a high rate of interest and the
borrower get it at a low rate," and this is as applicable to co-
operative banks as to individuals.

The man who borrows money of a co-operative bank at 7 per
cent. interest continues to pay that rate until his loan matures
or he shall have made a new contract. In the mean time a
separate account is kept of his dues paid in each month (really
partial payments on the loan), and it is the accumulation of
interest, profits divided, on this account, compounded either
quarterly, semi-annually or annually, according as new series
of shares are issued, that at maturity goes to reduce the
balance of interest in his two accounts.

As an illustration of the subject under discussion, we quote
a transaction to which our attention was recently called,
namely : —

A loan of $1,000 was made by a co-operative bank at 6 per
cent. interest, with an added monthly premium of 25 cents per
share, making the rate equivalent to $7\frac{1}{4}$ per cent. per annum.
This involved a monthly payment of dues on 5 shares, $5 ;

interest on $1,000 for a month, $5; premium, 25 cents a share on 5 shares, $1.25; an aggregate of $11.25; which was continued for a period of 132 months, when the shares matured, the whole amount paid during the term being:

Dues, $5 each month for 132 months, ...	$660 00
Interest, $5 each month for 132 months, . .	660 00
Premium, $1.25 each month for 132 months,. .	165 00
A total of, .	$1,485 00

These payments liquidated the loan of $1,000 and left a remainder of $485, which was said to represent the cost to the borrower for interest on the loan for 132 months.

The officers of the bank claimed that by this transaction the borrower had a loan of $1,000 for eleven years, at a cost of $485, and that the rate of interest was only about $4\frac{4}{10}$ per cent. per annum.

Such a statement is erroneous, for it will be seen at a glance from the foregoing statement that the interest (including premiums) paid by him was exactly $7\frac{1}{2}$ per cent., or $825, the difference of $340 being what his monthly payments of dues, $660 in all, had earned during the term; in short, the amount of $485 was merely the difference between what he paid the bank as interest on the money belonging to it, and what the bank allowed him as interest on the money it held belonging to him.

It is the usual custom among the banks to require the monthly payments to be made in advance; such being the case in the instance referred to, we claim that at no time did the borrower owe the bank the full sum of his loan, inasmuch as, before receiving the amount of $1,000, he had paid $5 in dues, and consequently for the first month of the term he owed the bank only $995, which was thereafter reduced each month by the sum of $5.

Treating the transaction in the same manner for the whole term of 132 months, we find that the borrower actually had the use of the following sums each for one month's time, viz. : —

$995	$895	$795	$695	$595	$495	$395
990	890	790	690	590	490	390
985	885	785	685	585	485	385
980	880	780	680	580	480	380
975	875	775	675	575	475	375
970	870	770	670	570	470	370
965	865	765	665	565	465	365
960	860	760	660	560	460	360
955	855	755	655	555	455	355
950	850	750	650	550	450	350
945	845	745	645	545	445	345
940	840	740	640	540	440	340
935	835	735	635	535	435	-
930	830	730	630	530	430	-
925	825	725	625	525	425	-
920	820	720	620	520	420	-
915	815	715	615	515	415	-
910	810	710	610	510	410	-
905	805	705	605	505	405	-
900	800	700	600	500	400	-

$18,950 + $16,950 + $14,950 + $12,950 + $10,950 + $8,950 + $4,410

say in all $88,110; the sum of $485 (or to be exact $484.60)
is equivalent to one month's interest on $88,110, at $6\frac{6}{10}$ per cent.
per annum, and we believe this fairly represents the rate per
cent. which the borrower paid for the money of which he had
the actual use.

Another bank in a printed report to its shareholders makes
a supposititious statement as to " what does it cost to borrow
money of a co-operative bank," and, assuming that shares will
mature in 132 months, makes it appear that a loan at $6\frac{1}{4}$ per
cent. will in the end cost the borrower only $3\frac{1}{6}$ per cent.

In view of the fact that during the year only one bank has
matured shares in as short a time as 132 months; that the
average of all shares matured during the year was over 138
months; that the bank mentioned has never matured any shares
at all; and that, if its profits are divided in the future at the
same rate as they have been heretofore, it will not be able to
mature its shares under 141 months, it will be seen that its
illustration is very misleading, and that it cannot fulfil any

such condition as the one held out as an inducement to borrow of a co-operative bank.

The co-operative bank system of this Commonwealth, so admirably planned at its inception, so carefully guarded by subsequent legislation, the past history of which has so clearly demonstrated its safety and its influence for good, is an agent for the accumulation of the savings of our people which cannot fail to commend itself to anyone who will carefully study its methods and its results, and the solid foundation on which it rests should not be undermined by any fictitious or misleading statements.

Such statements as those referred to savor too much of the style of the delusive bond schemes which wrought such mischief and entailed so much loss to the people of this Commonwealth a few years ago, and are unworthy of use by a co-operative bank, and in the end must tend to injure the institutions so doing.

We would recommend that each bank in its statements to the public should hereafter eliminate all theories and problematical results, and include only actual facts and figures derived from its own experience. Such a course, we believe, will redound to the benefit of the banks themselves as well as to the system, which has no more earnest advocates than are the members of this Board.

Annual Returns.

The statute (section 2, chapter 159, Acts of 1889) requires every co-operative bank to annually make a return to this Board within twenty days after the last business day of October, showing accurately the condition thereof at close of business on said day.

Some of the banks balance their accounts and post their books at the end of the calendar month and others at or soon after their monthly meeting; probably none of them include in their annual statement the amounts received in October on account of the November meeting; consequently exact compliance with the statute is the exception rather than the rule.

We think, if the law were amended so as to require all transactions up to the close of business on the last day of October, excepting only receipts of dues, interest, premiums and fines received on account of the November meeting, it would give more uniformity to these reports.

Although under the provisions of statute the reports should reach this Board not later than November 20, several were delayed the past year for thirty days and more after that date, notwithstanding repeated requests were made for an earlier rendering.

We believe that with very little exertion every bank can have its report returned at the stated time ; but there is at present no means for enforcing compliance with the statute, and we therefore recommend that a penalty be established for every day's delay, as is now in the case of railroad and gas companies.

COLLATERAL LOAN COMPANIES.

The Collateral Loan Company and the Workingmen's Loan Association, both of Boston, have been examined as usual by an expert accountant. Both companies continue the good work in which they have been engaged since their organization.

The first named loans mostly upon pledges of watches, jewelry, precious stones and wearing apparel, and during the term of twelve months has made nearly 40,000 loans; of which number 15,800 were for sums of $5 or less. The company has recently reduced its charge for interest to $1\frac{1}{2}$ per cent. net per month. While to the business community this may appear to be a high rate, it is probably as low as can be afforded, when the character of the company and the risk and expense of transacting its business are considered; and this is further evidenced by the fact that on 5,000 loans which have been settled during the year there has been an interest charge of only 10 cents on each.

The loans of the Workingmen's Loan Association are principally upon mortgages of household furniture, and range in amount from $25 upwards, the average being about $75. This company charges interest at the rate of 1 per cent. a month.

The class of people who patronize these companies obtain the accommodations they need at much less cost than if compelled to resort to individuals engaged in a similar line of business.

MORTGAGE LOAN COMPANIES.

The mortgage loan companies incorporated by this Commonwealth, and under the supervision of this Board, are

THE NATIONAL MORTGAGE AND DEBENTURE COMPANY and
THE GLOBE INVESTMENT COMPANY, both of Boston.

As permitted by statute and as has been the custom heretofore, the examination of these companies has been made by
expert accountants, and has been as thorough and careful as is
practicable in companies the bulk of whose business is trans-
acted beyond the confines of this Commonwealth.

The general depression in business throughout the country,
added to the short crops in those sections where the mortgages
of both companies are mostly placed, has delayed collections
and prevented sales of land.

The Globe Investment Company states that its business is
now in no manner involved with that of the company bearing
the same name organized under the laws of Nebraska, which,
it is claimed, is used simply as a means of readily handling
property conveyed to it by the Massachusetts company. The
future operations of this company must necessarily be depend-
ent upon circumstances. Continued failure of crops would
mean disaster, while two or three seasons of good crops would
undoubtedly create a demand for the lands it holds, and enable
its borrowers to meet their engagements, this in turn permitting
the company to fully meet its obligations.

FOREIGN COMPANIES.

The companies doing business in this Commonwealth at the date of this report under the provisions of chapter 310, Acts of 1890, were

THE MINNESOTA SAVING FUND AND INVESTMENT COMPANY, and
THE SECURITY SAVINGS AND LOAN ASSOCIATION, both of Minneapolis, Minn.

These companies have on deposit with the Treasurer and Receiver-General of the Commonwealth, for the benefit of the shareholders in Massachusetts, the following sums : —

Minnesota Saving Fund and Investment Company, .   . $53,969 98
Security Savings and Loan Association, ... 69,465 07

The companies continue to comply with all the requirements of the license granted them by this Board.   As has been stated in previous reports, an examination of the companies by this Board is not practicable, nor is it required by the statute.

The American Building Loan and Investment Society of Chicago is still in the hands of W. K. Sullivan, receiver.

The recommendation in our last report that the shareholders residing in this Commonwealth should take concerted action looking to the protection of their interests was not acted upon, owing, no doubt, to the class of people holding claims, and the added fact that they were scattered among a number of cities and towns with comparatively no very large amount at stake in one locality.

The United States district court has recently ordered a distribution of the deposit in the office of the State treasurer among those creditors in this Commonwealth who have proved their claims ; how much more these creditors will be able to recover will depend upon the realization of the general assets of the company and the action of the United States district court for the State of Illinois.

The present unfortunate position of the shareholders in this
company is an added illustration of the fact that it is generally
better to invest in our home institutions and receive a fair rate
of interest than to embark in enterprises located at distant
points, the nature of whose business and the character of
whose officers is not readily ascertained, and which frequently
terminate in disaster and loss.

During the year it was found that a company called the
Interstate Building and Loan Association of Bloomington, Ill.,
had opened an agency in one of the cities in the western part
of this Commonwealth, and was soliciting business there.
The company itself was at once notified that it must refrain
from transacting business in this Commonwealth; the agent
was also notified, and, being called upon by a member of this
Board, at once closed the office, having apparently up to that
time been ignorant of the fact that he was violating any law.

Several companies have made inquiries as to the conditions
upon which they could be permitted to do business in this
Commonwealth, but, upon being furnished with copies of the
statute, did not pursue the matter further.

CONCLUSION.

The financial statements of each of the institutions is contained in the following pages; the returns of the co-operative
banks include in each instance a statement of the receipts and
disbursements, which statements have not heretofore been included in the published reports.

In the Appendix will be found the laws relating to co-operative banks and mortgage loan and investment companies,
corrected to date.

Hon. Samuel O. Lamb, who was a member of the Board for
the entire period covered by this report, resigned his position
before the same was prepared, consequently his signature is not
affixed hereto.

STARKES WHITON,
WILLIAM D. T. TREFRY,
Commissioners.

ABSTRACT OF ANNUAL REPORTS

OF THE

CO-OPERATIVE BANKS,

SHOWING THEIR

CONDITION AT CLOSE OF BUSINESS

OCTOBER 31, 1894.

MADE IN CONFORMITY TO THE REQUIREMENTS OF CHAPTER 159
OF THE ACTS OF 1889.

ACUSHNET CO-OPERATIVE BANK — NEW BEDFORD.

Incorporated Nov. 15, 1889.   Commenced business Nov. 16, 1889.

RUFUS A. SOULE, *President.*   CHAS. R. PRICE, *Secretary.*

EDGAR LORD, *Treasurer.*

Names of security committee :
LOT B. BATES,   OLIVER P. BRIGHTMAN,
JASPER W. BRALEY.

Regular meetings the fourth Saturday of each month.

BALANCE SHEET OCTOBER 31, 1894.

ASSETS.		LIABILITIES.	
Loans on real estate, . .	$79,030 00	Dues capital, . .	$84,657 00
Loans on shares, . . .	6,670 00	Profits capital (all series), .	10,344 75
Permanent expense account, .	20 00	Surplus, ...	678 82
Unpaid interest, . . .	580 23	Guaranty fund, . .	297 88
Unpaid fines, ...	60 52	Forfeited share account, .	19 78
Unpaid dues, ...	1,104 00	Personal account, . . .	2 67
Suspense account, . . .	5 00		
Personal account, . . .	5 00		
Cash in hands of treasurer, .	8,526 15		
	$96,000 90		$96,000 90

Detailed Statement of Receipts and Disbursements for the Year ending Oct. 31, 1894.

RECEIPTS.		DISBURSEMENTS.	
From dues capital, .	$31,203 00	For real estate loans, . .	$27,800 00
interest, . . .	5,412 54	share loans, . . .	5,610 00
fines, ...	226 38	dues capital(withdrawn),	15,653 00
transfer fees, .	50	dues capital (retired), .	7,890 00
real estate loans repaid,	20,920 00	profits capital (with-	
share loans repaid, .	6,260 00	drawn), . . .	1,358 61
withdrawal profits, .	207 50	profits capital (retired),	1,024 59
personal accounts, .	88 09	temporary expenses, .	448 75
profits, . . .	05	fines, ...	3 15
		interest, ...	172 41
		personal accounts, .	665 22
Cash on hand Oct. 31, 1893, .	4,833 82	Cash on hand Oct. 31, 1894,	8,526 15
	$69,151 88		$69,151 88

Reconciliation of Share Account with Dues and Profits Capital.

DATE OF ISSUE.	Series.	Value per Share.	Shares in Force.	Total Value.		
Nov , 1889, .	1	$70 09	418	$29,297 62	Dues capital, as per general ledger, . .	
May, 1890, .	2	62 07	278	17,255 46		$84,657 00
Nov., 1890, .	3	54 31	140	7,603 40	Profits capital, as per general ledger, . .	
May, 1891, .	4	46 79	163	7,626 77		10,344 75
Nov., 1891, .	5	39 49	289	11,412 61		
May, 1892, .	6	32 41	207	6,708 87		
Nov., 1892, .	7	25 54	273	6,972 42		
May, 1893, .	8	18 86	229	4,318 94		
Nov., 1893, .	9	12 39	184	2,279 76		
May, 1894, .	10	6 10	229	1,396 90		
Dues paid in advance, .			.	129 00		
Total, ...				$95,001 75	Total, . . .	$95,001 75

Number of shares issued during the year, ... 539
Number of shares now in force, ... 2,410
Number of shares now borrowed upon, ... 743
Largest number of shares held by any one member, ... 25
Number of shares withdrawn during the year, ... 704
Number of shares retired during the year, ... 148
Highest premium received during the year, ... $0 22
Lowest premium received during the year, ... 01
Number of members withdrawn during the year, ... 84
Present number of members, ... 357
Present number of borrowers, ... 106
Present number of non-borrowers, ... 251
Number of loans secured by first mortgage of real estate, . . . 57
Number of loans on shares, ... 49
Largest loan to any one member, ... 5,000 00
Smallest loan to any one member, ... 10 00
Amount of expenses of the corporation for the year ending Oct. 31, 1893, 478 75
Date of examination by commissioner : October 1.

ALLSTON CO-OPERATIVE BANK — BOSTON.

Incorporated April 8, 1887.   Commenced business April 9, 1887.

HOMER ROGERS, *President.*   GEORGE F. TAFT, *Secretary.*
GEORGE F. TAFT, *Treasurer.*

Names of security committee:
JAMES I. WINGATE,   FREELON MORRIS,
S. W. BROWN, Jr.

Regular meetings the second Saturday of each month.

BALANCE SHEET OCTOBER 31, 1894.

ASSETS.		LIABILITIES.	
Loans on real estate, . .	$244,929 00	Dues capital, . .	$280,742 00
Loans on shares, . . .	18,055 00	Profits capital (all series), .	39,734 98
Permanent expense account, .	775 00	Interest, ...	5,728 07
Temporary expense account,	558 06	Premiums, ...	337 50
Real estate by foreclosure, .	3,851 72	Fines, ...	216 56
Unpaid interest, . . .	819 83	Transfer fees, . .	75
Unpaid premiums, . .	45 15	Surplus, . . .	15 51
Unpaid fines, ...	105 84	Guaranty fund, . .	1,451 75
Cash in hands of treasurer, .	60,485 43	Forfeited share account, .	913 95
		Withdrawal profits, .	483 96
	$329,625 03		$329,625 03

Detailed Statement of Receipts and Disbursements for the Year ending Oct. 31, 1894.

RECEIPTS.		DISBURSEMENTS.	
From dues capital, .	$89,725 00	For real estate loans, . .	$73,679 00
interest, . . .	17,421 10	share loans, . . .	13,535 00
premiums, . . .	1,078 70	dues capital(withdrawn),	40,753 00
fines, . . .	635 16	dues capital (forfeited),	1,242 00
transfer fees, . .	4 50	dues capital (retired), .	13,452 00
real estate loans repaid,	74,850 00	profits capital (with-	
share loans repaid, .	15,895 00	· drawn), . . .	4,653 89
withdrawal profits, .	1,124 51	profits capital (forfeited),	151 12
forfeiture profits, .	15 55	profits capital (retired),	2,453 70
forfeited shares, . .	305 23	temporary expenses, .	2,094 72
foreclosure expense, .	126 71	permanent expenses, .	30 25
temporary expense re-		forfeited shares, .	710 39
funded, . . .	315 65	foreclosure expense, .	255 92
Cash on hand Oct. 31, 1893, .	11,999 31	Cash on hand Oct. 31, 1894,	60,485 43
	$213,496 42		$213,496 42

Reconciliation of Share Account with Dues and Profits Capital.

Date of Issue.	Series.	Value per Share.	Shares in Force.	Total Value.		
April, 1887, .	1	$114 79	202	$23,187 58	Dues capital, as per general ledger, . .	$280,742 00
July, 1887, .	2	110 06	66	7,263 96	Profits capital, as per general ledger, . .	39,734 98
Jan., 1888, .	3	100 77	285	28,719 45	Unpaid dues, . . .	1,751 00
July, 1888, .	4	91 82	259	23,781 38		
Jan., 1889, .	5	83 12	625	51,950 00		
July, 1889, .	6	74 69	296	22,108 24		
Jan., 1890, .	7	66 58	303	20,173 74		
July, 1890, .	8	58 74	188	11,043 12		
Jan., 1891, .	9	51 11	583	29,797 13		
July, 1891, .	10	43 72	658	28,767 76		
Jan., 1892, .	11	36 58	621	22,716 18		
July, 1892, .	12	29 64	438	12,982 32		
Jan., 1893, .	13	22 92	760	17,419 20		
July, 1893, .	14	16 41	613	10,059 33		
Jan., 1894, .	15	10 11	872	8,815 92		
July, 1894, .	16	4 00	816	3,264 00		
Suspense profits, ...				1 67		
Dues paid in advance, . . .				177 00		
Total, . . .				$322,227 98	Total, . .	$322,227 98

Number of shares issued during the year, ... 1,828
Number of shares now in force, ... 7,585
Number of shares now borrowed upon, ... 1,663
Largest number of shares held by any one member, ... 25
Number of shares withdrawn during the year, ... 1,531
Number of shares forfeited during the year, ... 36
Number of shares retired during the year, ... 220
Highest premium received during the year, ... $0 10
Lowest premium received during the year, ... 05
Number of members withdrawn during the year, ... 152
Present number of members, ... 726
Present number of borrowers, ... 131
Present number of non-borrowers, ... 595
Number of loans secured by first mortgage of real estate, . . . 114
Number of loans on shares, ... 49
Largest loan to any one member, ... 5,000 00
Smallest loan to any one member, ... 50 00
Amount of expenses of the corporation for the year ending Oct. 31, 1894, . 1,907 76
Date of examination by commissioner: June 22.

AMESBURY CO-OPERATIVE BANK — AMESBURY.

Incorporated April 10, 1886.　Commenced business May 1, 1886.

WM. W. HAWKES, *President.*　　　　　PORTER SARGENT, *Secretary.*
PORTER SARGENT, *Treasurer.*

Names of security committee:

WM. W. HAWKES,	RICHARD E. BRIGGS,
GEORGE F. PIKE,	JOHN J. PREVAUX,
	JOHN CURRIER.

Regular meetings the first Monday of each month.

BALANCE SHEET OCTOBER 31, 1894.

ASSETS.		LIABILITIES.	
Loans on real estate, . .	$68,129 60	Dues capital, . . .	$70,464 00
Loans on shares, . . .	4,520 00	Profits capital (all series), .	12,711 79
Unpaid interest, . . .	1,039 22	Surplus, ...	2,259 45
Unpaid premiums, . .	153 75	Guaranty fund, . . .	1,071 64
Cash in hands of treasurer, .	12,698 10	Forfeited share account, .	33 79
	$86,540 67		$86,540 67

Detailed Statement of Receipts and Disbursements for the Year ending Oct. 31, 1894.

RECEIPTS.		DISBURSEMENTS.	
From dues capital, . .	$20,947 00	For real estate loans, . .	$18,025 00
interest, . . .	4,797 61	share loans, . . .	3,930 00
premiums, . . .	475 07	dues capital(withdrawn),	13,966 00
fines, ...	308 25	dues capital (forfeited),	10 00
transfer fees, . .	75	dues capital (retired), .	8,041 00
real estate loans repaid,	24,650 00	profits capital (with-	
share loans repaid, .	5,185 00	drawn), . . .	2,206 95
withdrawal profits, .	223 08	profits capital(forfeited),	45
forfeiture profits, . .	05	profits capital (retired), .	1,546 20
forfeited shares, . .	8 30	temporary expenses, .	675 59
Cash on hand Oct. 31, 1893, .	4,512 48	forfeited shares, . .	8 30
		Cash on hand Oct. 31, 1894, .	12,698 10
	$61,107 59		$61,107 59

Reconciliation of Share Account with Dues and Profits Capital.

DATE OF ISSUE.	Series.	Value per Share.	Shares in Force.	Total Value.		
May, 1886, .	1	$132 50	54	$7,155 00	Dues capital, as per general ledger, . .	$70,464 00
Nov., 1886, .	2	122 73	37	4,541 01		
May, 1887, .	3	113 24	84	9,512 16	Profits capital, as per general ledger, . .	12,711 79
Nov., 1887, .	4	104 03	95	9,882 85		
May, 1888, .	5	95 09	83	7,892 47	Unpaid dues, . . .	1,302 00
Nov., 1888, .	6	86 41	65	5,616 65		
May, 1889, .	7	77 98	80	6,238 40		
Nov., 1889, .	8	69 80	31	2,163 80		
May, 1890, .	9	61 85	84	5,195 40		
Nov., 1890, .	10	54 14	110	5,955 40		
May, 1891, .	11	46 65	80	3,732 00		
Nov., 1891, .	12	39 38	62	2,441 56		
May, 1892, .	13	32 32	113	3,652 16		
Nov., 1892, .	14	25 47	155	3,947 85		
May, 1893, .	15	18 82	124	2,333 68		
Nov., 1893, .	16	12 36	193	2,385 48		
May, 1894, .	17	6 09	288	1,753 92		
Dues paid in advance, . . .				78 00		
Total, ...				$84,477 79	Total, . . .	$84,477 79

Number of shares issued during the year, ... 487
Number of shares now in force, ... 1,738
Number of shares now borrowed upon, ... 489
Largest number of shares held by any one member, . . . 25
Number of shares withdrawn during the year, ... 325
Number of shares forfeited during the year, ... 5
Number of shares retired during the year, ... 113
Highest premium received during the year, ... $0 10
Lowest premium received during the year, ... 05
Number of members withdrawn during the year, ... 68
Present number of members, ... 270
Present number of borrowers, ... 63
Present number of non-borrowers, ... 207
Number of loans secured by first mortgage of real estate, . . . 53
Number of loans on shares, ... 10
Largest loan to any one member, ... 3,450 00
Smallest loan to any one member, ... 50 00
Amount of expenses of the corporation for the year ending Oct. 31, 1894, . 675 59
Date of examination by commissioner: September 11.

ARLINGTON CO-OPERATIVE BANK — ARLINGTON.

Incorporated Oct. 30, 1889. Commenced business Nov. 14, 1889.

GEO. D. MOORE, *President.* R. WALTER HILLIARD, *Secretary.*
WARREN A. PEIRCE, *Treasurer.*

Names of security committee:

GEO. D. MOORE, O. B. MARSTON,
L. C. TYLER.

Regular meetings the second Tuesday of each month.

BALANCE SHEET OCTOBER 31, 1894.

ASSETS.		LIABILITIES.	
Loans on real estate,	$81,700 00	Dues capital,	$77,696 00
Loans on shares,	2,437 00	Profits capital (all series),	9,305 64
Permanent expense account,	134 30	Surplus,	147 43
Unpaid interest,	14 23	Guaranty fund,	114 64
Unpaid premiums,	55	Forfeited share account,	5 80
Unpaid fines,	11 64		
Cash in hands of treasurer,	2,971 79		
	$87,269 51		$87,269 51

Detailed Statement of Receipts and Disbursements for the Year ending Oct. 31, 1894.

RECEIPTS.		DISBURSEMENTS.	
From dues capital,	$31,929 00	For real estate loans,	$30,000 00
interest,	4,592 11	share loans,	3,240 00
premiums,	264 90	dues capital (withdrawn),	10,563 00
fines,	83 87	profits capital (withdrawn),	996 38
transfer fees,	1 00		
real estate loans repaid,	6,000 00	temporary expenses,	488 79
share loans repaid,	4,625 00	permanent expenses,	34 50
withdrawal profits,	249 42		
Cash on hand Oct. 31, 1893,	549 16	Cash on hand Oct. 31, 1894,	2,971 79
	$48,294 46		$48,294 46

Reconciliation of Share Account with Dues and Profits Capital.

Date of Issue.	Series.	Value per Share.	Shares in Force.	Total Value.		
Nov., 1889, .	1	$70 59	291	$20,541 69	Dues capital, as per general ledger, . . .	$77,696 00
May, 1890, .	2	62 54	304	19,012 16		
Nov., 1890, .	3	54 72	126	6,894 72	Profits capital, as per general ledger, . .	9,305 64
May, 1891, .	4	47 13	91	4,288 83		
Nov., 1891, .	5	39 75	171	6,797 25	Unpaid dues, . .	434 00
May, 1892, .	6	32 60	299	9,747 40		
Nov., 1892, .	7	25 66	206	5,285 96		
May, 1893, .	8	18 93	319	6,038 67		
Nov., 1893, .	9	12 42	506	6,284 52		
May, 1894, .	10	6 11	404	2,468 44		
Dues paid in advance, . .				76 00		
Total, ...				$87,435 64	Total, . . .	$87,435 64

Number of shares issued during the year, ... 1,000
Number of shares now in force, ... 2,717
Number of shares now borrowed upon, ... 554
Largest number of shares held by any one member, . . . 25
Number of shares withdrawn during the year, ... 441
Highest per centum of interest received during the year: 9.
Lowest per centum of interest received during the year: 6.
Number of members withdrawn during the year, ... 40
Present number of members, ... 279
Present number of borrowers, ... 59
Present number of non-borrowers, ... 220
Number of loans secured by first mortgage of real estate, . . . 45
Number of loans on shares, ... 19
Largest loan to any one member, ... $5,000 00
Smallest loan to any one member, ... 35 00
Amount of expenses of the corporation for the year ending Oct. 31, 1894, . 501 48
Date of examination by commissioner: December 11.

ATHOL CO-OPERATIVE BANK—ATHOL.

Incorporated July 1, 1889.   Commenced business July 15, 1889.

GEORGE D. BATES, *President.*   C. F. RICHARDSON, *Secretary.*
                         C. F. RICHARDSON, *Treasurer.*

Names of security committee :

LEVI B. FAY,   LEROY C. PARMENTER,
                 ARTHUR F. TYLER.

Regular meetings the third Monday of each month.

BALANCE SHEET OCTOBER 31, 1894.

ASSETS.			LIABILITIES.		
Loans on real estate,	.	$49,400 00	Dues capital,	. . .	$46,736 00
Loans on shares,	. .	2,157 00	Profits capital (all series),	.	6,054 47
Permanent expense account,	.	20 00	Surplus,	. . . .	540 74
Unpaid interest,	. .	376 94	Guaranty fund,	. .	98 50
Unpaid premiums,	.	8 90	Forfeited share account,	.	99 93
Unpaid fines, .	. .	48 82			
Cash in hands of treasurer,	.	1,517 98			
		$53,529 64			$53,529 64

Detailed Statement of Receipts and Disbursements for the Year ending
Oct. 31, 1894.

RECEIPTS.			DISBURSEMENTS.		
From dues capital,	. .	$17,667 00	For real estate loans,	. .	$8,750 00
interest,	. . .	2,760 60	share loans,	. . .	2,775 00
premiums,	. . .	66 46	dues capital (withdrawn),		10,267 00
fines,	. . . .	206 96	dues capital (forfeited),		148 00
transfer fees,	. .	25	dues capital (retired),	.	2,739 00
real estate loans repaid,	.	4,550 00	profits capital (with-		
share loans repaid,	.	2,425 00	drawn), . . .		1,005 57
withdrawal profits,	.	143 12	profits capital (forfeited),		10 61
forfeiture profits,	.	7 45	profits capital (retired),		480 08
forfeited shares,	.	143 60	temporary expenses,	.	183 48
			forfeited shares,	.	48 15
			outstanding bills,	.	76 75
Cash on hand Oct. 31, 1893,	.	31 18	Cash on hand Oct. 31, 1894,		1,517 98
		$28,001 62			$28,001 62

Reconciliation of Share Account with Dues and Profits Capital.

DATE OF ISSUE.	Series.	Value per Share.	Shares in Force.	Total Value.		
July, 1889, .	1	$75 50	280	$21,140 00	Dues capital, as per general ledger, . .	$46,736 00
Jan., 1890, .	2	67 31	64	4,307 84		
July, 1890, .	3	59 41	51	3,029 91	Profits capital, as per general ledger, . .	6,054 47
Jan., 1891, .	4	51 73	130	6,724 90		
July, 1891, .	5	44 28	45	1,992 60	Unpaid dues, . .	669 00
Jan., 1892, .	6	37 07	90	3,336 30		
July, 1892, .	7	30 08	114	3,429 12		
Jan., 1893, .	8	23 28	194	4,516 32		
May, 1893, .	9	18 85	92	1,734 20		
Nov., 1893, .	10	12 38	171	2,116 98		
May, 1894, .	11	6 10	183	1,116 30		
Dues paid in advance, . . .				15 00		
Total, ...				$53,459 47	Total, . . .	$53,459 47

Number of shares issued during the year, ... 391
Number of shares now in force, ... 1,414
Number of shares now borrowed upon, ... 322
Largest number of shares held by any one member, . . . 25
Number of shares withdrawn during the year, ... 397
Number of shares forfeited during the year, ... 18
Number of shares retired during the year, ... 44
Highest per centum of interest received during the year: $10\frac{8}{10}$.
Lowest per centum of interest received during the year: 6.
Number of members withdrawn during the year, ... 58
Present number of members, ... 198
Present number of borrowers, ... 61
Present number of non-borrowers, ... 137
Number of loans secured by first mortgage of real estate, . . 61
Number of loans on shares, ... 15
Largest loan to any one member, ... $4,800 00
Smallest loan to any one member, ... 25 00
Amount of expenses of the corporation for the year ending Oct. 31, 1894, . 223 48
Date of examination by commissioner: February 19.

ATLANTIC CO-OPERATIVE BANK — LAWRENCE.

Incorporated March 26, 1891.   Commenced business April 30, 1891.

THOMAS BEVINGTON, *President.*   F. A. SHERMAN, *Secretary.*

W. D. CURRIER, *Treasurer.*

Names of security committee :

JOHN HAIGH,   THOMAS BEVINGTON,
SETH F. DAWSON,   ROBERT T. TODD,
JOHN O. BATTERSHILL.

Regular meetings the last Friday of each month.

BALANCE SHEET OCTOBER 31, 1894.

ASSETS.		LIABILITIES.	
Loans on real estate, . .	$34,950 00	Dues capital, . . .	$39,032 00
Loans on shares, . . .	4,750 00	Profits capital (all series), .	3,124 81
Permanent expense account,	127 39	Interest, ...	277 33
Unpaid interest, . . .	37 25	Premiums, ...	18 98
Unpaid premiums, . .	2 80	Fines, ...	12 66
Unpaid fines, ...	6 55	Transfer fees, . . .	25
		Surplus, ...	193 52
		Guaranty fund, . . .	118 19
		Forfeited share account, .	12 06
Cash in hands of treasurer, .	2,921 97	Withdrawal profits, .	6 16
	$42,795 96		$42,795 96

Detailed Statement of Receipts and Disbursements for the Year ending Oct. 31, 1894.

RECEIPTS.		DISBURSEMENTS.	
From dues capital, .	$18,367 00	For real estate loans, . .	$16,500 00
interest, . . .	2,090 29	share loans, . . .	6,300 00
premiums, . . .	186 29	dues capital (withdrawn),	5,603 00
fines, ...	60 19	dues capital (forfeited),	10 00
transfer fees, . .	2 50	profits capital (with-	
real estate loans repaid,	5,350 00	drawn), . . .	386 84
share loans repaid, .	4,500 00	profits capital (forfeited),	1 15
withdrawal profits, .	69 44	temporary expenses, .	186 00
forfeiture profits, .	29	permanent expenses, .	23 39
forfeited shares, . .	8 76		
Cash on hand Oct. 31, 1893, .	1,297 59	Cash on hand Oct 31, 1894,	2,921 97
	$31,932 35		$31,932 35

Reconciliation of Share Account with Dues and Profits Capital.

DATE OF ISSUE.	Series.	Value per Share.	Shares in Force.	Total Value.		
April, 1891, .	1	$47 64	344	$16,389 88	Dues capital, as per general ledger, . .	$39,032 00
July, 1891, .	2	44 01	36	1,584 54	Profits capital, as per general ledger, . .	3,124 81
Oct., 1891, .	3	40 41	93	3,758 60	Unpaid dues, . . .	144 00
Jan., 1892, .	4	36 88	42	1,549 17		
April, 1892, .	5	33 38	174	5,808 99		
July, 1892, .	6	29 93	23	688 50		
Oct., 1892, .	7	26 52	50	1,326 25		
Jan., 1893, .	8	23 16	138	3,196 77		
April, 1893, .	9	19 86	176	3,496 24		
July, 1893, .	10	16 60	50	830 25		
Oct., 1893, .	11	13 39	42	562 59		
Jan., 1894, .	12	10 22	109	1,114 53		
April, 1894, .	13	7 10	176	1,250 48		
July, 1894, .	14	4 03	166	668 98		
Oct., 1894, .	15	1 00	65	65 00		
Dues paid in advance, . . .				10 00		
Suspense profits, ...				04		
Total, ...				$42,300 81	Total, . . .	$42,300 81

Number of shares issued during the year, ... 609
Number of shares now in force, ... 1,684
Number of shares now borrowed upon, ... 330
Largest number of shares held by any one member, . . . 25
Number of shares withdrawn during the year, ... 312
Number of shares forfeited during the year, ... 5
Highest per centum of interest received during the year: $7\frac{1}{5}$.
Lowest per centum of interest received during the year: 6.
Number of members withdrawn during the year, ... 53
Present number of members, ... 210
Present number of borrowers, ... 42
Present number of non-borrowers, ... 168
Number of loans secured by first mortgage of real estate, . . . 26
Number of loans on shares, ... 16
Largest loan to any one member, ... $4,000 00
Smallest loan to any one member, ... 50 00
Amount of expenses of the corporation for the year ending Oct. 31, 1894, . 286 00
Date of examination by commissioner: June 7.

ATTLEBOROUGH CO-OPERATIVE BANK — ATTLEBOROUGH.

Incorporated July 18, 1892. Commenced business Aug. 17, 1892.

WILLIAM L. ELLIOT, *President.* HARRY E. CARPENTER, *Secretary.*
HARRY E. CARPENTER, *Treasurer.*

Names of security committee:
FRED L. TORREY, M. F. ASHLEY,
A. N. BROWNELL.

Regular meetings the third Wednesday of each month.

BALANCE SHEET OCTOBER 31, 1894.

ASSETS.			LIABILITIES.		
Loans on real estate,	$3,200	00	Dues capital,	$5,135	00
Loans on shares,	695	00	Profits capital (all series),	259	39
Permanent expense account,	200	00	Interest,	54	68
Temporary expense account,	26	00	Premiums,		87
Unpaid interest,	7	22	Fines,		90
Unpaid premiums,		08	Surplus,	3	08
Unpaid fines,	11	82	Guaranty fund,	7	00
			Forfeited share account,	29	28
Cash in hands of treasurer,	1,350	57	Withdrawal profits,		49
	$5,490	69		$5,490	69

Detailed Statement of Receipts and Disbursements for the Year ending Oct. 31, 1894.

RECEIPTS.			DISBURSEMENTS.		
From dues capital,	$2,836	00	For real estate loans,	$1,400	00
interest,	219	15	share loans,	410	00
premiums,	7	06	dues capital (withdrawn),	1,396	00
fines,	32	39	profits capital (withdrawn),	55	39
real estate loans repaid,	1,200	00			
share loans repaid,	380	00	temporary expenses,	70	25
sundries,	1	00			
Cash on hand Oct. 31, 1893,	6	61	Cash on hand Oct. 31, 1894,	1,350	57
	$4,682	21		$4,682	21

Reconciliation of Share Account with Dues and Profits Capital.

DATE OF ISSUE.	Series.	Value per Share.	Shares in Force.	Total Value.		
Aug., 1892, .	1	$28 38	174	$4,938 12	Dues capital, as per general ledger, . .	$5,135 00
Feb., 1893, .	2	21 82	10	218 20		
Aug., 1893, .	3	15 36	18	276 48	Profits capital, as per general ledger, . .	259 39
Feb., 1894, .	4	9 09	51	463 59		
Aug., 1894, .	5	3 00	12	36 00	Unpaid dues, . .	538 00
Total, ...				$5,932 39	Total, . . .	$5,932 39

Number of shares issued during the year, ... 81
Number of shares now in force, ... 265
Number of shares now borrowed upon, ... 62
Largest number of shares held by any one member, ... 25
Number of shares withdrawn during the year, ... 120
Number of shares forfeited during the year, ... 16
Highest per centum of interest received during the year : $6\frac{3}{10}$.
Lowest per centum of interest received during the year : 6.
Number of members withdrawn during the year, ... 32
Present number of members, ... 45
Present number of borrowers, ... 15
Present number of non-borrowers, ... 30
Number of loans secured by first mortgage of real estate, . . . 3
Number of loans on shares, ... 12
Largest loan to any one member, ... $1,400 00
Smallest loan to any one member, ... 20 00
Amount of expenses of the corporation for the year ending Oct. 31, 1894, . 85 08
Date of examination by commissioner : August 1.

BALDWINSVILLE CO-OPERATIVE BANK — BALDWINS-VILLE.

Incorporated July 16, 1889. Commenced business July 24, 1889.

H. M. SMALL, *President.* GEORGE E. BRYANT, *Secretary.*
GEORGE E. BRYANT, *Treasurer.*

Names of security committee:

GEORGE PARTRIDGE, E. N. MULLINS,
E. L. THOMPSON.

Regular meetings the fourth Wednesday of each month.

BALANCE SHEET OCTOBER 31, 1894.

ASSETS.		LIABILITIES.	
Loans on real estate, . .	$16,300 00	Dues capital, . . .	$18,550 00
Loans on shares, . . .	1,160 00	Profits capital (all series), .	2,355 37
Permanent expense account, .	63 79	Interest, ...	198 70
Temporary expense account,	16 64	Premiums, ...	23 47
Unpaid fines, . . .	21 24	Surplus, ...	227 08
Note of town of Templeton;		Guaranty fund, . . .	172 00
Mass., ...	1,500 00	Withdrawal profits, . .	6 84
Cash in hands of treasurer, .	2,471 79		
	$21,533 46		$21,533 46

Detailed Statement of Receipts and Disbursements for the Year ending Oct. 31, 1894.

RECEIPTS.		DISBURSEMENTS.	
From dues capital, . .	$5,106 00	For real estate loans, . .	$4,450 00
interest, . . .	1,003 38	share loans, . . .	1,750 00
premiums, . . .	88 06	dues capital (withdrawn),	2,296 00
fines, ...	48 86	profits capital (with-	
real estate loans repaid,	2,400 00	drawn), . . .	276 51
share loans repaid, .	1,370 00	temporary expenses, .	53 46
withdrawal profits, .	69 15		
Cash on hand Oct. 31, 1893, .	1,212 31	Cash on hand Oct. 31, 1894,	2,471 79
	$11,297 76		$11,297 76

Reconciliation of Share Account with Dues and Profits Capital.

DATE OF ISSUE.	Series.	Value per Share.	Shares in Force.	Total Value.		
July, 1889, .	1	$73 84	174	$12,848 16	Dues capital, as per general ledger, . .	$18,550 00
Jan., 1890, .	2	65 94	8	527 52		
July, 1890, .	3	58 24	27	1,572 48	Profits capital, as per general ledger, . .	2,355 37
Jan., 1891, .	4	50 75	35	1,776 25		
July, 1891, .	5	43 45	10	434 50	Unpaid dues, . . .	403 00
Jan., 1892, .	6	36 41	57	2,075 37		
July, 1892, .	7	29 55	29	856 95		
Jan., 1893, .	8	22 88	21	480 48		
July, 1893, .	9	16 40	17	278 80		
Jan., 1894, .	10	10 11	26	262 86		
July, 1894, .	11	4 00	40	160 00		
Dues paid in advance, . . .				35 00		
Total, ...				$21,308 37	Total, . . .	$21,308 37

Number of shares issued during the year, ... 78
Number of shares now in force, ... 444
Number of shares now borrowed upon, ... 120
Largest number of shares held by any one member, ... 25
Number of shares withdrawn during the year, ... 58
Highest per centum of interest received during the year: $6\frac{1}{2}$.
Lowest per centum of interest received during the year: 6.
Number of members withdrawn during the year, ... 12
Present number of members, ... 78
Present number of borrowers, ... 21
Present number of non-borrowers, ... 57
Number of loans secured by first mortgage of real estate, . . . 17
Number of loans on shares, ... 4
Largest loan to any one member, ... $2,000 00
Smallest loan to any one member, ... 50 00
Amount of expenses of the corporation for the year ending Oct. 31, 1894. . 68 41
Date of examination by commissioner: February 6.

BERKSHIRE COUNTY CO-OPERATIVE BANK — NORTH ADAMS.

Incorporated Nov. 8, 1890. Commenced business Nov. 19, 1890.

GEORGE H. KEARN, *President.*   C. W. FORD, *Secretary.*

C. W. FORD, *Treasurer.*

Names of security committee:

R. E. SCHOULER,   W. C. ELLIS,

M. R. FORD.

Regular meetings the third Monday of each month.

BALANCE SHEET OCTOBER 31, 1894.

ASSETS.			LIABILITIES.		
Loans on real estate, . .	$25,450	00	Dues capital, . . .	$27,680	00
Loans on shares, ...	2,495	00	Profits capital (all series), .	2,173	02
Permanent expense account,	337	40	Surplus, ...	21	45
Personal note,* . . .	60	00	Guaranty fund, . . .	25	11
Cash in hands of treasurer, .	1,557	18			
	$29,899	58		$29,899	58

* This illegal investment has been eliminated from the assets.

Detailed Statement of Receipts and Disbursements for the Year ending Oct. 31, 1894.

RECEIPTS.			DISBURSEMENTS.		
From dues capital, . .	$13,346	00	For real estate loans, . .	$11,100	00
interest, . . .	1,427	83	share loans, . . .	3,195	00
premiums, . . .	10	64	dues capital (withdrawn), .	3,262	00
fines, ...	47	96	profits capital (with-		
transfer fees, . .	3	00	drawn), . . .	168	84
real estate loans repaid,	2,900	00	temporary expenses, .	271	00
share loans repaid, .	1,750	00	note, ...	60	00
withdrawal profits, .	50	18			
Cash on hand Oct. 31, 1893, .	78	41	Cash on hand Oct. 31, 1894,	1,557	18
	$19,614	02		$19,614	02

Reconciliation of Share Account with Dues and Profits Capital.

DATE OF ISSUE.	Series.	Value per Share.	Shares in Force.	Total Value.		
Nov., 1890, .	1	$53 02	300	$15,906 00	Dues capital, as per general ledger, . . .	$27,680 00
April 1891, .	2	47 22	10	472 20	Profits capital, as per general ledger, . .	
Nov., 1891, .	3	39 08	40	1,563 20		2,173 02
May, 1892, .	4	32 16	36	1,157 76	Unpaid dues, . .	20 00
Nov., 1892, .	5	25 37	177	4,490 49		
May, 1893, .	6	18 76	120	2,251 20		
Nov., 1893, .	7	12 34	194	2,393 96		
May, 1894, .	8	6 09	269	1,638 21		
Total, ...				$29,873 02	Total, . . .	$29,873 02

Number of shares issued during the year, ... 559	
Number of shares now in force, ... 1,146	
Number of shares now borrowed upon, ... 319	
Largest number of shares held by any one member, ... 25	
Number of shares withdrawn during the year, ... 192	
Highest per centum of interest received during the year: 7½.	
Lowest per centum of interest received during the year: 6.	
Number of members withdrawn during the year, ... 25	
Present number of members, ... 136	
Present number of borrowers, ... 43	
Present number of non-borrowers, ... 93	
Number of loans secured by first mortgage of real estate, . . . 26	
Number of loans on shares, ... 17	
Largest loan to any one member, ...	$3,000 00
Smallest loan to any one member, ...	25 00
Amount of expenses of the corporation for the year ending Oct. 31, 1894,	291 00
Date of examination by commissioner: February 26.	

BEVERLY CO-OPERATIVE BANK — BEVERLY.

Incorporated Aug. 25, 1888.   Commenced business Sept. 18, 1888.

GEORGE P. BROWN, *President.*   HARRIE L. OBER, *Secretary.*
CHARLES F. LEE, *Treasurer.*

Names of security committee :
GEORGE P. BROWN,   GEORGE BUTMAN,
JOHN R. MOULTON.

Regular meetings the third Tuesday of each month.

BALANCE SHEET OCTOBER 31, 1894.

ASSETS.		LIABILITIES.	
Loans on real estate,	$101,200 00	Dues capital,	$91,261 00
Loans on shares,	1,860 00	Profits capital (all series),	12,525 45
Permanent expense account,	354 25	Interest,	79 39
Unpaid premiums,	15 45	Transfer fees,	25
Unpaid fines,	47 06	Surplus,	733 03
Cash in hands of treasurer,	1,711 66	Guaranty fund,	358 31
		Forfeited share account,	136 30
		Withdrawal profits,	94 69
	$105,188 42		$105,188 42

Detailed Statement of Receipts and Disbursements for the Year ending Oct. 31, 1894.

RECEIPTS.		DISBURSEMENTS.	
From dues capital,	$28,957 00	For real estate loans,	$31,000 00
interest,	5,499 01	share loans,	1,585 00
premiums,	323 67	dues capital (withdrawn),	9,332 00
fines,	271 51	dues capital (retired),	5,465 00
transfer fees,	1 25	profits capital (withdrawn),	1,053 48
real estate loans repaid,	11,775 00	profits capital (retired),	1,028 80
share loans repaid,	3,245 00	temporary expenses,	409 12
withdrawal profits,	250 62	permanent expenses,	14 25
real estate by foreclosure,	228 10		
sale of envelopes,	29 10		
Cash on hand Oct. 31, 1893,	1,019 05	Cash on hand Oct. 31, 1894,	1,711 66
	$51,599 31		$51,599 31

Reconciliation of Share Account with Dues and Profits Capital.

DATE OF ISSUE.	Series.	Value per Share.	Shares in Force.	Total Value.		
Sept., 1888, .	1	$88 58	389	$34,457 62	Dues capital, as per general ledger, . .	$91,261 00
Mar., 1889, .	2	80 14	178	14,264 92		
Sept., 1889, .	3	71 94	80	5,755 20	Profits capital, as per general ledger, . .	12,525 45
Mar., 1890, .	4	63 98	106	6,781 88		
Sept., 1890, .	5	56 25	129	7,256 25	Unpaid dues, . . .	1,554 00
Mar., 1891, .	6	48 74	121	5,897 54		
Sept., 1891, .	7	41 45	137	5,678 65		
Mar., 1892, .	8	34 37	233	8,008 21		
Sept., 1892, .	9	27 50	228	6,270 00		
Mar., 1893, .	10	20 84	235	4,897 40		
Sept., 1893, .	11	14 38	196	2,818 48		
Mar., 1894, .	12	8 10	333	2,697 30		
Sept., 1894, .	13	2 00	221	442 00		
Dues paid in advance, . . .				115 00		
Total, ...				$105,340 45	Total, . . .	$105,340 45

Number of shares issued during the year, ... 618
Number of shares now in force, ... 2,586
Number of shares now borrowed upon, ... 625
Largest number of shares held by any one member, ... 25
Number of shares withdrawn during the year, ... 304
Number of shares retired during the year, ... 87
Highest per centum of interest received during the year: 6_{16}^{9}.
Lowest per centum of interest received during the year : 6.
Number of members withdrawn during the year, ... 102
Present number of members, ... 410
Present number of borrowers, ... 97
Present number of non-borrowers, ... 313
Number of loans secured by first mortgage of real estate, . . . 90
Number of loans on shares, ... 22
Largest loan to any one member, ... $4,500 00
Smallest loan to any one member, ... 20 00
Amount of expenses of the corporation for the year ending Oct. 31, 1894, . 440 02
Date of examination by commissioner: February 26.

BOSTON CO-OPERATIVE BANK—BOSTON.

Incorporated April 30, 1888. Commenced business May 2, 1888.

EUGENE M. SMITH, *President.*   GEORGE T. BOSSON, *Secretary.*
GEORGE T. BOSSON, *Treasurer.*

Names of security committee:

GEORGE T. BOSSON,   EUGENE M. SMITH,
HENRY M. SANDERS.

Regular meetings the first Monday of each month.

BALANCE SHEET OCTOBER 31, 1894.

ASSETS.			LIABILITIES.		
Loans on real estate, . .	$134,575	00	Dues capital, . . .	$142,151	00
Loans on shares, . . .	9,715	00	Profits capital (all series), .	23,649	61
Permanent expense account,	270	14	Surplus, ...	2,017	65
Unpaid interest, . . .	1,187	23	Guaranty fund, . . .	821	12
Unpaid premiums, . .	375	75	Forfeited share account, .	27	92
Unpaid fines, ...	491	58			
Suspense account, . . .	8	19			
Russell estate, . . .	1	00			
Cash in hands of treasurer, .	22,043	41			
	$168,667	30		$168,667	30

Detailed Statement of Receipts and Disbursements for the Year ending Oct. 31, 1894.

RECEIPTS.			DISBURSEMENTS.		
From dues capital, . .	$54,211	00	For real estate loans, . .	$39,975	00
interest, . . .	9,728	04	share loans, . . .	9,545	00
premiums, . . .	1,339	80	dues capital(withdrawn),	39,168	00
fines, ...	682	15	dues capital (forfeited),	197	00
transfer fees, . .	5	75	dues capital (retired), .	8,402	00
real estate loans repaid,	54,200	00	profits capital (with-		
share loans repaid, .	6,835	00	drawn), . . .	5,135	64
withdrawal profits, .	1,334	89	profits capital(forfeited),	28	27
forfeited shares, . .	82	32	profits capital (retired),	1,849	14
real estate, . . .	74	57	temporary expenses, .	1,366	46
suspense, . . .	6	00	permanent expenses, .	480	25
			forfeited shares, . .	80	65
			real estate, . . .	43	12
			suspense, . . .	225	50
			profit and loss, . .	27	89
Cash on hand Oct. 31, 1893, .	67	81	Cash on hand Oct. 31, 1894, .	22,043	41
	$128,567	33		$128,567	33

Reconciliation of Share Account with Dues and Profits Capital.

DATE OF ISSUE.	Series.	Value per Share.	Shares in Force.	Total Value.		
May, 1888, .	1	$98 65	314	$30,976 10	Dues capital, as per general ledger, . . .	$142,151 00
Nov., 1888, .	2	89 38	198	17,697 24		
May, 1889, .	3	80 45	194	15,607 30	Profits capital, as per general ledger, . .	23,649 61
Nov., 1889, .	4	71 82	137	9,839 34		
May, 1890, .	5	63 48	369	23,424 12	Unpaid dues, . .	1,723 00
Nov., 1890, .	6	55 42	127	7,038 34		
May, 1891, .	7	47 62	232	11,047 84		
Nov., 1891, .	8	40 10	287	11,508 70		
May, 1892, .	9	32 82	356	11,683 92		
Nov., 1892..	10	25 80	324	8,359 20		
May, 1893, .	11	19 01	503	9,562 03		
Nov., 1893, .	12	12 45	360	4,482 00		
May, 1894, .	13	6 12	1,029	6,297 48		
Total, ...				$167,523 61	Total, . . .	$167,523 61

Number of shares issued during the year, ... 1,671
Number of shares now in force, ... 4,430
Number of shares now borrowed upon, ... 1,025
Largest number of shares held by any one member, . . . 25
Number of shares withdrawn during the year, ... 1,421
Number of shares forfeited during the year, ... 11
Number of shares retired during the year, ... 121
Highest premium received during the year, ... $0 80
Lowest premium received during the year, ... 05
Number of members withdrawn during the year, ... 146
Present number of members, ... 515
Present number of borrowers, ... 93
Present number of non-borrowers, ... 422
Number of loans secured by first mortgage of real estate, . . . 72
Number of loans on shares, ... 37
Largest loan to any one member, ... 5,000 00
Smallest loan to any one member, ... 50 00
Amount of expenses of the corporation for the year ending Oct. 31, 1894, . 1,646 57
Date of examination by commissioner: November 26.

BRAINTREE CO-OPERATIVE BANK — BRAINTREE.

Incorporated June 24, 1889. Commenced business Oct. 15, 1889.

JAMES T. STEVENS, *President.*   CHARLES B. CUMMINGS, *Secretary.*
CHARLES B. CUMMINGS, *Treasurer.*

Names of security committee :
ANSEL O. CLARK,   F. A. HOBART,
JAMES T. STEVENS.

Regular meetings the third Tuesday of each month.

BALANCE SHEET OCTOBER 31, 1894.

ASSETS.			LIABILITIES.		
Loans on real estate,	.	$27,700 00	Dues capital,	. . .	$27,241 00
Loans on shares,	. . .	2,870 00	Profits capital (all series),	.	3,339 18
Permanent expense account,	.	55 00	Interest,	. . : .	574 57
Forfeiture profits,	. .	20	Premiums,	. . . .	29 79
Cash in hands of treasurer,	.	1,003 74	Fines,	. . . .	20 26
			Surplus,	. . .	244 42
			Guaranty fund,	. .	52 60
			Forfeited share account,	.	72 72
			Withdrawal profits,	. .	52 54
			Suspense account,	. .	1 86
		$31,628 94			$31,628 94

Detailed Statement of Receipts and Disbursements for the Year ending Oct. 31, 1894.

RECEIPTS.			DISBURSEMENTS.		
From dues capital,	.	$7,246 00	For real estate loans,	. .	$8,890 00
interest,	. .	1,666 60	share loans,	. . .	3,000 00
premiums,	. .	93 74	dues capital (withdrawn),		3,939 00
fines,	. . .	108 43	dues capital (forfeited),		25 00
real estate loans repaid,		3,600 00	profits capital (withdrawn),		411 18
share loans repaid,	.	2,735 00	profits capital (forfeited),		1 90
withdrawal profits,	.	102 95	temporary expenses,	.	165 50
forfeiture profits,	.	48	Cash on hand Oct. 31, 1894,		1,003 74
Cash on hand Oct. 31, 1893,	.	1,883 12			
		$17,436 32			$17,436 32

Reconciliation of Share Account with Dues and Profits Capital.

DATE OF ISSUE.	Series.	Value per Share.	Shares in Force.	Total Value.		
Oct., 1889, .	1	$69 63	272	$18,939 36	Dues capital, as per general ledger, . . .	$27,241 00
Dec., 1889, .	2	66 99	36	2,411 64		
June, 1890, .	3	59 26	47	2,785 22	Profits capital, as per general ledger, . .	3,339 18
Dec., 1890, .	4	51 76	23	1,190 48		
June, 1891, .	5	44 46	30	1,333 80	Unpaid dues, . .	689 00
Dec., 1891, .	6	37 39	48	1,794 72		
June, 1892, .	7	30 52	28	854 56		
Dec., 1892, .	8	23 85	24	572 40		
June, 1893, .	9	17 38	40	695 20		
Dec., 1893, .	10	11 10	38	421 80		
June, 1894, .	11	5 00	49	245 00		
Dues paid in advance, . . .				25 00		
Total, ...				$31,269 18	Total, . . .	$31,269 18

Number of shares issued during the year, ... 87
Number of shares now in force, ... 635
Number of shares now borrowed upon, . . : . . . 246
Largest number of shares held by any one member, . . . 25
Number of shares withdrawn during the year, ... 127
Number of shares forfeited during the year, ... 5
Highest premium received during the year, ... $0 05
Lowest premium received during the year, ... 05
Number of members withdrawn during the year, ... 15
Present number of members, ... 106
Present number of borrowers, ... 40
Present number of non-borrowers, ... 66
Number of loans secured by first mortgage of real estate, . . . 29
Number of loans on shares, ... 15
Largest loan to any one member, ... 2,000 00
Smallest loan to any one member, ... 15 00
Amount of expenses of the corporation for the year ending Oct. 31, 1894, . 185 68
Date of examination by commissioner: November 16.

CAMBRIDGE CO-OPERATIVE BANK — EAST CAMBRIDGE.

Incorporated Sept. 5, 1877.   Commenced business Sept. 12, 1877.

Rufus R. Wade, *President.*   John H. Ponce, *Secretary.*
John Loughrey, *Treasurer.*

Names of security committee:

John Loughrey,   George S. Keeler,
Charles A. Messer.

Regular meetings the second Wednesday of each month.

BALANCE SHEET OCTOBER 31, 1894.

ASSETS.		LIABILITIES.	
Loans on real estate,	$33,100 00	Dues capital,	$31,603 00
Loans on shares,	3,990 00	Profits capital (all series),	5,817 13
Permanent expense account,	22 76	Interest,	688 50
Temporary expense account,	116 33	Premiums,	67 72
Unpaid dues,	343 00	Fines,	21 08
Unpaid interest,	205 40	Guaranty fund,	114 43
Unpaid premiums,	20 95	Forfeited share account,	9 66
Unpaid fines,	21 04	Profit and loss,	71 65
Sundry balances,	1 05	Suspense,	7 00
Cash in hands of treasurer,	579 64		
	$38,400 17		$38,400 17

Detailed Statement of Receipts and Disbursements for the Year ending Oct. 31, 1894.

RECEIPTS.		DISBURSEMENTS.	
From dues capital,	$7,949 00	For real estate loans,	$5,000 00
interest,	1,923 18	share loans,	1,895 00
premiums,	192 32	dues capital (withdrawn),	4,518 00
fines,	80 26	dues capital (matured),	1,425 00
real estate loans repaid,	1,300 00	profits capital (withdrawn),	564 46
share loans repaid,	2,120 00	profits capital (matured),	588 85
withdrawal profits,	188 08	temporary expenses,	362 99
personal account,	4 00	permanent expenses,	6 50
		int. on matured shares,	40 10
		sundry balances,	5 87
Cash on hand Oct. 31, 1893,	1,229 57	Cash on hand Oct. 31, 1894,	579 64
	$14,986 41		$14,986 41

Reconciliation of Share Account with Dues and Profits Capital.

DATE OF ISSUE.	Series.	Value per Share.	Shares in Force.	Total Value.		
Jan., 1884, .	25	$177 08	9	$1,593 72	Dues capital, as per general ledger, . .	$31,603 00
April, 1884, .	26	171 87	10	1,718 70	Profits capital, as per general ledger, . .	5,817 13
July, 1884, .	27	166 60	6	999 60		
Jan., 1885, .	29	156 45	3	469 35		
April, 1885, .	30	151 37	5	756 85		
Jan., 1886, .	32	136 47	42	5,731 74		
July, 1886, .	33	126 87	6	761 22		
Jan., 1887, .	34	117 42	19	2,230 98		
July, 1887, .	35	108 26	13	1,407 38		
Jan., 1888, .	36	99 30	24	2,383 20		
July, 1888, .	37	90 63	5	453 15		
Jan., 1889, .	38	82 24	29	2,384 96		
July, 1889, .	39	74 08	21	1,555 68		
Jan., 1890, .	40	66 16	37	2,447 92		
July, 1890, .	41	58 40	27	1,576 80		
Jan., 1891, .	42	50 83	39	1,982 37		
July, 1891, .	43	43 47	71	3,086 37		
Jan., 1892, .	44	36 41	53	1,929 73		
July, 1892, .	45	29 53	41	1,210 73		
Jan., 1893, .	46	22 85	69	1,576 65		
July, 1893, .	47	16 37	22	360 14		
Jan., 1894, .	48	10 09	65	655 85		
July, 1894, .	49	4 00	33	132 00		
Suspense profits, . .				15 04		
Total, ...				$37,420 13	Total, . . .	$37,420 13

Number of shares issued during the year, ...	108
Number of shares now in force, ...	649
Number of shares now borrowed upon, ...	255
Largest number of shares held by any one member, . . .	25
Number of shares withdrawn during the year, . . .	144
Number of shares matured during the year, ...	10
Highest premium received during the year, ...	$0 10
Lowest premium received during the year, ...	05
Number of members withdrawn during the year, . . .	19
Present number of members, ...	92
Present number of borrowers, ...	40
Present number of non-borrowers, ...	52
Number of loans secured by first mortgage of real estate, . .	29
Number of loans on shares, ...	30
Largest loan to any one member, ...	3,000 00
Smallest loan to any one member, ...	15 00
Amount of expenses of the corporation for the year ending Oct. 31, 1894, .	377 74

Date of examination by commissioner: October 6.

CAMPELLO CO-OPERATIVE BANK—BROCKTON.

Incorporated Oct. 3, 1877.   Commenced business Oct. 8, 1877.

PRESTON B. KEITH, *President.*   WARREN T. COPELAND, *Secretary.*
WARREN T. COPELAND, *Treasurer.*

Names of security committee:

JOHN A. HOWARD,   NATHAN H. WASHBURN,
CHARLES H. COLE.

Regular meetings the second Monday of each month.

BALANCE SHEET OCTOBER 31, 1894.

ASSETS.		LIABILITIES.	
Loans on real estate,	$270,870 00	Dues capital,	$252,200 00
Loans on shares,	3,350 00	Profits capital (all series),	37,466 31
Permanent expense account,	280 00	Interest,	1,460 25
Temporary expense account,	118 82	Premiums,	366 26
Real estate by foreclosure,	2,781 44	Fines,	69 16
Unpaid interest,	1,529 00	Transfer fees,	1 00
Unpaid premiums,	382 41	Surplus,	2,145 59
Unpaid fines,	190 12	Guaranty fund,	750 00
Real estate mortgage,	1,000 00	Forfeited share account,	99 36
Cash in hands of treasurer,	14,458 26	Withdrawal profits,	370 83
		Interest on deposits,	31 29
	$294,960 05		$294,960 05

Detailed Statement of Receipts and Disbursements for the Year ending Oct. 31, 1894.

RECEIPTS.		DISBURSEMENTS.	
From dues capital,	$118,560 00	For real estate loans,	$64,620 00
interest,	18,608 03	share loans,	6,050 00
premiums,	4,558 71	dues capital (withdrawn),	54,468 00
fines,	882 69	dues capital (forfeited),	348 00
transfer fees,	11 00	dues capital (retired),	85,872 00
real estate loans repaid,	99,400 00	dues capital (matured),	5,016 00
share loans repaid,	8,300 00	profits capital (with-	
withdrawal profits,	1,580 56	drawn),	6,307 33
forfeiture profits,	26 73	profits capital (forfeited),	52 08
forfeited shares,	364 88	profits capital (retired),	18,379 54
foreclosures,	1,382 93	profits capital (matured),	2,834 04
public funds,	4,000 00	temporary expenses,	1,415 33
rent and rebate on in-		forfeited shares,	356 98
surance,	46 16	Interest on retired shares,	1,488 33
sale of real estate,	1,250 00	foreclosures,	2,292 32
		foreclosures, expenses,	74 91
		taxes and insurance,	19 75
		real estate,	150 00
Cash on hand Oct. 31, 1893,	5,231 18	Cash on hand Oct. 31, 1894,	14,458 26
	$264,202 87		$264,202 87

Reconciliation of Share Account with Dues and Profits Capital.

DATE OF ISSUE.	Series.	Value per Share.	Shares in Force.	Total Value.		
Oct., 1884, .	8	$180 87	63	$11,394 81	Dues capital, as per general ledger, .	$252,200 00
Oct., 1885, .	9	156 06	23	3,589 38	eral ledger, . .	
April, 1886, .	10	144 44	8	1,155 52	Profits capital, as per	
Oct., 1886, .	11	133 17	21	2,796 57	general ledger, . .	37,466 31
April, 1887, .	12	122 38	25	3,050 50	Unpaid dues, . . .	2,253 00
Oct., 1887, .	13	111 97	34	3,806 98		
April, 1888, .	14	101 95	43	4,383 85		
Oct., 1888, .	15	92 30	32	2,953 60		
April, 1889, .	16	83 00	59	4,897 00		
Oct , 1889, .	17	74 05	332	24,584 60		
April, 1890, .	18	65 43	469	30,686 67		
Oct., 1890, .	19	57 12	559	31,930 08		
April, 1891, .	20	49 12	617	30,307 04		
Oct., 1891, .	21	41 43	789	32,688 27		
April, 1892, .	22	34 03	761	25,896 83		
Oct., 1892, .	23	26 92	1,078	29,019 76		
April, 1893, .	24	20 07	1,131	22,699 17		
Oct., 1893, .	25	13 47	1,040	14,008 80		
April, 1894, .	26	7 12	1,349	9,604 88		
Oct., 1894, .	27	1 00	1,631	1,631 00		
Dues paid in advance, . . .				825 00		
Total, ...				$291,919 31	Total, ...	$291,919 31

Number of shares issued during the year, ... 3,582
Number of shares now in force, ... 10,064
Number of shares now borrowed upon, ... 1,542
Largest number of shares held by any one member, ... 25
Number of shares withdrawn during the year, ... 2,390
Number of shares forfeited during the year, ... 18
Number of shares retired during the year, ... 1,300
Number of shares matured during the year, ... 38
Highest premium received during the year, ... $0 25
Lowest premium received during the year, ... 25
Number of members withdrawn during the year, ... 290
Present number of members, ... 1,093
Present number of borrowers, ... 214
Present number of non-borrowers, ... 879
Number of loans secured by first mortgage of real estate, . . . 201
Number of loans on shares, ... 27
Largest loan to any one member, ... 5,000 00
Smallest loan to any one member, ... 50 00
Amount of expenses of the corporation for the year ending Oct. 31, 1894, . 1,455 33
Date of examination by commissioner: March 8.

CANTON CO-OPERATIVE BANK — CANTON.

Incorporated Jan. 10, 1891.   Commenced business Feb. 10, 1891.

EPHRAIM B. THORNDIKE, *President.*   JOSEPH W. WATTLES, Jr., *Secretary.*
JOSEPH W. WATTLES, Jr., *Treasurer.*

Names of security committee :

CHARLES GALLIGAN,   ⋅ WM. W. BROOKS,
JOSEPH W. WATTLES.

Regular meetings the second Tuesday of each month.

BALANCE SHEET OCTOBER 31, 1894.

ASSETS.		LIABILITIES.	
Loans on real estate, . .	$56,900 00	Dues capital, . . .	$52,427 00
Loans on shares, . . .	630 00	Profits capital (all series), .	4,420 80
Permanent expense account,.	35 00	Interest, ...	974 70
Temporary expense account,	8 00	Premiums, ...	84 00
Unpaid interest, . . .	281 50	Fines, ...	32 35
Unpaid premiums, . ⋅ .	34 80	Surplus, ...	332 17
Unpaid fines, ...	26 21	Guaranty fund, . . .	137 02
Cash in hands of treasurer, .	. 575 18	Withdrawal profits, . .	82 65
	$58,490 69		$58,490 69

Detailed Statement of Receipts and Disbursements for the Year ending Oct. 31, 1894.

RECEIPTS.		DISBURSEMENTS.	
From dues capital, . .	$23,274 00	For real estate loans, . .	$22,950 00
interest, . . .	3,016 18	share loans, . . .	1,750 00
premiums, . . .	252 60	dues capital (withdrawn),	11,073 00
fines, ...	95 43	profits capital (with-	
transfer fees, . .	1 00	drawn, . . .	915 97
real estate loans repaid,	9,050 00	temporary expenses, .	221 10
share loans repaid, .	1,500 00		
withdrawal profits, .	229 35		
Cash on hand Oct. 31, 1893, .	66 69	Cash on hand Oct. 31, 1894,	575 18
	$37,485 25		$37,485 25

Reconciliation of Share Account with Dues and Profits Capital.

DATE OF ISSUE.	Series.	Value per Share.	Shares In Force.	Total Value.		
Feb., 1891, .	1	$50 20	325	$16,315 00	Dues capital, as per general ledger, . .	$52,427 00
Aug., 1891, .	2	42 78	374	15,999 72		
Feb., 1892, .	3	35 59	307	10,926 13	Profits capital, as per general ledger, . .	4,420 80
Aug , 1892, .	4	28 65	164	4,698 60		
Feb., 1893, .	5	21 93	185	4,057 05	Unpaid dues, . .	359 00
Aug., 1893, .	6	15 42	116	1,788 72		
Feb., 1894, .	7	9 11	278	2,532 58		
Aug., 1894, .	8	3 00	237	711 00		
Dues paid in advance, . . .				178 00		
Total, ...				$57,206 80	Total, . . .	$57,206 80

Number of shares issued during the year, ... 619
Number of shares now in force, ... 1,986
Number of shares now borrowed upon, ... 338
Largest number of shares held by any one member, . . . 25
Number of shares withdrawn during the year, ... 456
Highest premium received during the year, ... $0 10
Lowest premium received during the year, ... 05
Number of members withdrawn during the year, ... 51
Present number of members, ... 259
Present number of borrowers, ... 52
Present number of non-borrowers, ... 207
Number of loans secured by first mortgage of real estate, . . . 66
Number of loans on shares, ... 6
Largest loan to any one member, ... 2,800 00
Smallest loan to any one member, ... 30 00
Amount of expenses of the corporation for the year ending Oct. 31, 1894, . 251 10
Date of examination by commissioner: June 14.

CITIZENS' CO-OPERATIVE BANK — HAVERHILL.

Incorporated Aug. 22, 1887.   Commenced business Sept. 12, 1887.

GEO. H. CARLETON, *President.*   JAMES W. GOODWIN, *Secretary.*
                    JAMES W. GOODWIN, *Treasurer.*

Names of security committee:

JOSHUA M. STORER,   JOHN A. GALE,
          GEORGE M. GOODWIN.

Regular meetings the second Monday of each month.

BALANCE SHEET OCTOBER 31, 1894.

ASSETS.		LIABILITIES.	
Loans on real estate, . .	$83,885 00	Dues capital, . . .	$79,586 00
Loans on shares, . . .	4,880 00	Profits capital (all series), .	11,203 99
Unpaid interest, . . .	163 04	Premiums, ...	3 95
Cash in hands of treasurer, .	4,473 15	Fines, ...	2 28
		Surplus, ...	1,080 81
		Guaranty fund, . . .	255 24
		Forfeited share account, .	1,207 47
		Withdrawal profits, . .	13 95
		Forfeiture profits, . .	47 50
	$93,401 19		$93,401 19

Detailed Statement of Receipts and Disbursements for the Year ending Oct. 31, 1894.

RECEIPTS.		DISBURSEMENTS.	
From dues capital, . .	$29,153 00	For real estate loans, . .	$20,859 98
interest, . . .	5,251 36	share loans, . . .	6,067 00
premiums, . . .	97 10	dues capital(withdrawn),	23,834 00
fines, ...	157 00	dues capital (forfeited),	1,306 00
real estate loans repaid,	28,809 98	dues capital (retired), .	7,968 00
share loans repaid, .	3,817 00	profits capital (with-	
withdrawal profits, .	211 11	drawn), . . .	2,053 93
forfeiture profits, . .	120 90	profits capital (forfeited),	175 52
forfeited shares, . .	1,176 77	profits capital (retired),	1,542 52
		temporary expenses, .	900 00
		forfeited shares, . .	100 00
Cash on hand Oct. 31, 1893, .	485 88	Cash on hand Oct. 31, 1894,	4,473 15
	$69,280 10		$69,280 10

Reconciliation of Share Account with Dues and Profits Capital.

DATE OF ISSUE.	Series.	Value per Share.	Shares in Force.	Total Value.		
Sept., 1887, .	1	$104 21	249	$25,948 29	Dues capital, as per general ledger, . .	$79,586 00
April, 1888, .	2	94 34	90	8,490 60	Profits capital, as per general ledger, . .	
Oct., 1888, .	3	86 08	84	7,230 72		11,203 99
April, 1889, .	4	78 00	57	4,446 00	Unpaid dues, . .	1,168 00
Oct., 1889, .	5	70 10	25	1,752 50		
April, 1890, .	6	62 38	91	5,676 58		
Oct., 1890, .	7	54 84	122	6,690 48		
April, 1891, .	8	47 48	116	5,507 68		
Oct., 1891, .	9	40 30	110	4,433 00		
April, 1892, .	10	33 30	205	6,826 50		
Oct., 1892, .	11	26 48	216	5,719 68		
April, 1893, .	12	19 84	189	3,749 76		
Oct., 1893, .	13	13 38	240	3,211 20		
April, 1894, .	14	7 10	280	1,988 00		
Oct., 1894, .	15	1 00	176	176 00		
Dues paid in advance, . . .				111 00		
Total, ...				$91,957 99	Total, . . .	$91,957 99

Number of shares issued during the year, ... 585
Number of shares now in force, ... 2,250
Number of shares now borrowed upon, ... 671
Largest number of shares held by any one member, . . . 25
Number of shares withdrawn during the year, ... 807
Number of shares forfeited during the year, ... 61
Number of shares retired during the year, ... 98
Highest per centum of interest received during the year: 6.
Lowest per centum of interest received during the year: 6.
Number of members withdrawn during the year, ... 75
Present number of members, ... 256
Present number of borrowers, ... 67
Present number of non-borrowers, ... 189
Number of loans secured by first mortgage of real estate, . . . 52
Number of loans on shares, ... 15
Largest loan to any one member, ... $5,000 00
Smallest loan to any one member, ... 10 00
Amount of expenses of the corporation for the year ending Oct. 31, 1894, . 980 24
Date of examination by commissioner: May 31.

CITY CO-OPERATIVE BANK — HOLYOKE.

Incorporated July 16, 1889.   Commenced business July 23, 1889.

A. F. Richard, *President.*   Pierre Bonvouloir, *Secretary.*
                      Pierre Bonvouloir, *Treasurer.*

Names of security committee :

Daniel Proulx,   A. F. Gingras,
                  John St. John.

Regular meetings the fourth Tuesday of each month.

BALANCE SHEET OCTOBER 31, 1894.

ASSETS.		LIABILITIES.	
Loans on real estate,	$30,650 00	Dues capital,	$43,920 00
Loans on shares,	15,250 00	Profits capital (all series),	4,516 62
Temporary expense account,	123 88	Interest,	1,101 94
Unpaid interest,	69 13	Fines,	38 78
Unpaid fines,	4 68	Transfer fees,	50
Cash in hands of treasurer,	3,858 84	Surplus,	162 97
		Guaranty fund,	110 00
		Withdrawal profits,	105 72
	$49,956 53		$49,956 53

Detailed Statement of Receipts and Disbursements for the Year ending Oct. 31, 1894.

RECEIPTS.		DISBURSEMENTS.	
From dues capital,	$15,076 00	For real estate loans,	$8,750 00
interest,	2,750 43	share loans,	11,100 00
fines,	79 64	dues capital (withdrawn),	10,070 00
transfer fees,	50	profits capital (with-	
real estate loans repaid,	12,200 00	drawn),	943 82
share loans repaid,	4,250 00	temporary expenses,	250 75
withdrawal profits,	234 04		
treasurer's book sold,	50		
Cash on hand Oct. 31, 1893,	382 30	Cash on hand Oct. 31, 1894,	3,858 84
	$34,973 41		$34,973 41

Reconciliation of Share Account with Dues and Profits Capital.

DATE OF ISSUE.	Series.	Value per Share.	Shares in Force.	Total Value.		
July, 1889, .	1	$73 52	210	$15,439 20	Dues capital, as per general ledger, . . .	$43,920 00
Jan., 1890, .	2	65 64	106	6,957 84		
July, 1890, .	3	58 05	26	1,509 30	Profits capital, as per general ledger, . .	4,516 62
Jan., 1891, .	4	50 58	163	8,244 54		
July, 1891, .	5	43 32	83	3,595 56	Unpaid dues, . . .	221 00
Jan., 1892, .	6	36 27	87	3,155 49		
July, 1892, .	7	29 43	114	3,355 02		
Jan., 1893, .	8	22 79	163	3,714 77		
July, 1893, .	9	16 34	101	1,650 34		
Jan., 1894, .	10	10 08	57	574 56		
July, 1894, .	11	4 00	114	456 00		
Dues paid in advance, . .				5 00		
Total, ...				$48,657 62		$48,657 62

Number of shares issued during the year, ... 202
Number of shares now in force, ... 1,224
Number of shares now borrowed upon, ... 647
Largest number of shares held by any one member, . . . 25
Number of shares withdrawn during the year, ... 383
Highest per centum of interest received during the year: 6.
Lowest per centum of interest received during the year: 6.
Number of members withdrawn during the year, ... 66
Present number of members, ... 196
Present number of borrowers, ... 75
Present number of non-borrowers, ... 121
Number of loans secured by first mortgage of real estate, . . . 37
Number of loans on shares, ... 115
Largest loan to any one member, ... $5,000 00
Smallest loan to any one member, ... 25 00
Amount of expenses of the corporation for the year ending Oct. 31, 1894, . 320 25
Date of examiation by commissioner: March 19.

CLINTON CO-OPERATIVE BANK — CLINTON.

Incorporated Sept. 23, 1887.   Commenced business Oct. 20, 1887.

DANIEL B. INGALLS, *President.*   WALTER R. DAME, *Secretary.*
THOMAS S. DAVIS, *Treasurer.*

Names of security committee:
GEORGE P. FRENCH,   LYMAN LEIGHTON,
HENRY C. GREELY.

Regular meetings the third Thursday of each month.

BALANCE SHEET OCTOBER 31, 1894.

ASSETS.		LIABILITIES.	
Loans on real estate, . .	$127,135 00	Dues capital, . . .	$123,455 00
Loans on shares, . . .	5,915 00	Profits capital (all series), .	18,874 99
Permanent expense account, .	150 00	Interest, ...	821 77
Temporary expense account, .	75 27	Fines, ...	33 58
Unpaid interest, . . .	519 76	Transfer fees, . .	25
Cash in hands of treasurer, .	10,162 96	Withdrawal profits, . .	48 21
		Guaranty fund, . .	361 41
		Surplus, . . .	355 54
		Forfeited share account, .	5 74
		Security committee, .	1 50
	$143,957 99		$143,957 99

Detailed Statement of Receipts and Disbursements for the Year ending Oct. 31, 1894.

RECEIPTS.		DISBURSEMENTS.	
From dues capital, .	$38,476 00	For real estate loans, . .	$41,200 00
interest, . . .	8,161 72	share loans, . . .	5,145 00
fines, . . .	197 03	dues capital (withdrawn),	18,233 00
transfer fees, .	2 75	dues capital (retired), .	6,726 00
real estate loans repaid,	29,900 00	profits capital (with-	
share loans repaid, .	6,045 00	drawn), . .	1,932 78
withdrawal profits, .	281 47	profits capital (retired), .	1,376 83
		temporary expenses, .	570 51
Cash on hand Oct. 31, 1893, .	2,283 11	Cash on hand Oct. 31, 1894,	10,162 96
	$85,347 08		$85,347 08

Reconciliation of Share Account with Dues and Profits Capital.

DATE OF ISSUE.	Series.	Value per Share.	Shares in Force.	Total Value.		
Oct., 1887, .	1	$105 92	191	$20,230 72	Dues capital, as per general ledger, . .	$123,455 00
April, 1888, .	2	96 79	118	11,421 22		
Oct., 1888, .	3	87 97	148	13,019 56	Profits capital, as per general ledger, . .	18,874 99
April, 1889, .	4	79 43	221	17,554 03		
Oct., 1889, .	5	71 17	196	13,949 32	Unpaid dues, . .	765 00
April, 1890, .	6	63 18	180	11,372 40		
Oct., 1890, .	7	55 43	200	11,086 00		
April, 1891, .	8	47 90	145	6,945 50		
Oct., 1891, .	9	40 57	273	11,075 61		
April, 1892, .	10	33 47	241	8,066 27		
Oct., 1892, .	11	26 59	255	6,780 45		
April, 1893, .	12	19 89	302	6,006 78		
Oct., 1893, .	13	13 39	187	2,503 93		
April, 1894, .	14	7 10	382	2,712 20		
Oct., 1894, .	15	1 00	253	253 00		
Dues paid in advance, . .				118 00		
Total, ...				$143,094 99	Total, . . .	$143,094 99

Number of shares issued during the year, ... 742
Number of shares now in force, ... 3,292
Number of shares now borrowed upon, ... 945
Largest number of shares held by any one member, . . . 25
Number of shares withdrawn during the year, ... 726
Number of shares retired during the year, ... 87
Highest per centum of interest received during the year : 13.
Lowest per centum of interest received during the year : 6.
Number of members withdrawn during the year, ... 126
Present number of members, ... 475
Present number of borrowers, ... 126
Present number of non-borrowers, ... 349
Number of loans secured by first mortgage of real estate, . . . 108
Number of loans on shares, ... 39
Largest loan to any one member, ... $4,900 00
Smallest loan to any one member, ... 50 00
Amount of expenses of the corporation for the year ending Oct. 31, 1894, . 570 51
Date of examination by commissioner : April 16.

COLUMBIAN CO-OPERATIVE BANK — CAMBRIDGE.

Incorporated May 6, 1892. Commenced business June 6, 1892.

ALPHEUS B. ALGER, *President.*   WILLIAM E. BURRAGE, *Secretary.*
WILLIAM E. BURRAGE, *Treasurer.*

Names of security committee :

JAMES A. DOW,   DANA W. HYDE,
CHARLES E. HANCOCK,   LEVI HAWKES,
ISAAC S. PEAR.

Regular meetings the first Monday of each month.

BALANCE SHEET OCTOBER 31, 1894.

ASSETS.		LIABILITIES.	
Loans on real estate,	$27,390 00	Dues capital,	$33,848 00
Loans on shares,	300 00	Profits capital (all series),	1,202 36
Permanent expense account,	216 50	Interest,	626 06
Temporary expense account,	40 47	Premiums,	45 30
Real estate by foreclosure,	2,093 99	Fines,	86 75
Unpaid interest,	255 80	Transfer fees,	50
Unpaid premiums,	13 15	Surplus,	37 17
Unpaid fines,	44 68	Guaranty fund,	15 32
City of Cambridge, four per cent. bonds,	3,217 83	Forfeited share account,	92 77
Cash in hands of secretary,	2,409 85	Withdrawal profits,	28 04
	$35,982 27		$35,982 27

Detailed Statement of Receipts and Disbursements for the Year ending Oct. 31, 1894.

RECEIPTS.		DISBURSEMENTS.	
From dues capital,	$19,514 00	For real estate loans,	$13,000 00
interest,	1,319 22	share loans,	760 00
premiums,	104 29	dues capital(withdrawn),	6,018 00
fines,	148 08	dues capital (forfeited),	92 00
transfer fees,	1 50	profits capital (withdrawn),	202 90
real estate loans repaid,	4,710 00	profits capital (forfeited),	5 66
share loans repaid,	580 00	temporary expenses,	195 64
withdrawal profits,	55 35	forfeited shares,	105 72
forfeiture profits,	5 24	real estate by foreclosure,	2,148 74
forfeited shares,	198 49	city of Cambridge bonds,	3,217 83
sale of desk,	35 00	surplus,	9 06
real estate by foreclosure,	54 75	profits,	15 24
surplus, to correct error,	15 24		
Cash on hand Oct. 31, 1893,	1,439 48	Cash on hand Oct. 31, 1894,	2,409 85
	$28,180 64		$28,180 64

Reconciliation of Share Account with Dues and Profits Capital.

DATE OF ISSUE.	Series.	Value per Share.	Shares in Force.	Total Value.		
June, 1892, .	1	$30 26	689	$20,849 14	Dues capital, as per general ledger, . .	$33,848 00
Dec., 1892, .	2	23 76	264	6,272 64		
June, 1893, .	3	17 36	333	5,780 88	Profits capital, as per general ledger, . .	1,202 36
Dec., 1893, .	4	11 10	137	1,520 70		
June, 1894, .	5	5 00	243	1,215 00	Unpaid dues, . .	812 00
Dues paid in advance, . . .				224 00		
Total, ...				$35,862 36	Total, . . .	$35,862 36

Number of shares issued during the year, ...	447	
Number of shares now in force, ...	1,666	
Number of shares now borrowed upon, ...	184	
Largest number of shares held by any one member, . . .	25	
Number of shares withdrawn during the year, ...	393	
Number of shares forfeited during the year, ...	57	
Highest premium received during the year, ...		$0 20
Lowest premium received during the year, ...		05
Number of members withdrawn during the year, ...	53	
Present number of members, ...	249	
Present number of borrowers, ...	13	
Present number of non-borrowers, ...	236	
Number of loans secured by first mortgage of real estate, . . .	16	
Number of loans on shares, ...	2	
Largest loan to any one member, ...		3,000 00
Smallest loan to any one member, ...		100 00
Amount of expenses of the corporation for the year ending Oct. 31, 1894, .		224 14

Date of examination by commissioner: May 15.

DANVERS CO-OPERATIVE BANK — DANVERS.

Incorporated Aug. 24, 1892. Commenced business Aug. 29, 1892.

SAMUEL L. SAWYER, *President.*   A. G. ALLEN, Jr., *Secretary.*
A. G. ALLEN, Jr., *Treasurer.*

Names of security committee:

HENRY NEWHALL,   J. W. WOODMAN,
J. F. PORTER.

Regular meetings the last Monday of each month.

BALANCE SHEET OCTOBER 31, 1894.

ASSETS.		LIABILITIES.	
Loans on real estate, . .	$24,300 00	Dues capital, . . .	$25,003 00
Loans on shares, . . .	925 00	Profits capital (all series), .	1,159 83
Permanent expense account,	170 00	Interest, ...	346 93
Temporary expense account,	57 61	Premiums, ...	36 77
Unpaid interest, . . .	10 66	Fines, ...	17 18
Unpaid premiums,	4 20	Surplus, ...	171 96
Unpaid fines, ...·	16 64	Guaranty fund, . . .	25 00
Cash in hands of treasurer, .	1,287 13	Withdrawal profits, . .	10 57
	$26,771 24		$26,771 24

Detailed Statement of Receipts and Disbursements for the Year ending Oct. 31, 1894.

RECEIPTS.		DISBURSEMENTS.	
From dues capital, . .	$14,136 00	For real estate loans, . .	$10,400 00
interest, . . .	1,272 82	share loans, . . .	1,570 00
premiums, . . .	138 82	dues capital (withdrawn),	4,928 00
fines, ...	87 92	profits capital (withdrawn), . . .	173 47
share loans repaid, .	1,005 00	temporary expenses, .	193 66
withdrawal profits, .	43 64	Cash on hand Oct. 31, 1894,	1,287 13
Cash on hand Oct. 31, 1893, .	1,868 06		
	$18,552 26		$18,552 26

Reconciliation of Share Account with Dues and Profits Capital.

Date of Issue.	Series.	Value per Share.	Shares in Force.	Total Value.		
Aug., 1892, .	1	$28 44	648	$18,429 12	Dues capital as per general ledger, .	$25,003 00
Feb., 1893, .	2	21 81	210	4,580 10		
Aug., 1893, .	3	15 36	122	1,873 92	Profits capital as per general ledger, . .	1,159 83
Feb., 1894, .	4	9 09	141	1,281 69		
Aug., 1894, .	5	3 00	105	318 00	Unpaid dues, . .	339 00
Dues paid in advance, . . .				19 00		
Total, ...				$26,501 03		$26,501 03

Number of shares issued during the year, ... 247
Number of shares now in force, ... 1,227
Number of shares now borrowed upon, ... 186
Largest number of shares held by any one member, . . . 25
Number of shares withdrawn during the year, ... 322
Highest premium received during the year, ... $0 25
Lowest premium received during the year, ... 05
Number of members withdrawn during the year, ... 49
Present number of members, ... 184
Present number of borrowers, ... 25
Present number of non-borrowers, ... 159
Number of loans secured by first mortgage of real estate, . . . 16
Number of loans on shares, ... 9
Largest loan to any one member, ... 2,600 00
Smallest loan to any one member, ... 50 00
Amount of expenses of the corporation for the year ending Oct. 31, 1894, . 213 66
Date of examination by commissioner: February 6.

DEAN CO-OPERATIVE BANK — FRANKLIN.

Incorporated June 15, 1889. Commenced business July 2, 1889.

Geo. W. Wiggin, *Vice-President.* William A. Wyckoff, *Secretary.*
William A. Wyckoff, *Treasurer.*

Names of security committee:

Wm. E. Nason, Chas. A. Wight,
O. B. Carter.

Regular meetings the first Tuesday of each month.

Balance Sheet October 31, 1894.

Assets.		Liabilities.	
Loans on real estate, . .	$21,688 93	Dues capital, . . .	$23,223 00
Loans on shares, . . .	1,710 00	Profits capital (all series). .	2,580 50
Permanent expense account, .	100 00	Interest, ...	456 88
Temporary expense account, .	16 68	Premiums, ...	44 52
Real estate by foreclosure, .	2,192 01	Fines, ...	2 50
Cash in hands of treasurer, .	970 73	Surplus, ...	108 04
		Guaranty fund, . . .	170 00
		Withdrawal profits, . .	14 54
		Rentals, ...	78 37
	$26,678 35		$26,678 35

Detailed Statement of Receipts and Disbursements for the Year ending Oct. 31, 1894.

Receipts.		Disbursements.	
From dues capital, . .	$7,231 00	For real estate loans, . .	$7,788 93
interest, . . .	1,321 21	share loans, . . .	1,725 00
premiums, . . .	129 80	dues capital (withdrawn),	3,338 00
fines, ...	9 63	profits capital (withdrawn), . . .	264 54
real estate loans repaid,	4,000 00	temporary expenses, .	50 04
share loans repaid, .	1,200 00	real estate foreclosure, .	2,192 01
withdrawal profits, .	38 25		
rentals, . . .	153 37		
Cash on hand Oct. 31, 1893, .	2,245 99	Cash on hand Oct. 31, 1894,	970 73
	$16,329 25		$16,329 25

Reconciliation of Share Account with Dues and Profits Capital.

DATE OF ISSUE.	Series.	Value per Share.	Shares in Force.	Total Value.		
July, 1889, .	1	$72 76	227	$16,516 52	Dues capital, as per general ledger, . .	$23,223 00
Oct., 1889, .	2	69 00	5	345 00		
Jan., 1890, .	3	65 27	12	783 24	Profits capital, as per general ledger, . .	2,580 50
July, 1890, .	4	57 91	6	347 46		
Jan., 1891, .	5	50 66	11	557 26	Unpaid dues,. . .	67 00
July, 1891, .	6	43 43	37	1,606 91		
Jan., 1892, .	7	36 39	57	2,074 23		
July, 1892, .	8	29 52	38	1,121 76		
Jan., 1893, .	9	22 80	51	1,162 80		
July, 1893, .	10	16 37	34	556 58		
Jan., 1894, .	11	10 11	34	343 74		
July, 1894, .	12	4 00	101	404 00		
Dues paid in advance, . . .				51 00		
Total, ...				$25,870 50	Total, . . .	$25,870 50

Number of shares issued during the year, ... 180
Number of shares now in force, ... 613
Number of shares now borrowed upon, ... 175
Largest number of shares held by any one member, . . . 25
Number of shares withdrawn during the year, ... 160
Highest per centum of interest received during the year: 7.
Lowest per centum of interest received during the year: 6½.
Number of members withdrawn during the year, ... 21
Present number of members, ... 97
Present number of borrowers, ... 27
Present number of non-borrowers, ... 70
Number of loans secured by first mortgage of real estate, . . . 12
Number of loans on shares, ... 15
Largest loan to any one member, ... $4,000 00
Smallest loan to any one member, ... 25 00
Amount of expenses of the corporation for the year ending Oct. 31, 1894, . 100 04
Date of examination by commissioner: February 1.

DEDHAM CO-OPERATIVE BANK — DEDHAM.

Incorporated Feb. 11, 1886.   Commenced business Feb. 16, 1886.

F. F. FAVOR, *President.*   C. H. J. KIMBALL, *Secretary.*
T. P. MURRAY, *Treasurer.*

Names of security committee :
WILLIAM G. WARE,   JOHN WARDLE, Jr.,
OTIS W. WITHINGTON.

Regular meetings the third Tuesday of each month.

BALANCE SHEET OCTOBER 31, 1894.

ASSETS.		LIABILITIES.	
Loans on real estate,	$30,715 00	Dues capital,	$29,624 00
Loans on shares,	1,965 00	Profits capital (all series),	4,394 54
Unpaid interest,	137 00	Surplus,	698 36
Unpaid premiums,	7 15	Guaranty fund,	120 18
Unpaid fines,	16 82	Forfeited share account,	132 42
Cash in hands of treasurer,	2,128 53		
	$34,969 50		$34,969 50

Detailed Statement of Receipts and Disbursements for the Year ending Oct. 31, 1894.

RECEIPTS.		DISBURSEMENTS.	
From dues capital,	$10,836 00	For real estate loans,	$4,300 00
interest,	1,908 68	share loans,	1,385 00
premiums,	115 95	dues capital (withdrawn),	7,274 00
fines,	47 12	dues capital (forfeited),	300 00
real estate loans repaid,	3,100 00	dues capital (retired),	1,982 00
share loans repaid,	2,545 00	profits capital (withdrawn),	817 56
withdrawal profits,	214 55		
forfeited shares,	132 42	profits capital (forfeited),	33 80
temporary expense,	33 85	profits capital (retired),	568 80
		temporary expenses,	148 30
		forfeited shares,	6 58
Cash on hand Oct. 31, 1893,	11 00	Cash on hand Oct. 31, 1894,	2,128 53
	$18,944 57		$18,944 57

Reconciliation of Share Account with Dues and Profits Capital.

DATE OF ISSUE.	Series.	Value per Share.	Shares in Force.	Total Value.		
Feb., 1886, .	1	$137 36	23	$3,159 28	Dues capital, as per general ledger, . . .	$29,624 00
May, 1886, .	2	132 53	7	927 71		
Nov., 1886, .	3	123 07	3	369 21	Profits capital, as per general ledger, . .	4,394 54
May, 1887, .	4	113 27	12	1,359 24		
Nov., 1887, .	5	104 05	4	416 20	Unpaid dues, . .	205 00
May, 1888, .	6	95 11	29	2,758 19		
Nov., 1888, .	7	86 43	7	605 01		
May, 1889, .	8	78 00	41	3,198 00		
Nov., 1889, .	9	69 81	20	1,396 20		
May, 1890, .	10	61 86	59	3,649 74		
Nov., 1890, .	11	54 15	52	2,815 80		
May, 1891, .	12	46 66	61	2,846 26		
Nov., 1891, .	13	39 39	75	2,954 25		
May, 1892, .	14	32 33	67	2,166 11		
Nov., 1892, .	15	25 48	67	1,707 16		
May, 1893, .	16	18 83	107	2,014 81		
Nov., 1893, .	17	12 37	81	1,001 97		
May, 1894, .	18	6 10	144	878 40		
Total, ...				$34,223 54	Total, . . .	$34,223 54

Number of shares issued during the year, ... 252
Number of shares now in force, ... 859
Number of shares now borrowed upon, ... 212
Largest number of shares held by any one member, . . . 25
Number of shares withdrawn during the year, ... 225
Number of shares forfeited during the year, ... 10
Number of shares retired during the year, ... 20
Highest per centum of interest received during the year : 10.
Lowest per centum of interest received during the year : $6\frac{8}{10}$.
Number of members withdrawn during the year, ... 33
Present number of members, ... 162
Present number of borrowers, ... 47
Present number of non-borrowers, ... 115
Number of loans secured by first mortgage of real estate, . . . 30
Number of loans on shares, ... 20
Largest loan to any one member, ... $3,000 00
Smallest loan to any one member, ... 15 00
Amount of expenses of the corporation for the year ending Oct. 31, 1894, . 148 30
Date of examination by commissioner : December 4.

DORCHESTER CO-OPERATIVE BANK — BOSTON.

Incorporated Aug. 21, 1890.   Commenced business Sept. 10, 1890.

AMOR L. HOLLINGSWORTH, *President.*   WM. H. KENNEDY, *Secretary.*
FRANK E. BRIGHAM, *Treasurer.*

Names of security committee:

SAMUEL GANNETT,   LABAN PRATT,
J. HOMER PIERCE,   CHAS. B. FOX,
R. D. MOSSMAN.

Regular meetings the second Wednesday of each month.

BALANCE SHEET OCTOBER 31, 1894.

ASSETS.		LIABILITIES.	
Loans on real estate, . .	$79,700 00	Dues capital, . . .	$75,634 00
Loans on shares, . . .	1,235 00	Profits capital (all series), .	7,637 55
Permanent expense account, .	210 28	Interest, ...	764 16
Temporary expense account,	136 00	Premiums, ...	41 11
Cash in hands of treasurer, .	3,172 08	Fines, ...	28 78
		Surplus, ...	165 68
		Guaranty fund, . . .	124 74
		Forfeited share account, .	14 39
		Withdrawal profits, . .	42 95
	$84,453 36		$84,453 36

Detailed Statement of Receipts and Disbursements for the Year ending Oct. 31, 1894.

RECEIPTS.		DISBURSEMENTS.	
From dues capital, . .	$26,968 00	For real estate loans, . .	$25,100 00
interest, . .	4,258 97	share loans, . . .	685 00
premiums, . .	218 20	dues capital (withdrawn),	8,947 00
fines, . .	162 52	dues capital (forfeited),	310 00
transfer fees, . .	25	profits capital (with-	
real estate loans repaid,	1,650 00	drawn), . . .	709 39
share loans repaid, .	540 00	profits capital (forfeited),	33 70
withdrawal profits, .	185 77	temporary expenses, .	423 50
forfeited shares, . .	333 17	forfeited shares, . .	480 78
Cash on hand Oct. 31, 1893, .	5,544 57	Cash on hand Oct. 31, 1894,	3,172 08
	$39,861 45		$39,861 45

Reconciliation of Share Account with Dues and Profits Capital.

DATE OF ISSUE.	Series.	Value per Share.	Shares in Force.	Total Value.	
Sept., 1890, .	1	$56 09	818	$46,051 32	Dues capital, as per general ledger, . . $75,634 00
Mar., 1891, .	2	48 71	258	12,574 26	
Sept., 1891, .	3	41 45	99	4,060 56	Profits capital, as per general ledger, . . 7,637 55
Mar., 1892, .	4	34 37	282	9,664 81	
Sept., 1892, .	5	27 49	130	3,482 08	Unpaid dues, . . . 1,636 00
Mar., 1893, .	6	20 84	120	2,493 24	
Sept., 1893, .	7	14 38	302	4,338 58	
Mar., 1894, .	8	8 10	216	1,746 70	
Sept., 1894, .	9	2 00	138	276 00	
Dues paid in advance, .			.	220 00	
Total, ...			.	$84,907 55	Total, . . . $84,907 55

Number of shares issued during the year, ... 488
Number of shares now in force, ... 2,363
Number of shares now borrowed upon, ... 522
Largest number of shares held by any one member, ... 25
Number of shares withdrawn during the year, ... 372
Number of shares forfeited during the year, ... 10
Highest premium received during the year, ... $0 10
Lowest premium received during the year, ... 05
Number of members withdrawn during the year, ... 51
Present number of members, ... 295
Present number of borrowers, ... 51
Present number of non-borrowers, ... 244
Number of loans secured by first mortgage of real estate, . . . 44
Number of loans on shares, ... 7
Largest loan to any one member, ... 4,400 00
Smallest loan to any one member, ... 60 00
Amount of expenses of the corporation for the year ending Oct. 31, 1894, . 451 50
Date of examination by commissioner: June 27.

ECONOMY CO-OPERATIVE BANK — MERRIMAC.

Incorporated July 26, 1889. Commenced business Aug. 12, 1889.

GEORGE ADAMS, *President.*   BAILEY SARGENT, *Secretary.*
                    BAILEY SARGENT, *Treasurer.*

Names of security committee:
ISAAC B. LITTLE,   FRANK E. PEASE,
                    GEORGE W. DAVIS.

Regular meetings the second Monday of each, month.

BALANCE SHEET OCTOBER 31, 1894.

ASSETS.		LIABILITIES.	
Loans on real estate, . .	$28,000 00	Dues capital, . . .	$28,935 00
Loans on shares, . . .	1,060 00	Profits capital (all series), .	3,361 39
Permanent expense account,	125 00	Interest, ...	258 25
Temporary expense account,	53 73	Premiums, ...	13 60
Real estate by foreclosure, .	745 43	Fines, ...	16
Cash in hands of treasurer, .	4,176 13	Surplus, ...	330 63
		Guaranty fund, . . .	70 00
		Withdrawal profits, . .	32 69
		Forfeiture profits, . .	93
		Retired share account, .	1,157 64
	$34,160 29		$34,160 29

*Detailed Statement of Receipts and Disbursements for the Year ending
Oct. 31, 1894.*

RECEIPTS.		DISBURSEMENTS.	
From dues capital, . .	$9,700 00	For real estate loans, . .	$5,200 00
interest, . . .	1,730 84	share loans, . . .	1,450 00
premiums, . . .	112 55	dues capital(withdrawn),	6,352 00
fines, ...	79 87	dues capital (forfeited),	92 00
transfer fees, . .	50	dues capital (retired), .	1,001 00
real estate loans repaid,	5,550 00	profits capital (with-	
share loans repaid, .	1,440 00	drawn), . . .	625 10
withdrawal profits, .	62 54	profits capital (forfeited),	9 28
forfeiture profits, .	93	profits capital (retired),	156 64
retired share account, .	1,157 64	temporary expenses, .	160 23
		forfeited shares, . .	7 81
		real estate by foreclosure,	745 43
Cash on hand Oct. 31, 1893, .	140 75	Cash on hand Oct. 31, 1894, .	4,176 13
	$19,975 62		$19,975 62

Reconciliation of Share Account with Dues and Profits Capital.

Date of Issue.	Series.	Value per Share.	Shares in Force.	Total Value.		
Aug., 1889, .	1	$72 79	159	$11,573 61	Dues capital, as per general ledger, .	$28,935 00
Feb., 1890, .	2	64 85	44	2,853 40	Profits capital, as per general ledger, . .	3,361 39
Aug., 1890, .	3	57 14	83	4,742 62	Unpaid dues, . .	328 00
Feb., 1891, .	4	49 65	121	6,007 65		
Aug., 1891, .	5	42 38	41	1,737 58		
Feb., 1892, .	6	35 32	34	1,200 88		
Aug., 1892, .	7	28 47	81	2,306 07		
Feb., 1893, .	8	21 82	27	589 14		
Aug., 1893, .	9	15 36	71	1,090 56		
Feb., 1894, .	10	9 09	32	290 88		
Aug., 1894, .	11	3 00	60	180 00		
Dues paid in advance, . . .				52 00		
Total, ...				$32,624 39	Total, . . .	$32,624 39

Number of shares issued during the year, ... 93
Number of shares now in force, ... 753
Number of shares now borrowed upon, ... 187
Largest number of shares held by any one member, . . . 25
Number of shares withdrawn during the year, ... 230
Number of shares forfeited during the year, ... 4
Number of shares retired during the year, ... 16
Highest premium received during the year, ... $0 05
Lowest premium received during the year, ... 05
Number of members withdrawn during the year, ... 34
Present number of members, ... 125
Present number of borrowers, ... 37
Present number of non-borrowers, ... 88
Number of loans secured by first mortgage of real estate, . . . 30
Number of loans on shares, ... 7
Largest loan to any one member, ... 2,600 00
Smallest loan to any one member, ... 60 00
Amount of expenses of the corporation for the year ending Oct. 31, 1894, . 235 23
Date of examination by commissioner: July 20.

ENTERPRISE CO-OPERATIVE BANK — EAST BOSTON.

Incorporated March 31, 1888.   Commenced business April 3, 1888.

JOSHUA N. TAYLOR, *President.*   HORACE B. BUTLER, *Secretary.*
HORACE B. BUTLER, *Treasurer.*

Names of security committee:

JAMES TOWNSEND,   WM. G. EMERY,
CHARLES T. WITT.

Regular meetings the third Wednesday of each month.

BALANCE SHEET OCTOBER 31, 1894.

ASSETS.		LIABILITIES.	
Loans on real estate, . .	$230,870 00	Dues capital, . . .	$230,585 00
Loans on shares, ...	17,625 00	Profits capital (all series), .	33,461 31
Temporary expense account,	141 80	Interest, ...	851 91
Real estate by foreclosure, .	2,554 37	Premiums, ...	70 15
Unpaid fines, ...	35 75	Transfer fees, . . .	75
Cash in hands of treasurer, .	16,743 01	Guaranty fund, . . .	1,200 00
		Forfeited share account, .	441 30
		Withdrawal profits, . .	101 46
		Surplus, ...	745 25
		Forfeiture profits, . .	3 08
		Retired shares, . .	509 72
	$267,969 93		$267,969 93

Detailed Statement of Receipts and Disbursements for the Year ending Oct. 31, 1894.

RECEIPTS.		DISBURSEMENTS.	
From dues capital, . .	$82,180 00	For real estate loans, . .	$76,030 00
interest, . . .	15,374 02	share loans, ...	14,800 00
premiums, . . .	1,892 95	dues capital (withdrawn),	41,810 00
fines, ...	518 22	dues capital (forfeited),	1,165 00
transfer fees, . .	8 75	dues capital (retired), .	10,538 00
real estate loans repaid,	53,260 00	profits capital (with-	
share loans repaid, .	8,075 00	drawn), . . .	5,397 65
withdrawal profits, .	442 47	profits capital (forfeited),	163 24
forfeiture profits, .	70 84	profits capital (retired),	2,289 16
forfeited shares, . .	916 80	temporary expenses, .	1,549 79
real estate, . . .	2,621 80	forfeited shares, . .	553 12
security committee, .	45 00	security committee, .	52 50
retired shares, . .	12,840 36	real estate, . . .	3,129 25
Cash on hand Oct. 31, 1893, .	8,305 15	retired shares, . . .	12,330 64
		Cash on hand Oct. 31, 1894,	16,743 01
	$186,551 36		$186,551 36

Reconciliation of Share Account with Dues and Profits Capital.

Date of Issue.	Series.	Value per Share.	Shares in Force.	Total Value.		
April, 1888, .	1	$97 58	309	$30,152 22	Dues capital, as per general ledger, . .	$230,585 00
Oct., 1888, .	2	88 74	312	27,686 88		
April, 1889, .	3	80 14	523	41,913 22	Profits capital, as per general ledger, . .	33,461 31
Oct., 1889, .	4	71 79	323	23,188 17		
April, 1890, .	5	63 69	401	25,539 69	Unpaid dues, . .	1,106 00
Oct., 1890, .	6	55 83	285	15,911 55		
April, 1891, .	7	48 20	467	22,509 40		
Oct., 1891, .	8	40 80	278	11,342 40		
April, 1892, .	9	33 60	628	21,100 80		
Oct., 1892, .	10	26 64	571	15,211 44		
April, 1893, .	11	19 91	614	12,224 74		
Oct., 1893, .	12	13 40	778	10,425 20		
April, 1894, .	13	7 10	966	6,858 60		
Oct., 1894, .	14	1 00	615	615 00		
Dues paid in advance, . .				473 00		
Total, ...				$265,152 31	Total, . .	$265,152 31

Number of shares issued during the year, ... 1,991
Number of shares now in force, ... 7,070
Number of shares now borrowed upon, ... 1,815
Largest number of shares held by any one member, ... 25
Number of shares withdrawn during the year, ... 1,272
Number of shares forfeited during the year, ... 61
Number of shares retired during the year, ... 147
Highest premium received during the year, ... $0 15
Lowest premium received during the year, ... 05
Number of members withdrawn during the year, ... 124
Present number of members, ... 661
Present number of borrowers, ... 183
Present number of non-borrowers, ... 478
Number of loans secured by first mortgage of real estate, . . . 117
Number of loans on shares, ... 66
Largest loan to any one member, ... 5,000 00
Smallest loan to any one member, ... 25 00
Amount of expenses of the corporation for the year ending Oct. 31, 1894, . 1,549 79
Date of examination by commissioner : December 17.

EQUITABLE CO-OPERATIVE BANK—LYNN.

Incorporated September, 1877. Commenced business October, 1877.

JAMES H. RICHARDS, *President.*   BENJAMIN E. PORTER, *Secretary.*

BENJAMIN E. PORTER, *Treasurer.*

Names of security committee:

THOMAS E. WARD,   EDWARD N. HAINES,

BENJAMIN E. PORTER.

Regular meetings the first Monday of each month.

BALANCE SHEET OCTOBER 31, 1894.

ASSETS.		LIABILITIES.	
Loans on real estate,	$288,515 28	Dues capital, . . .	$287,940 83
Loans on shares, . . .	14,993 00	Profits capital (all series), .	40,037 78
Permanent expense account, .	344 60	Surplus, ...	1,834 78
Temporary expense account,	207 39	Guaranty fund, . . .	1,111 00
Real estate by foreclosure, .	4,787 81	Forfeited share account, .	49 79
Suspense account, . . .	80 03		
Unpaid interest, . . .	519 44		
Mortgages, ...	7,500 00		
Cash in hands of treasurer, .	14,026 63		
	$330,974 18		$330,974 18

Detailed Statement of Receipts and Disbursements for the Year ending Oct. 31, 1894.

RECEIPTS.		DISBURSEMENTS.	
From dues capital, . .	$106,837 00	For real estate loans, . .	$56,203 35
interest, . . .	18,069 62	share loans, . . .	14,830 00
fines, ...	829 55	dues capital (withdrawn),	67,442 00
real estate loans repaid,	35,974 00	dues capital (forfeited),	114 00
share loans repaid, .	16,931 00	dues capital (matured),	4,004 00
rent, ...	100 00	profits capital (withdrawn), . .	7,608 06
		profits capital (forfeited),	60 48
		profits capital (matured),	1,701 28
		temporary expenses, .	1,543 41
		permanent expenses, .	90 00
		forfeited shares, . .	4 18
		real estate by foreclosure,	3,667 80
		mortgages, . . .	7,500 00
		suspense, . . .	179 00
Cash on hand Oct. 31, 1893, .	233 02	Cash on hand Oct. 31, 1894,	14,026 63
	$178,974 19		$178,974 19

Reconciliation of Share Account with Dues and Profits Capital.

DATE OF ISSUE.	Series.	Value per Share.	Shares in Force.	Total Value.		
Oct., 1883, .	12	$185 24	24	$4,445 76	Dues capital, as per general ledger, . .	$287,940 83
April, 1884, .	13	174 23	27	4,704 21		
Oct., 1884, .	14	163 51	44	7,194 44	Profits capital, as per	
April, 1885, .	15	153 02	27	4,131 54	general ledger, . .	40,037 78
Oct., 1885, .	16	142 88	52	7,429 76	Unpaid dues, . . .	1,403 17
April, 1886, .	17	133 06	35	4,657 10		
Oct., 1886, .	18	123 39	71	8,760 69		
April, 1887, .	19	114 00	89	10,146 00		
Oct., 1887, .	20	104 88	114	11,956 32		
April, 1888, .	21	96 00	176	16,896 00		
Oct., 1888, .	22	87 34	115	10,044 10		
April, 1889, .	23	78 96	236	18,634 56		
Oct , 1889, .	24	70 77	262	18,541 74		
April, 1890, .	25	62 81	334	20,978 54		
Oct., 1890, .	26	55 09	462	25,451 58		
April, 1891, .	27	47 62	662	31,524 44		
Oct., 1891, .	28	40 36	711	28,695 96		
April, 1892, .	29	33 31	865	28,813 15		
Oct., 1892, .	30	26 47	1,152	30,493 44		
April, 1893, .	31	19 81	794	15,729 14		
Oct., 1893, .	32	13 36	738	9,859 68		
April, 1894, .	33	7 09	1,307	9,266 63		
Oct., 1894, .	34	1 00	1,027	1,027 00		
Total, ...				$329,381 78	Total, . . .	$329,381 78

Number of shares issued during the year, ...	2,556	
Number of shares now in force, ...	9,324	
Number of shares now borrowed upon, ...	2,433	
Largest number of shares held by any one member, ...	25	
Number of shares withdrawn during the year, ...	2,606	
Number of shares forfeited during the year, ...	18	
Number of shares matured during the year, ...	28	
Highest premium received during the year, ...		$0 21
Lowest premium received during the year, ...		01
Number of members withdrawn during the year, ...	137	
Present number of members, ...	1,225	
Present number of borrowers, ...	306	
Present number of non-borrowers, ...	919	
Number of loans secured by first mortgage of real estate, . . .	215	
Number of loans on shares, ...	91	
Largest loan to any one member, ...		5,000 00
Smallest loan to any one member, ...		10 00
Amount of expenses of the corporation for the year ending Oct. 31, 1894, .		1,643 41

Date of examination by commissioner: April 9.

EQUITY CO-OPERATIVE BANK — WORCESTER.

Incorporated Feb. 9, 1887.   Commenced business March 17, 1887.

CHAS. L. GATES, *President.*   T. J. HASTINGS, *Secretary.*
T. J. HASTINGS, *Treasurer.*

Names of security committee:
DANIEL PARLIN,   E. J. BARDWELL,
URGEL JAQUES.

Regular meetings the Thursday preceding the third Monday of each month.

BALANCE SHEET OCTOBER 31, 1894.

ASSETS.		LIABILITIES.	
Loans on real estate, . .	$236,000 00	Dues capital, . . .	$208,467 00
Loans on shares, . . .	7,600 00	Profits capital (all series), .	36,204 60
Temporary expense account,	181 21	Interest, ...	2,445 13
Cash in hands of treasurer, .	5,126 19	Fines, ...	68 76
		Transfer fees, . . .	4 00
		Surplus, ...	1,041 27
		Guaranty fund, . .	610 00
		Forfeited share account, .	66 64
	$248,907 40		$248,907 40

Detailed Statement of Receipts and Disbursements for the Year ending Oct. 31, 1894.

RECEIPTS.		DISBURSEMENTS.	
From dues capital, .	$64,052 00	For real estate loans, . .	$92,350 00
interest, . . .	15,408 21	share loans, ...	7,630 00
fines, ...	510 58	dues capital (withdrawn),	37,565 00
transfer fees, . .	14 00	dues capital (forfeited),	137 00
real estate loans repaid,	72,150 00	dues capital (retired), .	17,630 00
share loans repaid, .	7,800 00	profits capital (withdrawn), . .	4,835 40
withdrawal profits, .	588 23	profits capital (forfeited),	9 57
forfeiture profits, . .	2 35	profits capital (retired),	4,691 40
forfeited shares, . .	139 18	temporary expenses, .	980 52
expense account, . .	66 33	forfeited shares, . .	133 90
Cash on hand Oct. 31, 1893, .	10,358 10	Cash on hand Oct. 31, 1894,	5,126 19
	$171,088 98		$171,088 98

Reconciliation of Share Account with Dues and Profits Capital.

Date of Issue.	Series.	Value per Share.	Shares in Force.	Total Value.		
Mar., 1887, .	1	$117 90	443	$52,229 70	Dues capital, as per general ledger, . . .	$208,467 00
Sept., 1887, .	2	108 34	155	16,792 70		
Mar , 1888, .	3	99 04	272	26,938 88	Profits capital, as per general ledger, . .	36,204 60
Sept., 1888, .	4	90 04	96	8,643 84		
Mar., 1889, .	5	81 31	223	18,132 13	Unpaid dues, . .	1,731 00
Sept., 1889, .	6	72 87	205	14,938 35		
Mar., 1890, .	7	64 70	332	21,480 40		
Sept., 1890, .	8	56 80	163	9,258 40		
Mar., 1891, .	9	49 15	398	19,561 70		
Sept , 1891, .	10	41 75	263	10,980 25		
Mar., 1892, .	11	34 58	401	13,866 58		
Sept., 1892, .	12	27 64	300	8,292 00		
Mar., 1893, .	13	20 92	609	12,740 28		
Sept., 1893, .	14	14 41	386	5,562 26		
Mar., 1894, .	15	8 11	683	5,539 13		
Sept., 1894, .	16	2 00	551	1,102 00		
Dues paid in advance, . .				344 00		
Total, ...				$246,402 60	Total, . . .	$246,402 60

Number of shares issued during the year, ...	1,525
Number of shares now in force, ...	5,480
Number of shares now borrowed upon, ...	1,472
Largest number of shares held by any one member, . .	. 25
Number of shares withdrawn during the year, ...	1,394
Number of shares forfeited during the year, ...	. 12
Number of shares retired during the year, ...	. 210

Highest per centum of interest received during the year : 9½.
Lowest per centum of interest received during the year : 6.

Number of members withdrawn during the year, ...	148
Present number of members, ...	588
Present number of borrowers, ...	150
Present number of non-borrowers, ...	438
Number of loans secured by first mortgage of real estate, . .	163
Number of loans on shares, ...	38
Largest loan to any one member, ...	$5,000 00
Smallest loan to any one member, ...	50 00
Amount of expenses of the corporation for the year ending Oct. 31, 1894, .	914 19

Date of examination by commissioner : May 7.

EVERETT CO-OPERATIVE BANK — EVERETT.

Incorporated Sept. 24, 1890.   Commenced business Oct. 14, 1890.

EDWARD C. MEAD, *President.*   CHAS. E. JENNINGS, *Secretary.*
CHARLES E. JENNINGS, *Treasurer.*

Names of security committee :
JAMES E. FREEMAN,   NATHANIEL A. DILL,
GEO. E. SMITH.

Regular meetings the second Tuesday of each month.

BALANCE SHEET OCTOBER 31, 1894.

ASSETS.		LIABILITIES.	
Loans on real estate, . .	$41,961 00	Dues capital, . . .	$49,851 00
Loans on shares, . . .	8,445 00	Profits capital (all series), .	5,142 72
Temporary expense account,	76 00	Interest, ...	216 45
Unpaid fines, ...	1 72	Premiums, ...	11 35
Cash in hands of treasurer, .	5,477 65	Surplus, ...	369 19
		Guaranty fund, . . .	293 45
		Forfeited share account, .	39 06
		Withdrawal profits, . .	38 15
	$55,961 37		$55,961 37

Detailed Statement of Receipts and Disbursements for the Year ending Oct. 31, 1894.

RECEIPTS.		DISBURSEMENTS.	
From dues capital, . .	$18,198 00	For real estate loans, . .	$11,361 00
interest, . . .	2,902 06	share loans, . . .	5,870 00
premiums, . . .	173 40	dues capital (withdrawn),	8,673 00
fines, ...	74 53	dues capital (forfeited),	285 00
transfer fees, . .	75	profits capital (with-	
real estate loans repaid,	3,700 00	drawn, . . .	781 34
share loans repaid, .	4,169 00	profits capital (forfeited),	41 15
withdrawal profits, .	198 90	temporary expenses, .	228 80
forfeiture profits, . .	10 29	forfeited shares, . .	303 16
forfeited shares, . .	303 16		
Cash on hand Oct. 31, 1893, .	3,291 01	Cash on hand Oct. 31, 1894,	5,477 65
	$33,021 10		$33,021 10

Reconciliation of Share Account with Dues and Profits Capital.

DATE OF ISSUE.	Series.	Value per Share.	Shares in Force.	Total Value.		
Oct., 1890, .	1	$55 23	419	$23,141 37	Dues capital, as per general ledger, . .	$49,851 00
April, 1891, .	2	47 74	304	14,512 96		
Oct., 1891, .	3	40 46	165	6,675 90	Profits capital, as per general ledger, . .	5,142 72
April, 1892, .	4	33 39	110	3,672 90		
Oct., 1892, .	5	26 52	79	2,095 08	Unpaid dues, . .	207 00
April, 1893, .	6	19 85	81	1,607 85		
Oct., 1893, .	7	13 38	117	1,565 46		
April, 1894, .	8	7 10	242	1,718 20		
Oct., 1894, .	9	1 00	71	71 00		
Dues paid in advance, . . .				140 00		
Total, ...				$55,200 72	Total, . . .	$55,200 72

Number of shares issued during the year, ... 432
Number of shares now in force, ... 1,588
Number of shares now borrowed upon, ... 450
Largest number of shares held by any one member, . . . 25
Number of shares withdrawn during the year, ... 322
Number of shares forfeited during the year, ... 15
Highest premium received during the year, ... $0 05
Lowest premium received during the year, ... 05
Number of members withdrawn during the year, ... 28
Present number of members, ... 165
Present number of borrowers, ... 36
Present number of non-borrowers, ... 129
Number of loans secured by first mortgage of real estate, . . . 23
Number of loans on shares, ... 34
Largest loan to any one member, ... 4,000 00
Smallest loan to any one member, ... 45 00
Amount of expenses of the corporation for the year ending Oct. 31, 1894, . 228 80
Date of examination by commissioner: April 26.

FALL RIVER CO-OPERATIVE BANK — FALL RIVER.

Incorporated Dec. 1, 1888.   Commenced business Dec. 12, 1888.

JOHN BARLOW, *President.*   GEORGE O. LATHROP, *Secretary.*

RODOLPHUS N. ALLEN, *Treasurer.*

Names of security committee:

JOHN BARLOW,   CHAS. F. TRIPP,

HENRY WARING.

Regular meetings the second Wednesday of each month.

BALANCE SHEET OCTOBER 31, 1894.

ASSETS.		LIABILITIES.	
Loans on real estate,	$179,800 00	Dues capital,	$163,817 00
Loans on shares,	3,200 00	Profits capital (all series),	17,750 65
Temporary expense account,	89 72	Interest,	1,609 41
Real estate loans by foreclosure,	2,279 46	Fines,	3 18
Profit and loss,	14 48	Surplus,	999 25
Cash in hands of secretary,	65 55	Guaranty fund,	1,363 36
Cash in hands of treasurer,	93 64		
	$185,542 85		$185,542 85

Detailed Statement of Receipts and Disbursements for the Year ending Oct. 31, 1894.

RECEIPTS.		DISBURSEMENTS.	
From dues capital,	$67,922 00	For real estate loans,	$100,400 00
interest,	11,612 88	share loans,	2,450 00
fines,	350 26	dues capital (withdrawn),	43,315 00
real estate loans repaid,	73,150 00	dues capital (forfeited),	892 00
share loans repaid,	1,250 00	profits capital (withdrawn),	3,802 04
forfeited shares,	181 85	profits capital (forfeited),	74 05
real estate by foreclosure,	90 96	temporary expenses,	736 49
profits returned,	5 55	forfeited shares,	205 54
unknown account,	10 54	interest,	454 05
profit and loss,	60 21	real estate by foreclosure,	2,370 42
		unknown account,	28 09
		profit and loss,	14 78
Cash on hand Oct. 31, 1893,	267 40	Cash on hand Oct. 31, 1894,	159 19
	$154,901 65		$154,901 65

Reconciliation of Share Account with Dues and Profits Capital.

DATE OF ISSUE.	Series.	Value per Share.	Shares in Force.	Total Value.		
Dec., 1888, .	1	$84 22	404	$34,024 88	Dues capital, as per general ledger, . . .	$163,817 00
Mar., 1889, .	2	79 99	125	9,998 75		
Sept., 1889, .	3	71 80	174	12,493 20	Profits capital, as per	
Mar., 1890, .	4	63 85	262	16,728 70	general ledger, . .	17,750 65
Sept., 1890, .	5	56 14	234	13,136 76	Unpaid dues, . . .	1,293 00
Mar., 1891, .	6	48 65	423	20,578 95		
Sept., 1891, .	7	41 38	166	6,869 08		
Mar., 1892, .	8	34 32	640	21,964 80		
Sept., 1892, .	9	27 47	592	16,262 24		
Mar., 1893, .	10	20 82	714	14,865 48		
Sept., 1893, .	11	14 36	431	6,189 16		
Mar., 1894, .	12	8 09	985	7,968 65		
Sept., 1894, .	13	2 00	719	1,438 00		
Dues paid in advance, . . .				342 00		
Total, ...				$182,860 65		$182,860 65

Number of shares issued during the year, ... 2,044
Number of shares now in force, ... 5,869
Number of shares now borrowed upon, ... 1,147
Largest number of shares held by any one member, ... 25
Number of shares withdrawn during the year, ... 2,023
Number of shares forfeited during the year, ... 43
Highest premium received during the year, ... $0 30
Lowest premium received during the year, ... 08
Number of members withdrawn during the year, ... 179
Present number of members, ... 620
Present number of borrowers, ... 125
Present number of non-borrowers, ... 495
Number of loans secured by first mortgage of real estate, . . . 111
Number of loans on shares, ... 17
Largest loan to any one member, ... 5,000 00
Smallest loan to any one member, ... 50 00
Amount of expenses of the corporation for the year ending Oct. 31, 1894, . 836 49
Date of examination by commissioner : September 14.

FEDERAL CO-OPERATIVE BANK — BOSTON.

Incorporated Jan. 29, 1890. Commenced business Feb. 6, 1890.

WM. O. BLAKE, *President.*   WM. WARDWELL, *Secretary.*
WM. WARDWELL, *Treasurer.*

Names of security committee:

FRANK W. ELDREDGE,   ALEX B. WILSON,
FRANCIS G. WASHBURN,   L. W. BLANCHARD,
WM. B. HAYFORD,   CHAS. P. RENFREW,
FRANK PIERCE BROWN.

Regular meetings the first Thursday of each month.

BALANCE SHEET OCTOBER 31, 1894.

ASSETS.		LIABILITIES.	
Loans on real estate, . .	$32,720 00	Dues capital, . . .	$36,963 00
Loans on shares, . . .	1,675 00	Profits capital (all series), .	3,423 08
Temporary expense account, .	73 09	Surplus, ...	91 43
Real estate by foreclosure, .	2,033 07	Guaranty fund, . . .	230 00
Unpaid interest, . . .	202 94	Forfeited share account, .	17 83
Unpaid fines, ...	19 31		
Cash in hands of treasurer, .	4,001 93		
	$40,725 34		$40,725 34

Detailed Statement of Receipts and Disbursements for the Year ending Oct. 31, 1894.

RECEIPTS.		DISBURSEMENTS.	
From dues capital, .	$18,489 00	For real estate loans, . .	$9,800 00
interest, . . .	1,961 76	share loans, . . .	2,170 00
premiums, . . .	24 58	dues capital (withdrawn),	7,252 00
fines, ...	59 23	dues capital (forfeited),	335 00
real estate loans repaid,	2,280 00	profits capital (with-	
share loans repaid, .	1,130 00	drawn), . . .	551 10
withdrawal profits, .	119 74	profits capital (forfeited),	6 63
forfeiture profits, .	6 63	temporary expenses, .	298 07
forfeited shares, .	351 13	forfeited shares, . .	340 56
real estate by foreclosure,	36 93	real estate, . . .	2,050 00
		insurance, etc., . .	20 00
Cash on hand Oct. 31, 1893, .	2,366 29	Cash on hand Oct. 31, 1894,	4,001 93
	$26,825 29		$26,825 29

Reconciliation of Share Account with Dues and Profits Capital.

DATE OF ISSUE.	Series.	Value per Share.	Shares in Force.	Total Value.		
Feb., 1890, .	1	$65 88	96	$6,324 48	Dues capital, as per gen-	
Aug., 1890, .	2	58 06	97	5,631 82	eral ledger, . . .	$36,963 00
Feb., 1891, .	3	50 45	38	1,917 10	Profits capital, as per	
Aug., 1891, .	4	43 05	127	5,467 35	general ledger, . .	3,423 08
Feb., 1892, .	5	35 88	152	5,453 76	Unpaid dues, . .	830 00
Aug., 1892, .	6	28 92	131	3,788 52		
Feb., 1893, .	7	22 15	219	4,850 85		
Aug., 1893, .	8	15 59	206	3,211 54		
Feb., 1894, .	9	9 22	393	3,623 46		
May, 1894, .	10	6 10	152	927 20		
Dues paid in advance, . . .				20 00		
Total, ...				$41,216 08	Total, . . .	$41,216 08

Number of shares issued during the year, ... 601
Number of shares now in force, ... 1,611
Number of shares now borrowed upon, ... 274
Largest number of shares held by any one member, . . . 25
Number of shares withdrawn during the year, . . . 359
Number of shares forfeited during the year, ... 24
Highest per centum of interest received during the year: $6\frac{1}{2}$.
Lowest per centum of interest received during the year: 6.
Number of members withdrawn during the year, . . . 61
Present number of members, ... 213
Present number of borrowers, ... 30
Present number of non-borrowers, ... 183
Number of loans secured by first mortgage of real estate, . . . 22
Number of loans on shares, ... 22
Largest loan to any one member, ... $3,000 00
Smallest loan to any one member, ... 10 00
Amount of expenses of the corporation for the year ending Oct. 31, 1894, . 298 07
Date of examination by commissioner: March 26.

FIDELITY CO-OPERATIVE BANK — FITCHBURG.

Incorporated April 25, 1888.   Commenced business May 8, 1888.

GEO. E. CLIFFORD, *President.*   W. G. HAYES, *Secretary.*

W. G. HAYES, *Treasurer.*

Names of security committee :

H. G. MORSE,   L. H. GOODNOW,

WM. EDWARDS.

Regular meetings the second Tuesday of each month.

BALANCE SHEET OCTOBER 31, 1894.

ASSETS.		LIABILITIES.	
Loans on real estate, . .	$257,525 00	Dues capital, . . .	$252,568 00
Loans on shares, . .	16,495 00	Profits capital (all series), .	36,813 50
Temporary expense account,	144 27	Interest, ...	2,733 53
Unpaid interest, . . .	2,800 00	Premiums, ...	29 52
Unpaid premiums, . .	70 00	Fines, ...	66 49
Unpaid fines, ...	100 00	Transfer fees, . . .	1 50
Cash in hands of treasurer, .	16,890 75	Surplus, ...	975 49
		Guaranty fund, . . .	700 00
		Forfeited share account, .	24 79
		Withdrawal profits, . .	112 20
	$294,025 02		$294,025 02

Detailed Statement of Receipts and Disbursements for the Year ending Oct. 31, 1894.

RECEIPTS.		DISBURSEMENTS.	
From dues capital, . .	$77,457 00	For real estate loans, . .	$79,150 00
interest, . .	15,395 65	share loans, . . .	24,320 00
premiums, . . .	367 10	dues capital (withdrawn),	32,867 00
fines, ...	445 35	dues capital (retired), .	15,615 00
transfer fees, . .	3 75	profits capital (withdrawn), . . .	3,280 26
real estate loans repaid,	47,025 00		
share loans repaid, .	26,025 00	profits capital (retired),	2,747 60
withdrawal profits, .	329 07	temporary expenses, .	1,144 23
		forfeited shares, . .	4 00
Cash on hand Oct. 31, 1893, .	8,970 92	Cash on hand Oct. 31, 1894,	16,890 75
	$176,018 84		$176,018 84

Reconciliation of Share Account with Dues and Profits Capital.

DATE OF ISSUE.	Series.	Value per Share.	Shares in Force.	Total Value.		
May, 1888, .	1	$94 32	962	$90,735 84	Dues capital, as per general ledger, . .	$252,568 00
Sept., 1888, .	2	88 56	254	22,494 24	eral ledger, . .	
Mar., 1889, .	3	80 13	379	30,369 27	Profits capital, as per	
Sept., 1889, .	4	71 93	267	19,205 31	general ledger, . .	36,813 50
Mar., 1890, .	5	63 97	246	15,736 62	Unpaid dues, . .	3,454 00
Sept., 1890, .	6	56 24	348	19,571 52		
Mar., 1891, .	7	48 74	484	23,590 16		
Sept., 1891, .	8	41 46	209	8,665 14		
Mar., 1892, .	9	34 39	642	22,078 38		
Sept., 1892, .	10	27 52	469	12,906 88		
Mar., 1893, .	11	20 85	596	12,426 60		
Sept., 1893, .	12	14 38	468	6,729 84		
Mar., 1894, .	13	8 10	857	6,941 70		
Sept., 1894, .	14	2 00	353	706 00		
Dues paid in advance, .			.	678 00		
Total, ...			.	$292,835 50	Total, . . .	$292,835 50

Number of shares issued during the year, ...   1,617
Number of shares now in force, ...   6,534
Number of shares now borrowed upon, ...   1,924
Largest number of shares held by any one member,   .   .   .   25
Number of shares withdrawn during the year, ...   1,498
Number of shares retired during the year, ...   230
Highest per centum of interest received during the year: $13\frac{6}{10}$.
Lowest per centum of interest received during the year: 6.
Number of members withdrawn during the year, ...   169
Present number of members, ...   768
Present number of borrowers, ...   240
Present number of non-borrowers, ...   528
Number of loans secured by first mortgage of real estate,   .   .   178
Number of loans on shares, ...   62
Largest loan to any one member, ... $4,600 00
Smallest loan to any one member, ...   15 00
Amount of expenses of the corporation for the year ending Oct. 31, 1894,   .   1,144 23
Date of examination by commissioner: April 6.

FITCHBURG CO-OPERATIVE BANK — FITCHBURG.

Incorporated Oct. 27, 1877.   Commenced business Nov. 8, 1877.

JABEZ FISHER, *President.*   JOSEPH F. SIMONDS, *Secretary.*

HARRISON BAILEY, *Treasurer.*

Names of security committee :

MARTIN WEBBER,   NATHANIEL VARNEY,

EDGAR S. MOULTON.

Regular meetings the third Thursday of each month.

BALANCE SHEET OCTOBER 31, 1894.

ASSETS.		LIABILITIES.	
Loans on real estate,	$532,790 00	Dues capital,	$492,072 00
Loans on shares,	23,950 00	Profits capital (all series),	104,279 21
Real estate by foreclosure,	2,406 13	Advance dues,	1,590 00
Unpaid dues,	9,517 12	Sundry persons,	49 58
Unpaid interest,	6,889 42	Incomplete loans,	50 00
Unpaid premiums,	89 26	Surplus,	1,224 18
Unpaid fines,	448 01	Guaranty fund,	2,401 03
Suspense,	1,020 58	Forfeited share account,	205 55
Personal accounts,	206 21	Personal accounts,	978 90
Cash in hands of treasurer,	25,533 72		
	$602,850 45		$602,850 45

Detailed Statement of Receipts and Disbursements for the Year ending Oct. 31, 1894.

RECEIPTS.		DISBURSEMENTS.	
From dues capital,	$123,562 00	For real estate loans,	$149,870 00
interest,	33,815 90	share loans,	19,580 00
premiums,	554 00	dues capital (withdrawn),	70,375 00
fines,	911 55	dues capital (forfeited),	3,174 00
transfer fees,	18 00	dues capital (retired),	24,303 00
real estate loans repaid,	157,335 00	dues capital (matured),	18,901 00
share loans repaid,	19,035 00	profits capital (withdrawn),	9,984 99
withdrawal profits,	1,008 49	profits capital (forfeited),	321 42
forfeiture profits,	32 14	profits capital (retired),	8,554 80
forfeited shares,	292 02	profits capital (matured),	8,229 60
expense,	40 00	temporary expenses,	1,393 44
suspense,	858 46	permanent expenses,	113 28
guaranty fund,	338 47	forfeited shares,	565 03
real estate by foreclosure,	1,665 43	interest,	823 61
personal accounts,	2,000 51	premiums and fines,	7 40
incomplete loans,	6,450 00	surplus,	970 07
		advance dues,	143 00
		real estate by foreclosure,	1,484 48
		personal accounts,	2,012 95
		incomplete loans,	6,400 00
Cash on hand Oct. 31, 1893,	4,823 82	Cash on hand Oct. 31, 1894,	25,533 72
	$352,740 79		$352,740 79

Reconciliation of Share Account with Dues and Profits Capital.

DATE OF ISSUE.	Series.	Value per Share.	Shares in Force.	Total Value.		
May, 1883, .	12	$199 30	50	$9,965 00	Dues capital, as per general ledger, . .	$492,072 00
Nov., 1883, .	13	187 49	131	24,561 19	eral ledger, . .	
May, 1884, .	14	176 02	138	24,290 76	Profits capital, as per	
Nov., 1884, .	15	164 89	112	18,467 68	general ledger, . .	104,279 21
May, 1885, .	16	154 10	101	15,564 10		
Nov., 1885, .	17	143 61	112	16,084 32		
May, 1886, .	18	133 42	206	27,484 52		
Nov., 1886, .	19	123 52	187	23,098 24		
May, 1887, .	20	113 94	473	53,893 62		
Nov., 1887, .	21	104 60	464.	48,534 40		
May, 1888, .	22	95 57	472	45,109 04		
Nov., 1888, .	23	86 82	363	31,515 66		
May, 1889, .	24	78 33	515	40,339 95		
Nov., 1889, .	25	70 10	565	39,606 50		
May, 1890, .	26	62 11	482	29,937 02		
Nov., 1890, .	27	54 35	497	27,011 95		
May, 1891, .	28	46 83	562	26,318 46		
Nov., 1891, .	29	39 52	590	23,316 80		
May, 1892, .	30	32 42	673	21,818 66		
Nov., 1892, .	31	25 54	873	22,296 42		
May, 1893, .	32	18 86	605	11,410 30		
Nov., 1893, .	33	12 38	784	9,705 92		
May, 1894, .	34	6 10	987	6,020 70		
Total, ...				$596,351 21	Total, . . .	$596,351 21

Number of shares issued during the year, ... 1,942
Number of shares now in force, ... 9,942
Number of shares now borrowed upon, ... 3,201
Largest number of shares held by any one member, ... 25
Number of shares withdrawn during the year, ... 2,122
Number of shares forfeited during the year, ... 95
Number of shares retired during the year, ...· . 217
Number of shares matured during the year, ... 134
Highest per centum of interest received during the year : $6\frac{96}{100}$.
Lowest per centum of interest received during the year : 6.
Number of members withdrawn during the year, ... 362
Present number of members, ... 1,296
Present number of borrowers, ... 516
Present number of non-borrowers, ... 780
Number of loans secured by first mortgage of real estate, . . . 550
Number of loans on shares, ... 185
Largest loan to any one member, ... $5,000 00
Smallest loan to any one member, ... 10 00
Amount of expenses of the corporation for the year ending Oct. 31, 1894, . 1,466 72
Date of examination by commissioner : April 6.

FOXBOROUGH CO-OPERATIVE BANK—FOXBOROUGH.

Incorporated Feb. 25, 1889.   Commenced business March 19, 1889.

A. F. Bemis, *President.*   F. S. Lane, *Secretary.*

F. S. Lane, *Treasurer.*

Names of security committeee :

| Wm. T. Cook, | Chas. C. Sumner, |
| Ezra Pickens, | Chas. H. Hartshorn. |

Regular meetings the third Wednesday of each month.

BALANCE SHEET OCTOBER 31, 1894.

ASSETS.			LIABILITIES.	
Loans on real estate, . .	$36,900 00	Dues capital, . . .	$35,867 00
Loans on shares, . . .	1,130 00	Profits capital (all series), .	4,445 55
Unpaid fines, ...	19 65	Interest, ...	14 24
Cash in hands of treasurer, .	3,075 34	Premiums, ...	2 10
		Surplus, ...	717 04
		Guaranty fund, . . .	71 64
		Withdrawal profits, . .	7 42
	$41,124 99		$41,124 99

Detailed Statement of Receipts and Disbursements for the Year ending Oct. 31, 1894.

RECEIPTS.			DISBURSEMENTS.	
From dues capital, .	$12,376 00	For real estate loans, . .	$18,400 00
interest, . . .	2,167 47	share loans, . . .	535 00
premiums, . . .	175 20	dues capital (withdrawn),	4,873 00
fines, ...	153 70	dues capital (forfeited),	144 00
transfer fees, . .	1 50	profits capital (withdrawn), . . .	449 92
real estate loans repaid,	10,400 00	profits capital (forfeited),	13 41
share loans repaid, .	385 00	temporary expenses, .	207 61
withdrawal profits, .	79 45	forfeited shares, . .	147 69
forfeiture profits, .	5 94	real estate by foreclosure,	1,811 47
forfeited shares, . .	147 69	sundries, . . .	100 37
profits overpaid, . .	20		
surplus, . . .	3 05		
real estate by foreclosure, . . .	1,811 47		
Cash on hand Oct. 31, 1893, .	2,051 14	Cash on hand Oct. 31, 1894, .	3,075 34
	$29,757 81		$29,757 81

Reconciliation of Share Account with Dues and Profits Capital.

DATE OF ISSUE.	Series.	Value per Share.	Shares in Force.	Total Value.		
Mar., 1889, .	1	$80 21	144	$11,550 24	Dues capital, as per gen-	
Sept., 1889, .	2	71 99	91	6,551 09	eral ledger, . .	$35,867 00
Mar., 1890, .	3	64 03	25	1,600 75	Profits capital, as per	
Sept , 1890, .	4	56 30	64	3,603 20	general ledger, . .	4,445 55
Mar., 1891, .	5	48 79	100	4,879 00	Unpaid dues, . . .	818 00
Sept., 1891, .	6	41 50	44	1,826 00		
Mar., 1892, .	7	34 43	121	4,166 03		
Sept., 1892, .	8	27 56	63	1,736 28		
Mar., 1893, .	9	20 88	117	2,442 96		
Sept., 1893, .	10	14 40	76	1,094 40		
Mar., 1894, .	11	8 10	156	1,263 60		
Sept., 1894, .	12	2 00	206	412 00		
Dues paid in advance, . . .				5 00		
Total, ...				$41,130 55	Total, . . .	$41,130 55

Number of shares issued during the year, ... 439
Number of shares now in force, ... 1,207
Number of shares now borrowed upon, ... 293
Largest number of shares held by any one member, . . . 25
Number of shares withdrawn during the year, ... 191
Number of shares forfeited during the year, ... 9
Highest premium received during the year, ... $0 20
Lowest premium received during the year, ... 05
Number of members withdrawn during the year, ... 22
Present number of members, ... 236
Present number of borrowers, ... 43
Present number of non-borrowers, ... 193
Number of loans secured by first mortgage of real estate, . . . 35
Number of loans on shares, ... 8
Largest loan to any one member, ... 2,800 00
Smallest loan to any one member, ... 30 00
Amount of expenses of the corporation for the year ending Oct. 31, 1894, . 207 61
Date of examination by commissioner : January 11.

GARDNER CO-OPERATIVE BANK — GARDNER.

Incorporated Jan. 14, 1889.   Commenced business March 12, 1889.

GUY W. GARLAND, *President.*   JAMES A. STILES, *Secretary.*
                    JAMES A. STILES, *Treasurer.*

Names of security committee:

GEORGE R. LOWE,   JONAS R. DAVIS,
            HENRY G. POLLARD.

Regular meetings the second Tuesday of each month.

BALANCE SHEET OCTOBER 31, 1894.

ASSETS.			LIABILITIES.		
Loans on real estate, . .	$82,420	67	Dues capital, . . .	$80,892	00
Loans on shares, . . .	3,909	00	Profits capital (all series), . .	11,238	46
Permanent expense account,	240	00	Interest, ...	985	72
Temporary expense account,	69	75	Premiums, ...	114	67
Real estate by foreclosure, .	5,339	34	Fines, ...	62	17
Unpaid interest, . . .	884	65	Transfer fees, . . .		50
Unpaid premiums, . .	101	60	Surplus, ...	634	31
Unpaid fines, ...	70	22	Guaranty fund, . . .	190	22
Cash in hands of treasurer, .	1,152	07	Forfeited share account, . .	18	69
			Withdrawal profits, . .	37	44
			Forfeiture profits, . . .	13	12
	$94,187	30		$94,187	30

Detailed Statement of Receipts and Disbursements for the Year ending Oct. 31, 1894.

RECEIPTS.			DISBURSEMENTS.		
From dues capital, . .	$26,022	00	For real estate loans, . .	$23,939	00
interest, . . .	5,133	83	share loans, . . .	3,909	00
premiums, . . .	599	45	dues capital (withdrawn),	13,219	00
fines, . . .	210	25	dues capital (forfeited),	542	00
transfer fees, . .	1	25	dues capital (retired), .	7,144	00
real estate loans repaid,	20,279	33	profits capital (with-		
share loans repaid, .	4,135	00	drawn), . . .	1,550	71
withdrawal profits, .	160	14	profits capital (forfeited),	78	75
forfeiture profits, .	33	31	profits capital (retired),	1,357	52
forfeited shares, . .	217	77	temporary expenses, .	359	61
real estate by fore-			forfeited shares, . .	208	19
closure, . . .	134	00	interest, . . .	7	27
			real estate by foreclosure,	3,619	93
Cash on hand Oct. 31, 1893, .	160	72	Cash on hand Oct. 31, 1894,	1,152	07
	$57,087	05		$57,087	05

Reconciliation of Share Account with Dues and Profits Capital.

DATE OF ISSUE.	Series.	Value per Share.	Shares in Force.	Total Value.		
Mar., 1889, .	1	$80 58	529	$42,626 82	Dues capital, as per general ledger, . .	$80,892 00
Sept., 1889, .	2	72 34	104	7,523 36		
Mar., 1890, .	3	64 31	102	6,559 62	Profits capital, as per general ledger, . .	11,238 46
Sept., 1890, .	4	56 49	62	3,502 38		
Mar., 1891, .	5	48 91	170	8,314 70	Unpaid dues, . .	1,202 00
Sept., 1891, .	6	41 55	97	4,030 35		
Mar., 1892, .	7	34 44	256	8,816 64		
Sept., 1892, .	8	27 55	111	3,058 05		
Mar., 1893, .	9	20 86	256	5,340 16		
Sept., 1893, .	10	14 38	101	1,452 38		
Mar., 1894, .	11	8 10	240	1,944 00		
Sept., 1894, .	12	2 00	61	122 00		

Dues paid in advance, . . .				42 00		
Total, ...				$93,332 46	Total, . . .	$93,332 46

Number of shares issued during the year, ... 385
Number of shares now in force, ... 2,089
Number of shares now borrowed upon, ... 533
Largest number of shares held by any one member, ... 25
Number of shares withdrawn during the year, ... 446
Number of shares forfeited during the year, ... 26
Number of shares retired during the year, ... 118
Highest premium received during the year, ... $0 50
Lowest premium received during the year, ... 02
Number of members withdrawn during the year, ... 85
Present number of members, ... 398
Present number of borrowers, ... 90
Present number of non-borrowers, ... 308
Number of loans secured by first mortgage of real estate, . . . 98
Number of loans on shares, ... 17
Largest loan to any one member, ... 3,000 00
Smallest loan to any one member, ... 20 00
Amount of expenses of the corporation for the year ending Oct. 31, 1894, . 419 61
Date of examination by commissioner : February 12.

GERMANIA CO-OPERATIVE BANK — BOSTON.

Incorporated Oct. 3, 1885. Commenced business Oct. 20, 1885.

JOSEPH TONDORF, *President.*   ANDREW M. DORR, *Secretary.*
MARTIN HASENFUSS, *Treasurer.*

Names of security committee:
HERMAN OBERMARD,   THEODOR FANDEL,
NICHOLAS SCHAAF.

Regular meetings the third Tuesday of each month.

BALANCE SHEET OCTOBER 31, 1894.

ASSETS.		LIABILITIES.	
Loans on real estate, . .	$182,050 00	Dues capital, . . .	$169,706 00
Loans on shares, . . .	6,050 00	Profits capital (all series), .	28,805 02
Permanent expense account, .	330 39	Interest, ...	962 47
Temporary expense account,	180 50	Fines, ...	14 49
Real estate by foreclosure, .	7,565 30	Surplus, ...	805 98
Cash in hands of secretary, .	37 98	Guaranty fund, . . .	1,767 38
Cash in hands of treasurer, .	6,127 47	Forfeited share account, .	20 36
		Withdrawal profits, .	259 94
	$202,341 64		$202,341 64

Detailed Statement of Receipts and Disbursements for the Year ending Oct. 31, 1894.

RECEIPTS.		DISBURSEMENTS.	
From dues capital, . .	$64,118 00	For real estate loans, . .	$32,950 00
interest, . . .	13,567 52	share loans, . . .	6,600 00
fines, ...	291 83	dues capital (withdrawn),	43,057 00
transfer fees, . .	3 50	dues capital (forfeited),	1,006 00
real estate loans repaid,	47,600 00	dues capital (retired), .	29,163 00
share loans repaid, .	6,550 00	profits capital (with-	
withdrawal profits, .	1,193 77	drawn), . . .	4,791 09
forfeiture profits, .	54 80	profits capital (forfeited),	219 63
forfeited shares, . .	1,083 29	profits capital (retired),	8,176 03
rents, ...	408 50	temporary expenses, .	1,334 95
		permanent expenses, .	67 65
		forfeited shares, . .	1,165 13
		taxes, ...	236 16
		insurance, . . .	44 00
Cash on hand Oct. 31, 1893, .	104 88	Cash on hand Oct. 31, 1894,	6,165 45
	$134,976 09		$134,976 09

Reconciliation of Share Account with Dues and Profits Capital.

DATE OF ISSUE.	Series.	Value per Share.	Shares in Force.	Total Value.		
Oct., 1885, .	1	$146 60	111	$16,272 60	Dues capital, as per general ledger, . . .	$169,706 00
April, 1886, .	2	136 30	105	14,311 50		
Oct., 1886, .	3	126 23	101	12,749 23	Profits capital, as per general ledger, . .	28,805 02
April, 1887, .	4	116 43	72	8,382 96		
Oct., 1887, .	5	106 98	80	8,558 40	Unpaid dues, . .	1,904 00
April, 1888, .	6	97 69	141	13,774 29		
Oct., 1888, .	7	88 79	139	12,341 81		
April, 1889, .	8	80 09	8	640 72		
Oct., 1889, .	9	71 64	118	8,453 52		
April, 1890, .	10	63 52	147	9,337 44		
Oct., 1890, .	11	55 65	287	15,971 55		
April, 1891, .	12	48 04	281	13,499 24		
Oct., 1891, .	13	40 68	292	11,878 56		
April, 1892, .	14	33 52	451	15,117 52		
Oct., 1892, .	15	26 62	429	11,419 98		
April, 1893, .	16	19 91	654	13,021 14		
Oct., 1893, .	17	13 41	537	7,201 17		
April, 1894, .	18	7 11	949	6,747 39		
Oct., 1894, .	19	1 00	717	717 00		
Dues paid in advance, . . .				19 00		
Total, ...				$200,415 02	Total, . . .	$200,415 02

Number of shares issued during the year, ... 1,921
Number of shares now in force, ... 5,619
Number of shares now borrowed upon, ... 1,174
Largest number of shares held by any one member, . . . 25
Number of shares withdrawn during the year, ... 1,873
Number of shares forfeited during the year, ... 32
Number of shares retired during the year, ... 337
Highest per centum of interest received during the year: 12.
Lowest per centum of interest received during the year: 6.
Number of members withdrawn during the year, ... 224
Present number of members, ... 664
Present number of borrowers, ... 131
Present number of non-borrowers, ... 533
Number of loans secured by first mortgage of real estate, . . 109
Number of loans on shares, ... 45
Largest loan to any one member, ... $5,000 00
Smallest loan to any one member, ... 50 00
Amount of expenses of the corporation for the year ending Oct. 31, 1894, . 1,454 25
Date of examination by commissioner: December 15.

GLOUCESTER CO-OPERATIVE BANK — GLOUCESTER.

Incorporated March 2, 1887.   Commenced business April 14, 1887.

W. FRANK PARSONS, *President.*   EVERETT LANE, *Secretary.*
EVERETT LANE, *Treasurer.*

Names of security committee:

EDWIN O. PARSONS,   HERBERT PRESSON,
JOS. C. SHEPHERD,   JOHN S. ROGERS,
CALVIN SARGENT.

Regular meetings the second Thursday of each month.

BALANCE SHEET OCTOBER 31, 1894.

ASSETS		LIABILITIES	
Loans on real estate,	$128,600 00	Dues capital,	$120,687 00
Loans on shares,	8,600 00	Profits capital (all series),	18,126 58
Unpaid interest,	284 75	Interest,	717 75
Unpaid premiums,	53 74	Premiums,	87 78
Unpaid fines,	38 38	Fines,	16 32
Cash in hands of treasurer,	4,786 71	Transfer fees,	25
		Surplus,	1,834 02
		Guaranty fund,	717 68
		Forfeited share account,	7 65
		Withdrawal profits,	168 55
	$142,363 58		$142,363 58

Detailed Statement of Receipts and Disbursements for the Year ending Oct. 31, 1894.

RECEIPTS		DISBURSEMENTS	
From dues capital,	$37,510 00	For real estate loans,	$32,000 00
interest,	8,053 23	share loans,	8,650 00
premiums,	1,045 06	dues capital (withdrawn),	11,699 00
fines,	305 34	dues capital (retired),	6,396 00
transfer fees,	3 25	profits capital (withdrawn),	1,297 84
real estate loans repaid,	8,100 00	profits capital (retired),	1,649 33
share loans repaid,	11,350 00	temporary expenses,	789 70
withdrawal profits,	324 24	Cash on hand Oct. 31, 1894,	4,786 71
Cash on hand Oct. 31, 1893,	577 46		
	$67,268 58		$67,268 58

Reconciliation of Share Account with Dues and Profits Capital.

DATE OF ISSUE.	Series.	Value per Share.	Shares in Force.	Total Value.		
April, 1887, .	1	$114 23	212	$24,216 76	Dues capital, as per general ledger, . . .	$120,687 00
Oct., 1887, .	2	105 03	93	9,767 79		
April, 1888, .	3	96 09	91	8,744 19	Profits capital, as per general ledger, . .	18,126 58
Oct., 1888, .	4	87 41	79	6,905 39		
April, 1889, .	5	78 98	136	10,741 28	Unpaid dues, . .	758 00
Oct., 1889, .	6	70 80	138	9,770 40		
April, 1890, .	7	62 85	198	12,444 30		
Oct.,. 1890, .	8	55 14	88	4,852 32		
April, 1891, .	9	47 65	306	14,580 90		
Oct., 1891, .	10	40 38	208	8,399 04		
April, 1892, .	11	33 32	281	9,362 92		
Oct., 1892, .	12	26 47	269	7,120 43		
April, 1893, .	13	19 82	337	6,679 34		
Oct., 1893, .	14	13 36	266	3,553 76		
April, 1894, .	15	7 09	264	1,871 76		
Oct., 1894, .	16	1 00	142	142 00		
Dues paid in advance, . . .				419 00		
Total, ...				$139,571 58	Total, . . .	$139,571 58

Number of shares issued during the year, ... 539
Number of shares now in force, ... 3,108
Number of shares now borrowed upon, ... 860
Largest number of shares held by any one member, ... 25
Number of shares withdrawn during the year, ... 440
Number of shares retired during the year, ... 71
Highest premium received during the year, ... $0 50
Lowest premium received during the year, ... 05
Number of members withdrawn during the year, ... 90
Present number of members, ... 535
Present number of borrowers, ... 156
Present number of non-borrowers, ... 379
Number of loans secured by first mortgage of real estate, . . . 138
Number of loans on shares, ... 46
Largest loan to any one member, ... 5,000 00
Smallest loan to any one member, ... 50 00
Amount of expenses of the corporation for the year ending Oct. 31, 1894, . 789 70
Date of examination by commissioner: March 2.

GRAFTON CO-OPERATIVE BANK — GRAFTON.

Incorporated Oct. 19, 1887.   Commenced business Nov. 10, 1887.

DANIEL N. GIBBS, *President.*   JOSEPH A. DODGE, *Secretary.*
JOSEPH A. DODGE, *Treasurer.*

Names of security committee:
HENRY F. WING,   ALBERT L. FISHER,
OLIVER M. WING.

Regular meetings the second Thursday of each month.

BALANCE SHEET OCTOBER 31, 1894.

ASSETS.		LIABILITIES.	
Loans on real estate,	$40,198 33	Dues capital,	$36,772 00
Loans on shares,	2,063 00	Profits capital (all series),	6,169 15
Unpaid interest,	96 07	Surplus,	638 67
Cash in hands of treasurer,	1,532 15	Guaranty fund,	309 73
	$43,889 55		$43,889 55

Detailed Statement of Receipts and Disbursements for the Year ending Oct. 31, 1894.

RECEIPTS.		DISBURSEMENTS.	
From dues capital,	$10,581 00	For real estate loans,	$4,415 00
interest,	2,527 89	share loans,	2,174 00
fines,	20 62	dues capital(withdrawn),	7,404 00
transfer fees,	2 00	profits capital (withdrawn),	1,132 38
real estate loans repaid,	1,050 00		
share loans repaid,	2,183 00	temporary expenses,	164 55
withdrawal profits,	126 86		
membership fees,	17 55		
suspense account,	65 17		
Cash on hand Oct. 31, 1893,	247 99	Cash on hand Oct. 31, 1894,	1,532 15
	$16,822 08		$16,822 08

Reconciliation of Share Account with Dues and Profits Capital.

DATE OF ISSUE.	Series.	Value per Share.	Shares in Force.	Total Value.		
Nov., 1887, .	1	$105 35	116	$12,220 60	Dues capital, as per general ledger, . .	$36,772 00
May, 1888, .	2	96 30	21	2,022 30		
Nov., 1888, .	3	87 53	33	2,888 49	Profits capital, as per general ledger, . .	6,169 15
May, 1889, .	4	79 02	20	1,580 40		
Nov., 1889, .	5	70 72	43	3,040 96	Unpaid dues, . .	151 00
May, 1890, .	6	62 59	55	3,442 45		
Nov., 1890, .	7	54 74	72	3,941 28		
May, 1891, .	8	47 12	56	2,638 72		
Nov., 1891, .	9	39 73	103	4,092 19		
May, 1892, .	10	32 57	73	2,377 61		
Nov., 1892, .	11	25 63	123	3,152 49		
May, 1893, .	12	18 91	31	586 21		
Nov., 1893, .	13	12 41	56	694 96		
May, 1894, .	14	6 11	59	360 49		
Dues paid in advance, . . .				53 00		
Total, ...				$43,092 15	Total, . . .	$43,092 15

Number of shares issued during the year, ... 117
Number of shares now in force, ... 861
Number of shares now borrowed upon, ... 291
Largest number of shares held by any one member, . . . 25
Number of shares withdrawn during the year, . . . 192
Highest per centum of interest received during the year : 7.
Lowest per centum of interest received during the year : 6.
Number of members withdrawn during the year, ... 39
Present number of members, ... 160
Present number of borrowers, ... 51
Present number of non-borrowers, ... 109
Number of loans secured by first mortgage of real estate, . . . 37
Number of loans on shares, ... 18
Largest loan to any one member, ... $4,000 00
Smallest loan to any one member, ... 10 00
Amount of expenses of the corporation for the year ending Oct. 31, 1894, . 164 55
Date of examination by commissioner : May 17.

GUARDIAN CO-OPERATIVE BANK — BOSTON.

Incorporated July 2, 1886.   Commenced business Aug. 6, 1886.

GAMALIEL BRADFORD, *President.*   DANIEL ELDREDGE, *Secretary.*
DANIEL ELDREDGE, *Treasurer.*

Names of security committee :

| JOHN K. FELLOWS, | JAMES M. SIMPSON, |
| HIRAM AMES, | WALTER H. ROBERTS. |

Regular meetings the first Friday of each month.

BALANCE SHEET OCTOBER 31, 1894.

ASSETS.		LIABILITIES.	
Loans on real estate, . .	$237,250 00	Dues capital, . . .	$233,760 00
Loans on shares, . . .	8,400 00	Profits capital (all series), .	30,895 65
Temporary expense account,	575 00	Interest, ...	6,538 99
Real estate by foreclosure, .	8,166 27	Premiums, ...	436 40
Unpaid interest, . . .	1,204 50	Fines, ...	330 25
Unpaid premium, . . .	80 05	Transfer fees, . . .	1 50
Unpaid fines, ...	125 36	Surplus, . . .	2,902 76
Cash in hands of treasurer, .	20,782 14	Guaranty fund, . . .	1,350 00
		Forfeited share account, .	15 06
		Withdrawal profits, .	352 71
	$276,583 32		$276,583 32

Detailed Statement of Receipts and Disbursements for the Year ending Oct. 31, 1894.

RECEIPTS.		DISBURSEMENTS.	
From dues capital, . .	$72,096 00	For real estate loans, . .	$65,950 00
interest, . . .	14,929 50	share loans, . . .	4,950 00
premiums, . . .	1,063 35	dues capital(withdrawn),	24,999 00
fines, ...	692 96	dues capital (forfeited),	154 00
transfer fees, . .	5 00	dues capital (retired), .	21,204 00
real estate loans repaid,	49,150 00	profits capital (withdrawn), .	3,172 25
share loans repaid, .	6,550 00	profits capital (forfeited),	19 26
withdrawal profits, .	792 88	profits capital (retired),	5,238 90
forfeiture profits, .	10 03	temporary expenses, .	2,142 57
forfeited shares, . .	52 35	forfeited shares, . .	90 63
retired shares, . .	24,548 72	interest, ...	157 00
real estate by foreclosure,	554 37	retired shares, . .	24,548 72
		real estate by foreclosure,	383 05
Cash on hand Oct. 31, 1893, .	3,346 36	Cash on hand Oct. 31, 1894,	20,782 14
	$173,791 52		$173,791 52

Reconciliation of Share Account with Dues and Profits Capital.

DATE OF ISSUE.	Series.	Value per Share.	Shares in Force.	Total Value.		
Aug., 1886, .	1	$125 23	29	$3,631 67	Dues capital as per general ledger, . .	$233,760 00
Dec., 1886, .	2	118 86	43	5,110 98		
June, 1887, .	3	109 57	283	31,008 31	Profits capital as per general ledger, .	30,895 65
Dec., 1887, .	4	100 57	222	22,326 54		
June, 1888, .	5	91 83	233	21,396 39	Unpaid dues, . .	1,971 00
Dec., 1888, .	6	83 35	308	25,671 80		
June, 1889, .	7	75 10	223	16,747 30		
Dec., 1889, .	8	67 10	275	18,452 50		
June, 1890, .	9	59 36	303	17,986 08		
Dec., 1890, .	10	51 80	252	13,053 60		
June, 1891, .	11	44 47	571	25,392 37		
Dec., 1891, .	12	37 37	302	11,285 74		
June, 1892, .	13	30 48	769	23,439 12		
Dec., 1892, .	14	23 82	548	13,053 36		
June, 1893, .	15	17 36	505	8,766 80		
Dec., 1893, .	16	11 09	501	5,556 09		
June 1894, .	17	5 00	639	3,195 00		
Dues paid in advance, . . .				553 00		
Total, ...				$266,626 65	Total, . . .	$266,626 65

Number of shares issued during the year, ... 1,197
Number of shares now in force, ... 6,006
Number of shares now borrowed upon, ... 1,449
Largest number of shares held by any one member, . . . 25
Number of shares withdrawn during the year, ... 760
Number of shares forfeited during the year, ... 7
Number of shares retired during the year, ... 240
Highest premium received during the year, ... $0 15
Lowest premium received during the year, ... 05
Number of members withdrawn during the year, ... 152
Present number of members, ... 793
Present number of borrowers, ... 143
Present number of non-borrowers, ..., ... 650
Number of loans secured by first mortgage of real estate, . . . 144
Number of loans on shares, ... 44
Largest loan to any one member, ... 5,000 00
Smallest loan to any one member, ... 50 00
Amount of expenses of the corporation for the year ending Oct. 31, 1894, . 2,142 57
Date of examination by commissioner: April 27.

HAVERHILL CO-OPERATIVE BANK — HAVERHILL.

Incorporated Aug. 20, 1877. Commenced business Sept. 3, 1877.

AMOS W. DOWNING, *President.* WILLIAM H. PAGE, *Secretary.*
WILLIAM H. PAGE, *Treasurer.*

Names of security committee:
IRA O. SAWYER, M. WARREN HANSCOM,
FRANK C. CAME.

Regular meetings the first Monday of each month.

BALANCE SHEET OCTOBER 31, 1894.

ASSETS.		LIABILITIES.	
Loans on real estate,	$401,100 00	Dues capital,	$367,911 00
Loans on shares,	7,600 00	Profits capital (all series),	74,638 10
Mortgage balance,	26 69	Surplus,	490 10
Real estate by foreclosure,	10,908 85	Guaranty fund,	3,500 00
Unpaid interest,	7,636 50	Forfeited share account,	287 38
Unpaid premiums,	708 75	Matured share account,	18,919 24
Unpaid fines,	378 08		
City of Haverhill, Mass., 4s,	15,000 00		
City of Quincy, Mass., 4s,	5,000 00		
City of Somerville, Mass., 4s,	7,000 00		
County of Aroostook, Me , 4½s,	5,000 00		
Cash in hands of treasurer,	5,386 95		
	$465,745 82		$465,745 82

Detailed Statement of Receipts and Disbursements for the Year ending Oct. 31, 1894.

RECEIPTS.		DISBURSEMENTS.	
From dues capital,	$102,689 00	For real estate loans,	$98,400 00
interest,	25,192 82	share loans,	12,150 00
premiums,	2,207 69	dues capital (withdrawn),	46,304 00
fines,	956 23	dues capital (forfeited),	3,086 00
transfer fees,	9 50	dues capital (retired),	11,073 00
real estate loans repaid,	82,000 00	dues capital (matured),	27,041 00
share loans repaid,	14,450 00	profits capital (withdrawn),	6,690 76
withdrawal profits,	668 59	profits capital (forfeited),	827 23
forfeiture profits,	82 71	profits capital (retired),	2,235 20
forfeited shares,	320 70	profits capital (matured),	13,003 70
real estate foreclosed,	8,836 40	temporary expenses,	2,212 17
mortgage balance,	82 50	forfeited shares,	358 67
retired share account,	12,805 13	matured shares,	15,851 84
matured share account,	34,771 08	retired shares,	12,887 99
bonds and notes,	15,000 00	bonds and notes,	33,248 19
surplus,	1 76	real estate foreclosed,	13,121 71
		mortgage balance,	13 50
Cash on hand Oct. 31, 1893,	3,817 80	Cash on hand Oct. 31, 1894,	5,386 95
	$303,891 91		$303,891 91

Reconciliation of Share Account with Dues and Profits Capital.

DATE OF ISSUE.	Series.	Value per Share.	Shares in Force.	Total Value.		
Jan., 1884, .	11	$188 46	81	$15,265 26	Dues capital, as per gen-	
Nov., 1884, .	12	168 55	115	19,383 25	eral ledger, . .	$367,911 00
May, 1885, .	13	157 13	66	10,370 58	Profits capital, as per	
Nov., 1885, .	14	146 13	127	18,558 51	general ledger, . .	74,638 10
May, 1886, .	15	135 48	158	21,405 84	Unpaid dues, . . .	6,860 00
Nov., 1886, .	16	125 19	227	28,418 13		
May, 1887, .	17	115 25	151	17,402 75		
Nov., 1887, .	18	105 67	176	18,597 92		
May, 1888, .	19	96 39	353	34,025 67		
Nov., 1888, .	20	87 41	434	37,935 94		
May, 1889, .	21	78 75	483	38,036 25		
Nov., 1889, .	22	70 37	246	17,311 02		
May, 1890, .	23	62 29	253	15,759 37		
Nov., 1890, .	24	54 47	704	38,346 88		
May, 1891, .	25	46 88	587	27,518 56		
Nov., 1891, .	26	39 53	591	23,362 23		
May, 1892, .	27	32 42	730	23,666 60		
Nov., 1892, .	28	25 53	479	12,228 87		
May, 1893, .	29	18 84	897	16,899 48		
Nov., 1893, .	30	12 36	739	9,134 04		
May, 1894, .	31	6 09	855	5,206 95		
Dues paid in advance, . . .				575 00		
Total, ...				$449,409 10	Total, . . .	$449,409 10

Number of shares issued during the year, ...   1,758
Number of shares now in force, ...   8,452
Number of shares now borrowed upon, ...   2,268
Largest number of shares held by any one member,   .   .   .   25
Number of shares withdrawn during the year,   .   .   .   1,536
Number of shares forfeited during the year, ...   86
Number of shares retired during the year, ...   160
Number of shares matured during the year, ...   199
Highest premium received during the year, ... $0 05
Lowest premium received during the year, ...   05
Number of members withdrawn during the year, ·   168
Present number of members,   .   .   ,.   1,162
Present number of borrowers, ...   314
Present number of non-borrowers, ...   848
Number of loans secured by first mortgage of real estate,   .   .   276
Number of loans on shares, ...   38
Largest loan to any one member, ...   5,000 00
Smallest loan to any one member, ...   50 00
Amount of expenses of the corporation for the year ending Oct. 31, 1894,   .   2,212 17
Date of examination by commissioner: May 31.

HENRY WILSON CO-OPERATIVE BANK — NATICK.

Incorporated Oct. 23, 1886.   Commenced business Nov. 12, 1886.

JOHN R. ADAMS, *President.*   ERDIX T. TURNER, *Secretary*
                    HARVEY H. WHITNEY, *Treasurer.*

Names of security committee:

J. E. SWEETLAND,	EDWARD MCMANUS,
A. P. CHENEY,	EDGAR S. DODGE,
JOSEPH WILDE.	

Regular meetings the second Friday of each month.

BALANCE SHEET OCTOBER 31, 1894.

ASSETS.		LIABILITIES.	
Loans on real estate, . .	$117,550 00	Dues capital, . . .	$114,947 00
Loans on shares, . .	6,550 00	Profits capital (all series), .	22,006 96
Permanent expense account, .	232 50	Guaranty fund, . . .	805 00
Real estate by foreclosure, .	4,025 00	Surplus, ...	1,414 79
Unpaid interest, . . .	1,739 05	Forfeited share account, .	18 38
Unpaid premiums, . .	139 20		
Unpaid fines, . . .	100 65		
Cash in hands of treasurer, .	8,855 73		
	$139,192 13		$139,192 13

Detailed Statement of Receipts and Disbursements for the Year ending Oct. 31, 1894.

RECEIPTS.		DISBURSEMENTS.	
From dues capital, .	$29,649 00	For real estate loans, . .	$29,600 00
interest, . . .	7,092 92	share loans, . . .	3,350 00
premiums, . . .	457 02	dues capital (withdrawn), .	10,839 00
fines, . . .	181.05	dues capital (retired), .	12,791 00
transfer fees, . .	1 25	profits capital (withdrawn), . . .	1,564 69
real estate loans repaid,	19,300 00	profits capital (retired),	2,713 86
share loans repaid, .	6,550 00	temporary expenses, .	483 38
withdrawal profits, .	336 13	permanent expenses, .	115 77
rent, . . .	163 00	Cash on hand Oct. 31, 1894, .	8,855 73
Cash on hand Oct. 31, 1893, .	6,583 06		
	$70,313 43		$70,313 43

Reconciliation of Share Account with Dues and Profits Capital.

DATE OF ISSUE.	Series.	Value per Share.	Shares in Force.	Total Value.		
Nov., 1886, .	1	$123 65	237	$29,305 05	Dues capital, as per general ledger, .	$114,947 00
May, 1887, .	2	113 97	112	12,764 64	eral ledger, .	
Nov., 1887, .	3	104 63	156	16,322 28	Profits capital, as per	
May, 1888, .	4	95 55	65	6,210 75	general ledger, . .	22,006 96
Nov., 1888, .	5	86 75	90	7,807 50	Unpaid dues, . .	2,988 00
May, 1889, .	6	78 21	116	9,072 36		
Nov., 1889, .	7	69 94	138	9,651 72		
May, 1890, .	8	61 95	180	11,151 00		
Nov., 1890, .	9	54 20	139	7,533 80		
May, 1891, .	10	46 69	138	6,443 22		
Nov., 1891, .	11	39 42	84	3,311 28		
May, 1892, .	12	32 37	175	5,664 75		
Nov., 1892, .	13	25 52	239	6,099 28		
May, 1893, .	14	18 85	207	3,901 95		
Nov., 1893, .	15	12 38	206	2,550 28		
May, 1894, .	16	6 10	351	2,141 10		
Dues paid in advance, . . .				11 00		
Total, ...				$139,941 96	Total, . . .	$139,941 96

Number of shares issued during the year, ... 590
Number of shares now in force, ... 2,633
Number of shares now borrowed upon, ... 752
Largest number of shares held by any one member, ... 25
Number of shares withdrawn during the year, ... 363
Number of shares retired during the year, ... 177
Highest premium received during the year, ... $0 05
Lowest premium received during the year, ... 05
Number of members withdrawn during the year, ... 72
Present number of members, ... 388
Present number of borrowers, ... 110
Present number of non-borrowers, ... 278
Number of loans secured by first mortgage of real estate, . . . 96
Number of loans on shares, ... 45
Largest loan to any one member, ... 5,000 00
Smallest loan to any one member, ... 50 00
Amount of expenses of the corporation for the year ending Oct. 31, 1894, . 538 38
Date of examination by commissioner: March 30.

HINGHAM CO-OPERATIVE BANK—HINGHAM.

Incorporated June 1, 1889. Commenced business June 5, 1889.

EBED L. RIPLEY, *President.* WALTER B. FOSTER, *Secretary.*
WALTER B. FOSTER, *Treasurer.*

Names of security committee:

E. WATERS BURR, C. SUMNER CUSHING,
FRANCIS M. RIPLEY, STETSON FOSTER,
EDWARD H. BARTLETT.

Regular meetings the first Wednesday of each month.

BALANCE SHEET OCTOBER 31, 1894.

ASSETS.		LIABILITIES.	
Loans on real estate,	$101,200 00	Dues capital,	$94,667 00
Loans on shares,	3,200 00	Profits capital (all series),	12,100 84
Permanent expense account,	108 00	Guaranty fund,	161 24
Unpaid interest,	124 75	Surplus,	48 03
Unpaid premiums,	10 95	Forfeited share account,	73 62
Unpaid fines,	17 04		
Cash in hands of treasurer,	2,389 99		
	$107,050 73		$107,050 73

Detailed Statement of Receipts and Disbursements for the Year ending Oct. 31, 1894.

RECEIPTS.		DISBURSEMENTS.	
From dues capital,	$34,042 00	For real estate loans,	$31,550 00
interest,	5,767 45	share loans,	2,250 00
premiums,	345 30	dues capital(withdrawn),	7,081 00
fines,	142 12	dues capital (retired),	7,820 00
transfer fees,	2 50	profits capital (withdrawn),	622 12
real estate loans repaid,	7,000 00	profits capital (retired),	1,293 50
share loans repaid,	3,550 00	temporary expenses,	480 35
withdrawal profits,	154 80	permanent expenses,	80 00
		forfeited shares,	3 12
		interest on retired shares,	83 05
Cash on hand Oct. 31, 1893,	2,648 96	Cash on hand Oct. 31, 1894,	2,389 99
	$53,653 13		$53,653 13

Reconciliation of Share Account with Dues and Profits Capital.

DATE OF ISSUE.	Series.	Value per Share.	Shares in Force.	Total Value.		
June, 1889, .	1	$77 51	311	$24,105 61	Dues capital, as per general ledger, .	$94,667 00
Nov., 1889, .	2	70 60	128	9,036 80	eral ledger, .	
May, 1890, .	3	62 55	193	12,072 15	Profits capital, as per	
Nov., 1890, .	4	54 70	174	9,517 80	general ledger, .	12,100 84
May, 1891, .	5	47 08	254	11,958 32	Unpaid dues, .	408 00
Nov., 1891, .	6	39 69	261	10,359 09		
May, 1892, .	7	32 54	417	13,569 18		
Nov., 1892, .	8	25 61	217	5,557 37		
May, 1893, .	9	18 89	258	4,873 62		
Nov., 1893, .	10	12 40	252	3,124 80		
May, 1894, .	11	6 10	451	2,751 10		
Dues paid in advance, . . .				250 00		
Total, ...				$107,175 84	Total, . . .	$107,175 84

Number of shares issued during the year, ... 713
Number of shares now in force, ... 2,916
Number of shares now borrowed upon, ... 717
Largest number of shares held by any one member, . . . 25
Number of shares withdrawn during the year, ... 305
Number of shares retired during the year, ... 132
Highest premium received during the year, ... $0 10
Lowest premium received during the year, ... 05
Number of members withdrawn during the year, . . . 52
Present number of members, ... 424
Present number of borrowers, ... 93
Present number of non-borrowers, ... 331
Number of loans secured by first mortgage of real estate, . . 88
Number of loans on shares, ... 18
Largest loan to any one member, ... 5,000 00
Smallest loan to any one member, ... 50 00
Amount of expenses of the corporation for the year ending Oct. 31, 1894, . 512 35
Date of examination by commissioner : October 12.

HOLBROOK CO-OPERATIVE BANK — HOLBROOK.

Incorporated May 11, 1888. Commenced business June 11, 1888.

E. Newton Thayer, *President.*   Geo. T. Wilde, *Secretary.*
Geo. T. Wilde, *Treasurer.*

Names of security committee:

Z. A. French,   A. C. Holbrook,
Howard Platts.

Regular meetings the second Tuesday of each month.

Balance Sheet October 31, 1894.

Assets.		Liabilities.	
Loans on real estate,	$33,300 00	Dues capital,	$33,034 00
Loans on shares,	2,550 00	Profits capital (all series),	5,039 51
Temporary expense account,	41 75	Interest,	970 15
Unpaid interest,	230 00	Premiums,	53 85
Unpaid premiums,	12 35	Fines,	61 82
Unpaid fines,	26 54	Withdrawal profits,	99 38
		Guaranty fund,	100 00
Cash in hands of treasurer,	3,709 28	Surplus,	511 21
	$39,869 92		$39,869 92

Detailed Statement of Receipts and Disbursements for the Year ending Oct. 31, 1894.

Receipts.		Disbursements.	
From dues capital,	$7,936 00	For real estate loans,	$8,200 00
interest,	2,179 06	share loans,	1,200 00
premiums,	120 55	dues capital(withdrawn),	4,960 00
fines,	130 92	profits capital (withdrawn),	571 29
transfer fees,	25		
real estate loans repaid,	7,050 00	temporary expenses,	102 76
share loans repaid,	915 00		
withdrawal profits,	142 86		
Cash on hand Oct. 31, 1893,	268 68	Cash on hand Oct. 31, 1894,	3,709 28
	$18,743 32		$18,743 32

Reconciliation of Share Account with Dues and Profits Capital.

DATE OF ISSUE.	Series.	Value per Share.	Shares in Force.	Total Value.			
June, 1888, .	1	$91 19	214	$19,514 66	Dues capital, as per general ledger, . .		$33,034 00
Dec., 1888, .	2	88 22	92	7,619 44			
June, 1889, .	3	74 79	13	972 27	Profits capital, as per general ledger, . .		5,039 51
Dec., 1889, .	4	66 85	45	3,008 25			
June, 1890, .	5	59 14	18	1,064 52	Unpaid dues, . .		369 00
Dec., 1890, .	6	51 66	13	671 58			
June, 1891, .	7	44 38	30	1,331 40			
Dec., 1891, .	8	37 32	34	1,268 88			
June, 1892, .	9	30 48	12	365 76			
Dec., 1892, .	10	23 82	59	1,405 38			
June, 1893, .	11	17 36	42	729 12			
Dec., 1893, .	12	11 09	25	277 25			
June, 1894, .	13	5 00	31	155 00			
Dues paid in advance, . . .				59 00			
Total, ...				$38,442 51	Total, . . .		$38,442 51

Number of shares issued during the year, ... 67
Number of shares now in force, ... 628
Number of shares now borrowed upon, ... 205
Largest number of shares held by any one member, . . . 20
Number of shares withdrawn during the year, ... 144
Highest premium received during the year, ... $0 05
Lowest premium received during the year, ... 05
Number of members withdrawn during the year, ... 21
Present number of members, ... 138
Present number of borrowers, ... 48
Present number of non-borrowers, ... 90
Number of loans secured by first mortgage of real estate, . . . 37
Number of loans on shares, ... 13
Largest loan to any one member, ... 3,000 00
Smallest loan to any one member, ... 25 00
Amount of expenses of the corporation for the year ending Oct. 31, 1894, . 102 75
Date of examination by commissioner : April 17.

HOLYOKE CO-OPERATIVE BANK—HOLYOKE.

Incorporated July 24, 1880.   Commenced business Aug. 25, 1880.

JOSEPH W. MOORE, *President.*   DWIGHT O. JUDD, *Secretary.*

DWIGHT O. JUDD, *Treasurer.*

Names of security committee :

JOHN H. MONTGOMERY,   THOMAS W. DOYLE,

W. H. BULLARD.

Regular meetings the fourth Wednesday of each month.

BALANCE SHEET OCTOBER 31, 1894.

ASSETS.		LIABILITIES.	
Loans on real estate, . .	$176,750 00	Dues capital, . . .	$174,327 00
Loans on shares, . . .	18,200 00	Profits capital (all series), .	36,014 65
Permanent expense account, .	78 92	Guaranty fund, . . .	679 06
Real estate by foreclosure, .	1,433 01	Surplus, . . .	1,147 92
Unpaid interest, . . .	491 00	Forfeited share account, .	34 05
Unpaid premiums, . .	5 04		
Unpaid fines, . . .	17 69		
Unpaid dues, . . .	813 00		
Furniture account, . .	400 00		
Cash in hands of treasurer, .	14,014 02		
	$212,202 68		$212,202 68

Detailed Statement of Receipts and Disbursements for the Year ending Oct. 31, 1894.

RECEIPTS.		DISBURSEMENTS.	
From dues capital, . .	$48,999 00	For real estate loans, . .	$46,700 00
interest, . . .	12,513 29	share loans, . .	15,950 00
premiums, . .	179 32	dues capital (withdrawn),	23,372 00
fines, ...	408 68	dues capital (forfeited),	1,587 00
transfer fees, . .	4 50	dues capital (matured),	20,020 00
real estate loans repaid,	42,800 00	profits capital (with-	
share loans repaid, .	22,550 00	drawn), . . .	2,987 07
withdrawal profits, .	748 65	profits capital (forfeited),	318 01
forfeiture profits, .	90 02	profits capital (matured),	8,912 71
forfeited shares, . .	1,514 29	temporary expenses, .	1,336 94
real estate, . .	7,799 67	permanent expenses, .	2 00
general expense, . .	61 50	forfeited shares, . .	1,502 61
		real estate, . . .	9,232 68
Cash on hand Oct. 31, 1893, .	8,266 12	Cash on hand Oct. 31, 1894,	14,014 02
	$145,935 04		$145,935 04

Reconciliation of Share Account with Dues and Profits Capital.

DATE OF ISSUE.	Series.	Value per Share.	Shares in Force.	Total Value.		
Nov., 1883, .	7	$186 27	109	$20,303 43	Dues capital, as per general ledger, . . .	$174,327 00
May, 1884, .	8	174 69	40	6,987 60	Profits capital, as per	
Nov., 1884, .	9	163 64	100	16,364 00	general ledger, . .	36,014 65
May, 1885, .	10	152 91	35	5,351 85		
Nov., 1885, .	11	142 47	54	7,693 38		
May, 1886, .	12	132 39	64	8,472 96		
Nov., 1886, .	13	122 62	68	8,338 16		
May, 1887, .	14	113 08	66	7,463 28		
Nov., 1887, .	15	103 87	161	16,723 07		
May, 1888, .	16	94 96	106	10,065 76		
Nov., 1888, .	17	86 29	139	11,994 31		
May, 1889, .	18	77 87	75	5,840 25		
Nov., 1889, .	19	69 69	126	8,780 94		
May, 1890, .	20	61 77	216	13,342 32		
Nov., 1890, .	21	54 06	200	10,812 00		
May, 1891, .	22	46 58	139	6,474 62		
Nov., 1891, .	23	39 32	241	9,476 12		
May, 1892, .	24	32 27	437	14,101 99		
Nov., 1892, .	25	25 44	317	8,064 48		
May, 1893, .	26	18 79	343	6,444 97		
Nov., 1893, .	27	12 34	290	3,578 60		
May, 1894, .	28	6 08	582	3,538 56		
Dues paid in advance, .			.	129 00		
Total, ...			.	$210,341 65	Total, . . .	$210,341 65

Number of shares issued during the year, ... 958
Number of shares now in force, ... 3,908
Number of shares now borrowed upon, ... 1,230
Largest number of shares held by any one member, ... 25
Number of shares withdrawn during the year, ... 753
Number of shares forfeited during the year, ... 58
Number of shares matured during the year, ... 143
Highest per centum of interest received during the year, . . . $0 10½
Lowest per centum of interest received during the year 06
Number of members withdrawn during the year, ... 145
Present number of members, ... 596
Present number of borrowers, ... 197
Present number of non-borrowers, ... 399
Number of loans secured by first mortgage of real estate, . . . 154
Number of loans on shares, ... 43
Largest loan to any one member, ... 4,200 00
Smallest loan to any one member, ... 50 00
Amount of expenses of the corporation for the year ending Oct. 31, 1894, . 1,293 73
Date of examination by commissioner: October 25.

HOME CO-OPERATIVE BANK — WORCESTER.

Incorporated June 10, 1882.   Commenced business June 16, 1882.

E. H. TOWNE, *President.*   T. J. HASTINGS, *Secretary.*

T. J. HASTINGS, *Treasurer.*

Names of security committee:

DANIEL PARLIN,   E. J. BARDWELL,

D. C. LEONARD.

Regular meetings the Friday preceding the third Monday of each month.

BALANCE SHEET OCTOBER 31, 1894.

ASSETS.		LIABILITIES.	
Loans on real estate, . .	$399,100 00	Dues capital, . . .	$362,515 00
Loans on shares, . . .	22,285 00	Profits capital (all series), .	70,439 98
Temporary expense account,	649 75	Interest, ...	8,031 80
Cash in hands of treasurer, .	25,796 96	Fines, ...	447 68
		Transfer fees, . . .	9 50
		Guaranty fund, . . .	1,500 00
		Surplus, ...	4,846 98
		Forfeited share account, .	40 77
	$447,831 71		$447,831 71

Detailed Statement of Receipts and Disbursements for the Year ending Oct. 31, 1894.

RECEIPTS.		DISBURSEMENTS.	
From dues capital, . .	$95,991 00	For real estate loans, . .	$121,400 00
interest, . . .	27,104 36	share loans, . . .	18,610 00
fines, . . .	1,150 92	dues capital(withdrawn),	64,424 00
transfer fees, . .	21 00	dues capital (forfeited),	42 00
real estate loans repaid,	152,050 00	dues capital (retired), .	17,396 00
share loans repaid, .	13,510 00	dues capital (matured),	19,855 00
withdrawal profits, .	1,496 36	profits capital (withdrawn), .	10,190 99
forfeiture profits, . .	0 95	profits capital (forfeited),	2 23
forfeited shares, . .	36 98	profits capital (retired), .	5,781 25
expense account, . .	145 13	profits capital (matured),	9,598 62
		temporary expenses, .	1,693 31
		forfeited shares, . .	32 06
Cash on hand Oct. 31, 1893,	3,315 72	Cash on hand Oct. 31, 1894, .	25,796 96
	$294,822 42		$294,822 42

Reconciliation of Share Account with Dues and Profits Capital.

DATE OF ISSUE.	Series.	Value per Share.	Shares in Force.	Total Value.		
June, 1883, .	3	$197 39	78	$15,395 64	Dues capital, as per general ledger, . . .	$362,515 00
Dec., 1883, .	4	185 42	63	11,681 46		
June, 1884, .	5	173 80	56	9,732 80	Profits capital, as per general ledger, . .	70,439 98
Dec., 1884, .	6	162 50	108	17,550 00		
June, 1885, .	7	151 57	110	16,672 70	Unpaid dues, . .	3,678 00
Dec., 1885, .	8	140 95	108	15,222 60		
June, 1886, .	9	130 68	215	28,096 20		
Dec., 1886, .	10	120 76	208	25,118 08		
June, 1887, .	11	111 11	254	28,221 94		
Dec., 1887, .	12	101 79	292	29,722 68		
June, 1888, .	13	92 80	225	20,880 00		
Dec., 1888, .	14	84 09	349	29,347 41		
June, 1889, .	15	75 69	281	21,268 80		
Dec., 1889, .	16	67 53	368	24,851 04		
June, 1890, .	17	59 66	407	24,281 62		
Dec., 1890, .	18	52 06	401	20,876 06		
June, 1891, .	19	44 69	463	20,691 47		
Dec., 1891, .	20	37 56	623	23,399 88		
June, 1892, .	21	30 63	590	18,071 70		
Dec., 1892, .	22	23 92	658	15,739 36		
June, 1893, .	23	17 41	399	6,946 59		
Dec., 1893, .	24	11 11	726	8,065 86		
June, 1894, .	25	5 00	875	4,375 00		
Dues paid in advance, . . .				424 00		
Total, ...				$436,632 98	Total, . . .	$436,632 98

Number of shares issued during the year, ... 1,749
Number of shares now in force, ... 7,857
Number of shares now borrowed upon, ... 2,535
Largest number of shares held by any one member, ... 25
Number of shares withdrawn during the year, ... 1,974
Number of shares forfeited during the year, ... 15
Number of shares retired during the year, ... 171
Number of shares matured during the year, ... 144
Highest per centum of interest received during the year: 8¼.
Lowest per centum of interest received during the year: 6.
Number of members withdrawn during the year, ... 199
Present number of members, ... 879
Present number of borrowers, ... 249
Present number of non-borrowers, ... 630
Number of loans secured by first mortgage of real estate, . . 235
Number of loans on shares, ... 84
Largest loan to any one member, ... $5,000 00
Smallest loan to any one member, ... 50 00
Amount of expenses of the corporation for the year ending Oct. 31, 1894, 1,548 18
Date of examination by commissioner: May 7.

HOMESTEAD CO-OPERATIVE BANK — BOSTON.

Incorporated Sept. 11, 1877.   Commenced business Sept. 12, 1877.

WALTER H. ROBERTS, *President.*   DANIEL ELDREDGE, *Secretary.*
DANIEL ELDREDGE, *Treasurer.*

Names of security committee:

JAMES M. SIMPSON,	JOHN K. FELLOWS,
JOHN D. CAMPBELL,	WALTER H. ROBERTS,
	WILLIS S. MASON.

Regular meetings the second Wednesday of each month.

BALANCE SHEET OCTOBER 31, 1894.

ASSETS.		LIABILITIES.	
Loans on real estate,	$362,700 00	Dues capital,	$326,714 00
Loans on shares,	13,050 00	Profits capital (all series),	69,800 69
Temporary expense account,	350 00	Interest,	4,210 31
Real estate by foreclosure,	3,170 25	Premiums,	398 45
Unpaid interest,	2,509 35	Fines,	218 86
Unpaid premiums,	262 80	Transfer fees,	2 25
Unpaid fines,	192 76	Withdrawal profits,	244 89
Mortgages,	9,930 00	Forfeiture profits,	4 35
Cash in hands of treasurer,	15,987 45	Guaranty fund,	1,928 73
		Surplus,	2,947 26
		Forfeited share account,	331 63
		Retired shares,	1,351 19
	$408,152 61		$408,152 61

Detailed Statement of Receipts and Disbursements for the Year ending Oct. 31, 1894.

RECEIPTS.		DISBURSEMENTS.	
From dues capital,	$87,839 00	For real estate loans,	$82,050 00
interest,	24,687 06	share loans,	16,200 00
premiums,	2,573 30	dues capital (withdrawn),	36,756 00
fines,	1,403 61	dues capital (forfeited),	2,321 00
transfer fees,	11 25	dues capital (retired),	43,393 00
real estate loans repaid,	81,150 00	dues capital (matured),	3,082 00
share loans repaid,	19,000 00	profits capital (withdrawn),	5,908 96
withdrawal profits,	1,477 00	profits capital (forfeited),	522 50
forfeiture profits,	136 42	profits capital (retired),	16,195 75
forfeited shares,	28 44	profits capital (matured),	1,519 84
mortgages,	3,690 00	temporary expenses,	2,121 58
retired shares,	58,193 49	surplus,	5 00
matured shares,	2,124 61	real estate by foreclosure,	14,785 01
real estate by foreclosure,	16,001 88	forfeited shares,	27 28
		matured shares,	2,728 25
		retired shares,	56,994 73
		mortgages,	2,730 00
		interest,	279 27
Cash on hand Oct. 31, 1893,	5,291 56	Cash on hand Oct. 31, 1894,	15,987 45
	$303,607 62		$303,607 62

Reconciliation of Share Account with Dues and Profits Capital.

DATE OF ISSUE.	Shares.	Value per Share.	Shares in Force.	Total Value.			
Sept , 1883, .	13	$199 85	29	$5,795 65	Dues capital, as per gen-		
Mar., 1884, .	14	187 03	54	10,099 62	eral ledger, . .		$326,714 00
Sept., 1884, .	15	174 76	25	4,369 00	Profits capital, as per		
Mar., 1885, .	16	162 97	75	12,222 75	general ledger, . .		69,800 69
Sept., 1885, .	17	151 59	24	3,638 16	Unpaid dues, . .		3,415 00
Mar., 1886, .	18	140 63	160	22,500 80			
Sept., 1886, .	19	130 04	237	30,819 48			
Mar , 1887, .	20	119 82	130	15,576 60			
Sept., 1887, .	21	109 93	177	19,457 61			
Mar., 1888, .	22	100 38	258	25,898 04			
Sept., 1888, .	23	91 16	590	53,784 40			
Mar., 1889, .	24	82 24	341	28,043 84			
Sept., 1889, .	25	73 63	328	24,150 64			
Mar., 1890, .	26	65 31	379	24,752 49			
Sept., 1890, .	27	57 27	395	22,621 65			
Mar., 1891, .	28	49 50	318	15,741 00			
Sept., 1891, .	29	41 99	501	21,036 99			
Mar., 1892, .	30	34 74	702	24,387 48			
Sept., 1892, .	31	27 74	419	11,623 06			
Mar., 1893, .	32	20 97	432	9,059 04			
Sept., 1893, .	33	14 43	469	6,767 67			
Mar., 1894, .	34	8 11	752	6,098 72			
Sept., 1894, .	35	2 00	576	1,152 00			
Dues paid in advance, . . .				333 00			
Total, ...				$399,929 69	Total, . . .		$399,929 69

Number of shares issued during the year, ...	1,500	
Number of shares now in force, ...	7,371	
Number of shares now borrowed upon, ...	2,118	
Largest number of shares held by any one member, . . .	25	
Number of shares withdrawn during the year, . . .	1,113	
Number of shares forfeited during the year, ...	100	
Number of shares retired during the year, ...	400	
Number of shares matured during the year, ...	23	
Highest premium received during the year, . -		$0 15
Lowest premium received during the year, ...		05
Number of members withdrawn during the year, ...	207	
Present number of members, ...	924	
Present number of borrowers, ...	245	
Present number of non-borrowers, ...	679	
Number of loans secured by first mortgage of real estate, . .	246	
Number of loans on shares, ...	63	
Largest loan to any one member, ...	4,800 00	
Smallest loan to any one member, ...	50 00	
Amount of expenses of the corporation for the year ending Oct. 31, 1894, .	2,121 58	

Date of examination by commissioner : April 27.

HOUSATONIC CO-OPERATIVE BANK — GREAT BARRINGTON.

Incorporated June 3, 1889. Commenced business July 1, 1889.

NATHANIEL WARNER, *President.*   MICHAEL J. LEAHY, *Secretary.*
TIMOTHY Z. POTTER, *Treasurer.*

Names of security committee:

TIMOTHY Z. POTTER,   E. S. THATCHER,
F. M. MOORE.

Regular meetings the first Monday of each month.

BALANCE SHEET OCTOBER 31, 1894.

ASSETS.		LIABILITIES.	
Loans on real estate,	$13,450 00	Dues capital,	$12,956 00
Loans on shares,	1,150 00	Profits capital (all series),	1,237 24
Temporary expense account,	8 50	Interest,	255 11
Cash in hands of treasurer,	113 21	Fines,	3 02
		Withdrawal profits,	33 13
		Guaranty fund,	39 16
		Surplus,	185 25
		Forfeited share account,	12 80
	$14,721 71		$14,721 71

Detailed Statement of Receipts and Disbursements for the Year ending Oct. 31, 1894.

RECEIPTS.		DISBURSEMENTS.	
From dues capital,	$4,715 00	For real estate loans,	$3,200 00
interest,	758 17	share loans,	650 00
fines,	9 62	dues capital (withdrawn),	3,159 00
real estate loans repaid,	500 00	profits capital (withdrawn),	238 72
share loans repaid,	750 00	temporary expenses,	48 50
withdrawal profits,	60 20	Cash on hand Oct. 31, 1894,	113 21
Cash on hand Oct. 31, 1893,	616 44		
	$7,409 43		$7,409 43

Reconciliation of Share Account with Dues and Profits Capital.

DATE OF ISSUE.	Series.	Value per Share.	Shares in Force.	Total Value.		
July, 1889, .	1	$72 14	106	$7,646 84	Dues capital, as per general ledger, . .	$12,956 00
Jan., 1890, .	2	64 74	17	1,100 58	eral ledger, . .	
July, 1890, .	3	57 15	2	114 30	Profits capital, as per	
Jan., 1891, .	4	49 89	17	848 13	general ledger, . .	1,237 24
July, 1891, .	5	42 84	15	642 60	Unpaid dues, . .	284 00
Jan., 1892, .	6	35 96	33	1,186 68		
July, 1892, .	7	29 26	31	907 06		
Jan., 1893, .	8	22 71	23	522 33		
July, 1893, .	9	16 32	49	799 68		
Jan., 1894, .	10	10 08	50	504 00		
July, 1894, .	11	4 00	48	192 00		
Suspense profits, ...				1 04		
Dues paid in advance, . . .				12 00		
Total, ...				$14,477 24	Total, . . .	$14,477 24

Number of shares issued during the year, ... 118
Number of shares now in force, ... 391
Number of shares now borrowed upon, ... 100
Largest number of shares held by any one member, ... 15
Number of shares withdrawn during the year, ... 147
Highest per centum of interest received during the year : 6.
Lowest per centum of interest received during the year : 5¼.
Number of members withdrawn during the year, ... 26
Present number of members, ... 108
Present number of borrowers, ... 25
Present number of non-borrowers, ... 81
Number of loans secured by first mortgage of real estate, . . . 16
Number of loans on shares, ... 9
Largest loan to any one member, ... $2,000 00
Smallest loan to any one member, ... 50 00
Amount of expenses of the corporation for the year ending Oct. 31, 1894, . 64 46
Date of examination by commissioner : August 16.

HUDSON CO-OPERATIVE BANK — HUDSON.

Incorporated Oct. 22, 1885.   Commenced business Nov. 19, 1885.

A. T. KNIGHT, *President.*   C. H. HILL, *Secretary.*

C. E. HALL, *Treasurer.*

Names of security committee:

R. HENRY HAPGOOD,   JOSIAH S. WELSH,

CHAS. F. WELCH.

Regular meetings the third Thursday of each month.

BALANCE SHEET OCTOBER 31, 1894.

ASSETS.		LIABILITIES.	
Loans on real estate, . .	$165,550 00	Dues capital, . . .	$152,750 00
Loans on shares, . .	7,575 00	Profits capital (all series), .	26,185 54
Permanent expense account, .	200 00	Guaranty fund, . .	774 58
Unpaid interest, . .	958 50	Surplus, ...	557 31
Cash in hands of treasurer, .	5,995 23	Forfeited share account, .	11 30
	$180,278 73		$180,278 73

Detailed Statement of Receipts and Disbursements for the Year ending Oct. 31, 1894.

RECEIPTS.		DISBURSEMENTS.	
From dues capital, . .	$50,407 00	For real estate loans, . .	$57,000 00
interest, . .	9,708 58	share loans, . . .	5,900 00
premiums, . . .	530 77	dues capital (withdrawn), .	22,223 00
fines, ...	441 19	dues capital (forfeited), .	15 00
transfer fees, . .	1 00	dues capital (retired), .	1,860 00
real estate loans repaid,	26,050 00	profits capital (with-	
share loans repaid,	5,675 00	drawn), . . .	2,497 46
withdrawal profits, .	619 17	profits capital (forfeited),	70
forfeiture profits, . .	1 52	profits capital (retired), .	471 64
forfeited shares, . .	15 00	temporary expenses, .	820 60
		forfeited shares, . .	86 10
Cash on hand Oct. 31, 1893, .	3,420 50	Cash on hand Oct. 31, 1894, .	5,995 23
	$96,869 73		$96,869 73

Reconciliation of Share Account with Dues and Profits Capital.

DATE OF ISSUE.	Series.	Value per Share.	Shares in Force.	Total Value.		
Nov., 1885, .	1	$145 29	103	$14,964 87	Dues capital, as per general ledger, . .	$152,750 00
May, 1886, .	2	134 60	22	2,961 20		
Nov., 1886, .	3	124 78	37	4,616 86	Profits capital, as per general ledger, . .	26,185 54
May, 1887, .	4	115 11	22	2,532 42		
Nov., 1887, .	5	105 73	148	15,648 04	Unpaid dues, . .	1,321 00
May, 1888, .	6	96 60	121	11,688 60		
Nov., 1888, .	7	87 74	105	9,212 70		
May, 1889, .	8	79 07	214	16,920 98		
Nov., 1889, .	9	70 72	220	15,558 40		
May, 1890, .	10	62 59	262	16,398 58		
Nov., 1890, .	11	54 70	241	13,182 70		
May, 1891, .	12	47 09	195	9,182 55		
Nov., 1891, .	13	39 71	222	8,815 62		
May, 1892, .	14	32 55	275	8,951 25		
Nov., 1892, .	15	25 62	399	10,222 38		
May, 1893, .	16	18 91	415	7,847 65		
Nov., 1893, .	17	12 41	680	8,438 80		
May, 1894, .	18	6 11	454	2,773 94		
Dues paid in advance, . . .				339 00		
Total, ...				$180,256 54	Total, . . .	$180,256 54

Number of shares issued during the year, ... 1,259
Number of shares now in force, ... 4,135
Number of shares now borrowed upon, ... 930
Largest number of shares held by any one member, . . . 25
Number of shares withdrawn during the year, ... 925
Number of shares forfeited during the year, ... 7
Number of shares retired during the year, ... 22
Highest per centum of interest received during the year: $7\frac{2}{10}$.
Lowest per centum of interest received during the year: 6.
Number of members withdrawn during the year, ... 80
Present number of members, ... 563
Present number of borrowers, ... 151
Present number of non-borrowers, ... 412
Number of loans secured by first mortgage of real estate, . . 135
Number of loans on shares, ... 23
Largest loan to any one member, ... $4,950 00
Smallest loan to any one member, ... 50 00
Amount of expenses of the corporation for the year ending Oct. 31, 1894, . 820 60
Date of examination by commissioner: February 2.

HYDE PARK CO-OPERATIVE BANK—HYDE PARK.

Incorporated March 26, 1886. Commenced business May 5, 1886.

GEORGE MILES, *President.*   THOMAS E. FAUNCE, *Secretary.*
THOMAS E. FAUNCE, *Treasurer.*

Names of security committee:

ELI B. TASKER,   ALONZO H. RICHARDSON,
HOWARD JENKINS.

Regular meetings the first Wednesday of each month.

BALANCE SHEET OCTOBER 31, 1894.

ASSETS.		LIABILITIES.	
Loans on real estate, .	$149,150 00	Dues capital, . . .	$135,849 00
Loans on shares, . . .	7,890 00	Profits capital (all series), .	20,018 94
Permanent expense account,	184 00	Interest, . - . .	1,016 31
Temporary expense account,	287 68	Premiums, ...	74 45
Unpaid fines, ...	0 91	Transfer fees, . . .	0 25
Cash in hands of treasurer, .	974 96	Withdrawal profits, . .	171 81
		Guaranty fund, . .	639 02
		Surplus, . . .	717 77
	$158,487 55		$158,487 55

Detailed Statement of Receipts and Disbursements for the Year ending Oct. 31, 1894.

RECEIPTS.		DISBURSEMENTS.	
From dues capital, . .	$47,061 00	For real estate loans, . .	$51,950 00
interest, . . .	8,899 26	share loans, . . .	8,230 00
premiums, . . .	841 05	dues capital (withdrawn),	29,123 00
fines, ...	400 81	dues capital (retired), .	670 00
transfer fees, . .	3 50	profits capital (withdrawn), . . .	3,584 69
real estate loans repaid,	29,300 00	profits capital (retired),	118 91
share loans repaid, .	8,640 00	temporary expenses, .	1,400 27
withdrawal profits, .	633 11	interest, ...	42 00
		premiums, . . .	4 20
Cash on hand Oct. 31, 1893, .	319 30	Cash on hand Oct. 31, 1894,	974 96
	$96,098 03		$96,098 03

Reconciliation of Share Account with Dues and Profits Capital.

DATE OF ISSUE.	Series.	Value per Share.	Shares in Force.	Total Value.		
May, 1886, .	1	$133 71	69	$9,225 99	Dues capital, as per general ledger, . .	$135,849 00
Mar., 1887, .	2	117 36	98	11,501 28	Profits capital, as per general ledger, . .	20,018 94
Sept., 1887, .	3	107 95	39	4,210 05	Unpaid dues, . . .	1,197 00
Mar., 1888, .	4	98 76	75	7,407 00		
Sept., 1888, .	5	89 84	93	8,355 12		
Mar., 1889, .	6	81 22	132	10,721 04		
Sept., 1889, .	7	72 82	116	8,447 12		
Mar., 1890, .	8	64 68	290	18,757 20		
Sept., 1890, .	9	56 80	188	10,678 40		
Mar., 1891, .	10	49 15	349	17,153 35		
Sept., 1891, .	11	41 75	294	12,274 50		
Mar., 1892, .	12	34 58	321	11,100 18		
Sept., 1892, .	13	27 65	316	8,737 40		
Mar., 1893, .	14	20 93	412	8,623 16		
Sept., 1893, .	15	14 42	309	4,455 78		
Mar., 1894, .	16	8 11	467	3,787 37		
Sept., 1894, .	17	2 00	537	1,074 00		
Dues paid in advance, . . .				556 00		
Total, ...				$157,064 94	Total, . . .	$157,064 94

Number of shares issued during the year, ... 1,185
Number of shares now in force, ... 4,105
Number of shares now borrowed upon, ... 1,050
Largest number of shares held by any one member, ... 25
Number of shares withdrawn during the year, . ·. . . 1,101
Number of shares retired during the year, ... 11
Highest premium received during the year, ... $0 20
Lowest premium received during the year, ... 0 05
Number of members withdrawn during the year, ... 109
Present number of members, ... 568
Present number of borrowers, ... 127
Present number of non-borrowers, ... 441
Number of loans secured by first mortgage of real estate, . . . 96
Number of loans on shares, ... 43
Largest loan to any one member, ... 4,500 00
Smallest loan to any one member, ... 20 00
Amount of expenses of the corporation for the year ending Oct. 31, 1894, . 1,437 42
Date of examination by commissioner: June 14.

LAFAYETTE CO-OPERATIVE BANK — FALL RIVER.

Incorporated April 11, 1894. Commenced business May 2, 1894.

JOHN B. CHAGNON, *President.*   WM. F. WINTER, *Secretary.*
WM. F. WINTER, *Treasurer.*

Names of security committee:

JOHN B. HUARD,   SAMUEL BENOIT,
EDMUND REEVES.

Regular meetings the first Wednesday of each month.

BALANCE SHEET OCTOBER 31, 1894.

ASSETS.		LIABILITIES.	
Loans on real estate,	$7,200 00	Dues capital,	$8,040 00
Permanent expense account,	208 42	Interest,	155 00
Temporary expense account,	72 80	Premiums,	20 50
Unpaid fines,	9 56	Fines,	27 46
Unpaid dues,	401 00	Advance dues,	10 00
Cash in hands of treasurer,	370 18	Appraisal fees,	9 00
	$8,261 96		$8,261 96

Detailed Statement of Receipts and Disbursements for the Year ending Oct. 31, 1894.

RECEIPTS.		DISBURSEMENTS.	
From dues capital,	$7,979 00	For real estate loans,	$8,400 00
interest,	155 00	dues capital(withdrawn),	330 00
premiums,	20 50	temporary expenses,	72 80
fines,	17 90	permanent expenses,	208 42
real estate loans repaid,	1,200 00	Cash on hand Oct. 31, 1894,	370 18
appraisal fees,	9 00		
	$9,381 40		$9,381 40

Reconciliation of Share Account with Dues and Profits Capital.

DATE OF ISSUE.	Series.	Value per Share.	Shares in Force.	Total Value.		
May, 1894, .	1	$6 00	1,340	$8,040 00	Dues capital, as per general ledger, .	$8,040 00
Total, ...				$8,040 00	Total, . . .	$8,040 00

Number of shares issued during the year, ... 1,424
Number of shares now in force, ... 1,340
Number of shares now borrowed upon, ... 37
Largest number of shares held by any one member, . . . 25
Number of shares withdrawn during the year, ... 84
Highest premium received during the year, ... $0 15
Lowest premium received during the year, ... 10
Number of members withdrawn during the year, ... 13
Present number of members, ... 179
Present number of borrowers, ... 3
Present number of non-borrowers, ... 176
Number of loans secured by first mortgage of real estate, . . . 3
Largest loan to any one member, ... 4,000 00
Smallest loan to any one member, ... 1,300 00
Amount of expenses of the corporation for the year ending Oct. 31, 1894, . 72 80
Date of examination by commissioner: August 27.

LAWRENCE CO-OPERATIVE BANK — LAWRENCE.

Incorporated March 12, 1888.   Commenced business April 6, 1888.

JAMES B. LYALL, *President.*   A. M. FAY, *Secretary.*
GEORGE W. HALL, *Treasurer.*

Names of security committee :

A. M. FAY,   OSCAR E. SPEAR,
COLIN KERR.

Regular meetings the first Friday of each month.

BALANCE SHEET OCTOBER 31, 1894.

ASSETS.		LIABILITIES.	
Loans on real estate, . .	$187,500 00	Dues capital, . . .	$168,400 00
Loans on shares, . . .	6,220 00	Profits capital (all series), .	23,523 98
Unpaid interest, . . .	936 79	Interest, ...	1,092 43
Unpaid premiums, . .	35 55	Premiums, ...	104 55
Unpaid fines, ...	107 50	Fines, ...	52 32
Cash in hands of secretary, .	1,257 54	Withdrawal profits, . .	52 16
Cash in hands of treasurer, .	103 95	Guaranty fund, . . .	765 00
		Surplus, ...	2,147 41
		Forfeited share account, .	23 48
	$196,161 33		$196,161 33

Detailed Statement of Receipts and Disbursements for the Year ending Oct. 31, 1894.

RECEIPTS.		DISBURSEMENTS.	
From dues capital, . .	$58,541 00	For real estate loans, . .	$89,750 00
interest, . . .	10,772 53	share loans, . . .	4,795 00
premiums, . . .	1,044 26	dues capital(withdrawn),	29,868 00
fines, ...	325 70	dues capital (retired), .	8,492 00
transfer fees, . .	2 25	profits capital (with-	
real estate loans repaid,	58,800 00	drawn), . . .	3,111 29
share loans repaid, .	5,960 00	profits capital (retired),	1,574 45
withdrawal profits, .	774 57	temporary expenses, .	751 08
profits, ...	27 00	forfeited shares, . .	16 84
		withdrawal profits, .	6 75
Cash on hand Oct. 31, 1893, .	3,479 59	Cash on hand Oct. 31, 1894,	1,361 49
	$139,726 90		$139,726 90

Reconciliation of Share Account with Dues and Profits Capital.

DATE OF ISSUE.	Series.	Value per Share.	Shares In Force.	Total Value.		
April, 1888, .	1	$96 89	193	$18,699 77	Dues capital, as per general ledger, . .	$168,400 00
Oct., 1888, .	2	88 34	142	12,544 28		
April, 1889, .	3	79 97	317	25,350 49	Profits capital, as per general ledger, . .	23,523 98
Oct., 1889, .	4	71 68	173	12,400 64		
April, 1890, .	5	63 81	331	24,311 61	Unpaid dues,. . .	1,689 00
Oct., 1890, .	6	56 00	209	11,704 00		
April, 1891, .	7	48 39	372	18,001 08		
Oct., 1891, .	8	40 97	434	17,780 98		
April, 1892, .	9	33 76	614	20,728 64		
Oct., 1892, .	10	26 78	614	16,442 92		
April, 1893, .	11	20 01	433	8,664 33		
Oct., 1893, .	12	13 46	218	2,934 28		
April, 1894, .	13	7 12	508	3,616 96		
Oct., 1894, .	14	1 00	370	370 00		
Dues paid in advance, . . .				63 00		
Total, ...				$193,612 98	Total, . . .	$193,612 98

Number of shares issued during the year, ... 921
Number of shares now in force, ... 4,978
Number of shares now borrowed upon, ... 1,185
Largest number of shares held by any one member, . . . 25
Number of shares withdrawn during the year, . . . 1,048
Number of shares retired during the year, ... 131
Highest premium received during the year, ... $0 25
Lowest premium received during the year, ... 05
Number of members withdrawn during the year, ... 179
Present number of members, ... 734
Present number of borrowers, ... 153
Present number of non-borrowers, ... 581
Number of loans secured by first mortgage of real estate, . . . 142
Number of loans on shares, ... 36
Largest loan to any one member, ... 5,000 00
Smallest loan to any one member, ... 10 00
Amount of expenses of the corporation for the year ending Oct. 31, 1894, . 751 08
Date of examination by commissioner: June 26.

LEOMINSTER CO-OPERATIVE BANK — LEOMINSTER.

Incorporated May 8, 1888.   Commenced business May 18, 1888.

JOEL G. TYLER, *President.*   ROBERT L. CARTER, *Secretary.*
ROBERT L. CARTER, *Treasurer.*

Names of security committee :
CHAS. E. BIGELOW,   HURLBURT L. HARRIS,
WILLARD F. LAWRENCE.

Regular meetings the third Friday of each month.

BALANCE SHEET OCTOBER 31, 1894.

ASSETS.			LIABILITIES.	
Loans on real estate, . .	$75,250 00		Dues capital, . . .	$71,557 00
Loans on shares, . . .	1,235 00		Profits capital (all series), .	10,335 55
Unpaid interest, . . .	592 70		Guaranty fund, . . .	304 00
Unpaid premiums, . .	92 58		Surplus, ...	952 44
Unpaid fines, ...	91 76			
Cash in hands of treasurer, .	5,886 95			
	$83,148 99			$83,148 99

Detailed Statement of Receipts and Disbursements for the Year ending Oct. 31, 1894.

RECEIPTS.			DISBURSEMENTS.	
From dues capital, . .	$24,124 00		For real estate loans, . .	$22,653 41
interest, . . .	4,298 17		share loans, . . .	1,180 00
premiums, . . .	382 60		dues capital (withdrawn),	18,285 00
fines, ...	99 47		dues capital (retired), .	2,034 00
transfer fees, . .	1 00		profits capital (withdrawn), . . .	1,909 22
real estate loans repaid,	19,730 00		profits capital (retired),	335 82
share loans repaid, .	1,635 00		temporary expenses, .	1,015 80
withdrawal profits, .	185 11		forfeited shares, . .	1 24
temporary expense, .	478 94		interest, ...	55 64
profit and loss, . .	56 24		profit and loss, . .	97 00
Cash on hand Oct. 31, 1893, .	2,463 55		Cash on hand Oct. 31, 1894,	5,886 95
	$53,454 08			$53,454 08

Reconciliation of Share Account with Dues and Profits Capital.

DATE OF ISSUE.	Series.	Value per Share.	Shares in Force.	Total Value.		
May, 1888, .	1	$95 27	207	$19,720 89	Dues capital, as per general ledger, . .	$71,557 00
Nov., 1888, .	2	86 57	100	8,657 00		
May, 1889, .	3	78 13	51	3,984 63	Profits capital, as per	
Nov., 1889, .	4	69 93	83	5,804 19	general ledger, . .	10,335 55
May, 1890, .	5	61 97	86	5,329 42	Unpaid dues, . .	2,252 00
Nov., 1890, .	6	54 24	159	8,624 16		
May, 1891, .	7	46 74	110	5,141 40		
Nov., 1891, .	8	39 46	154	6,076 84		
May, 1892, .	9	32 39	205	6,639 95		
Nov., 1892, .	10	25 52	216	5,512 32		
May, 1893, .	11	18 85	285	5,372 25		
Nov., 1893, .	12	12 38	115	1,423 70		
May, 1894, .	13	6 10	248	1,512 80		
Dues paid in advance, . . .				345 00		
Total, ...				$84,144 55		$84,144 55

Number of shares issued during the year, ... 422
Number of shares now in force, ... 2,019
Number of shares now borrowed upon, ... 550
Largest number of shares held by any one member, ... 25
Number of shares withdrawn during the year, ... 624
Number of shares retired during the year, ... 34
Highest premium received during the year, ... $0 25
Lowest premium received during the year, ... 05
Number of members withdrawn during the year, ... 52
Present number of members, ... 339
Present number of borrowers, ... 92
Present number of non-borrowers, ... 247
Number of loans secured by first mortgage of real estate, . . . 79
Number of loans on shares, ... 13
Largest loan to any one member, ... 3,550 00
Smallest loan to any one member, ... 50 00
Amount of expenses of the corporation for the year ending Oct. 31, 1894, . 626 24
Date of examination by commissioner: August 28.

LOWELL CO-OPERATIVE BANK—LOWELL.

Incorporated April 29, 1885.   Commenced business May 14, 1885.

ARTEMAS B. WOODWORTH, *President.*   GEO. W. BATCHELDER, *Secretary.*
DANIEL A. EATON, *Treasurer.*

Names of security committee:
JOSEPH L. SEDGLEY,   CALEB L. SMITH,
CHARLES H. BURTT.

Regular meetings the first Friday after the tenth of each month.

BALANCE SHEET OCTOBER 31, 1894.

ASSETS.			LIABILITIES.	
Loans on real estate, . .	$220,040	00	Dues capital, . . .	$199,778 00
Loans on shares, . . .	9,845	00	Profits capital (all series), .	39,248 72
Permanent expense account,	78	50	Interest, ...	148 60
Real estate by foreclosure, .	2,863	75	Premiums, ...	20 95
Unpaid interest, . . .	1,050	50	Fines, ...	16 04
Unpaid premiums, . . .	90	83	Transfer fees, . . .	0 50
Unpaid fines, ...	102	31	Guaranty fund, . . .	560 66
Cash in hands of secretary, .	15	62	Surplus, ...	335 37
Cash in hands of treasurer, .	6,209	59	Forfeited share account, .	187 26
	$240,296	10		$240,296 10

Detailed Statement of Receipts and Disbursements for the Year ending Oct. 31, 1894.

RECEIPTS.			DISBURSEMENTS.	
From dues capital, . .	$59,339	00	For real estate loans, . .	$54,800 00
interest, . . .	12,550	77	share loans, . . .	7,795 00
premiums, . . .	1,171	95	dues capital (withdrawn),	32,782 00
fines, ...	417	43	dues capital (forfeited),	175 00
transfer fees, . .	7	75	dues capital (retired), .	680 00
real estate loans repaid,	15,600	00	profits capital (with-	
share loans repaid, .	12,190	00	drawn), . . .	5,241 72
withdrawal profits, .	659	09	profits capital (forfeited),	26 20
forfeiture profits, . .	11	84	profits capital (retired),	138 20
forfeited shares, . .	187	26	temporary expenses, .	744 54
cash from over-payment,	2	55	permanent expenses, .	28 50
rent, ...	163	97	real estate, . . .	193 58
			interest on retired shares,	39 20
Cash on hand Oct. 31, 1893, .	6,567	54	Cash on hand Oct. 31, 1894,	6,225 21
	$108,869	15		$108,869 15

Reconciliation of Share Account with Dues and Profits Capital.

DATE OF ISSUE.	Series.	Value per Share.	Shares in Force.	Total Value.		
May, 1885, .	1	$159 28	107	$17,042 96	Dues capital, as per general ledger, . . .	$199,778 00
Nov., 1885, .	2	148 22	80	11,857 60	eral ledger, . . .	
May, 1886, .	3	137 48	43	5,910 78	Profits capital, as per	
Nov., 1886, .	4	127 06	122	15,501 32	general ledger, . .	39,248 72
May, 1887, .	5	116 90	66	7,715 40	Unpaid dues, . . .	1,338 00
Nov., 1887, .	6	107 10	97	10,388 70		
May, 1888, .	7	97 64	125	12,205 00		
Nov., 1888, .	8	88 52	182	16,110 64		
May, 1889, .	9	79 70	309	24,627 30		
Nov., 1889, .	10	71 16	154	10,958 64		
May, 1890, .	11	62 92	416	26,174 72		
Nov., 1890, .	12	54 96	195	10,717 20		
May, 1891, .	13	47 28	294	13,900 32		
Nov., 1891, .	14	39 85	299	11,915 15		
May, 1892, .	15	32 67	398	13,002 66		
Nov., 1892, .	16	25 71	478	12,289 38		
May, 1893, .	17	18 96	535	10,143 60		
Nov., 1893, .	18	12 43	491	6,103 13		
May, 1894, .	19	6 11	602	3,678 22		
Dues paid in advance, . . .				122 00		
Total, ...				$240,364 72	Total, ...	$240,364 72

Number of shares issued during the year, ... 1,177
Number of shares now in force, ... 4,993
Number of shares now borrowed upon, ... 1,387
Largest number of shares held by any one member, ... 25
Number of shares withdrawn during the year, ... 928
Number of shares forfeited during the year, ... 5
Number of shares retired during the year, ... 14
Highest premium received during the year, ... $0 40
Lowest premium received during the year, ... 0 05
Number of members withdrawn during the year, ... 97
Present number of members, ... 613
Present number of borrowers, ... 205
Present number of non-borrowers, ... 408
Number of loans secured by first mortgage of real estate, . . . 158
Number of loans on shares, ... 47
Largest loan to any one member, ... 5,000 00
Smallest loan to any one member, ... 50 00
Amount of expenses of the corporation for the year ending Oct. 31, 1894, . 766 54
Date of examination by commissioner : November 27.

LYNN CO-OPERATIVE BANK — LYNN.

Incorporated Nov. 18, 1891.   Commenced business Nov. 23, 1891.

JACOB M. LEWIS, *President.*   EDWIN C. LEWIS, *Secretary.*
JOSEPH W. HARDING, *Treasurer.*

Names of security committee :

FRED D. MAYO,	DAVID E. CONNOR,
CHAS. H. GOLDTHWAIT,	WM. H. SEVERANCE,
	F. F. LAWRENCE.

Regular meetings the first Monday of each month.

BALANCE SHEET OCTOBER 31, 1894.

ASSETS.		LIABILITIES.	
Loans on real estate, . .	$15,000 00	Dues capital, . . .	$16,639 00
Loans on shares, . .	1,225 00	Profits capital (all series), .	1,155 54
Permanent expense account,	170 00	Guaranty fund, . . .	20 00
Unpaid interest, . . .	71 00	Surplus, ...	228 00
Unpaid premiums, . .	3 65	Forfeited share account, .	155 92
Unpaid fines, ...	42 81		
Cash in hands of treasurer, .	1,686 00		
	$18,198 46		$18,198 46

Detailed Statement of Receipts and Disbursements for the Year ending Oct. 31, 1894.

RECEIPTS.		DISBURSEMENTS.	
From dues capital, . .	$8,109 00	For real estate loans, . .	$3,100 00
interest, . . .	855 68	share loans, . . .	645 00
premiums, . .	35 92	dues capital(withdrawn),	4,157 00
fines, ...	47 88	dues capital (forfeited),	65 00
real estate loans repaid,	200 00	profits capital (withdrawn), . . .	186 82
share loans repaid,	565 00	profits capital (forfeited),	6 10
forfeited shares, . .	71 10	temporary expenses, .	73 70
surplus, . . .	21 93	permanent expenses, .	75 00
		surplus, ...	30 00
Cash on hand Oct. 31, 1893, .	118 11	Cash on hand Oct. 31, 1894,	1,686 00
	$10,024 62		$10,024 62

Reconciliation of Share Account with Dues and Profits Capital.

DATE OF ISSUE.	Series.	Value per Share.	Shares in Force.	Total Value.		
Nov., 1891, .	1	$38 86	254	$9,870 44	Dues capital, as per general ledger, . .	$16,639 00
May, 1892, .	2	32 07	126	4,040 82		
Nov., 1892, .	3	25 39	55	1,396 45	Profits capital, as per	
May, 1893, .	4	18 80	60	1,128 00	general ledger, . .	1,155 54
Nov., 1893, .	5	12 36	103	1,273 08	Unpaid dues, . . .	496 00
May, 1894, .	6	6 09	75	456 75		
Dues paid in advance, . . .				125 00		
Total, ...				$18,290 54	Total, . . .	$18,290 54

Number of shares issued during the year, ... 214
Number of shares now in force, ... 673
Number of shares now borrowed upon, ... 144
Largest number of shares held by any one member, . . . 25
Number of shares withdrawn during the year, ... 214
Number of shares forfeited during the year, ... 5
Highest premium received during the year, ... $0 05
Lowest premium received during the year, ... 05
Number of members withdrawn during the year, ... 22
Present number of members, ... 71
Present number of borrowers, ... 16
Present number of non-borrowers, ... 55
Number of loans secured by first mortgage of real estate, . . . 11
Number of loans on shares, ... 6
Largest loan to any one member, ... 3,400 00
Smallest loan to any one member, ... 20 00
Amount of expenses of the corporation for the year ending Oct. 31, 1894, . 108 70
Date of examination by commissioner: April 24.

MALDEN CO-OPERATIVE BANK — MALDEN.

Incorporated April 27, 1887. Commenced business May 9, 1887.

Marcellus Coggan, *President.*   Lewis P. Brown, *Secretary.*
Lewis P. Brown, *Treasurer.*

Names of security committee:

Geo. S. Gould,	John E. Staples,
M. S. O'Donnell,	John E. Farnham,
Chas. A. Stiles,	James S. Webber.

Regular meetings the second Monday of each month.

BALANCE SHEET OCTOBER 31, 1894.

ASSETS.		LIABILITIES.	
Loans on real estate,	$196,523 73	Dues capital,	$185,662 00
Loans on shares,	13,310 00	Profits capital (all series),	34,032 83
Unpaid interest,	1,460 15	Guaranty fund,	951 20
Unpaid premiums,	128 75	Surplus,	1,251 04
Unpaid fines,	60 00	Forfeited share account,	73 58
Cash in hands of treasurer,	10,488 02		
	$221,970 65		$221,970 65

Detailed Statement of Receipts and Disbursements for the Year ending Oct. 31, 1894.

RECEIPTS.		DISBURSEMENTS.	
From dues capital,	$56,527 00	For real estate loans,	$50,423 04
interest,	11,430 67	share loans,	5,750 00
premiums,	1,138 34	dues capital (withdrawn),	18,942 00
fines,	222 29	dues capital (forfeited),	55 00
transfer fees,	1 00	dues capital (retired),	8,857 00
real estate loans repaid,	18,350 00	profits capital (withdrawn),	2,187 58
share loans repaid,	6,875 00	profits capital (forfeited),	8 30
withdrawal profits,	544 26	profits capital (retired),	2,242 20
forfeiture profits,	6 25	temporary expenses,	635 89
forfeited shares,	54 95	forfeited shares,	259 31
Cash on hand Oct. 31, 1893,	4,698 58	Cash on hand Oct 31, 1894,	10,488 02
	$99,848 34		$99,848 34

Reconciliation of Share Account with Dues and Profits Capital.

Date of Issue.	Series.	Value per Share.	Shares in Force.	Total Value.		
May, 1887, .	1	$116 96	258	$30,175 68	Dues capital, as per general ledger, .	$185,662 00
Nov., 1887, .	2	107 31	203	21,783 93		
May, 1888, .	3	97 73	251	24,530 23	Profits capital, as per general ledger, .	34,032 83
Nov., 1888, .	4	88 76	183	16,243 08		
May, 1889, .	5	79 90	302	24,129 80	Unpaid dues, .	2,491 00
Nov., 1889, .	6	71 36	147	10,489 92		
May, 1890, .	7	63 09	124	7,823 16		
Nov., 1890, .	8	55 07	189	10,408 23		
May, 1891, .	9	47 35	272	12,879 20		
Nov., 1891, .	10	39 89	404	16,115 56		
May, 1892, .	11	32 67	618	20,190 06		
Nov., 1892, .	12	25 69	386	9,916 34		
May, 1893, .	13	18 95	446	8,451 70		
Nov., 1893, .	14	12 42	421	5,228 82		
May, 1894, .	15	6 11	592	3,617 12		
Dues paid in advance, .				203 00		
Total, ...				$222,185 83	Total, . . .	$222,185 83

Number of shares issued during the year, ... 1,091
Number of shares now in force, ... 4,796
Number of shares now borrowed upon, ... 1,448
Largest number of shares held by any one member, . . . 25
Number of shares withdrawn during the year, ... 714
Number of shares forfeited during the year, ... 5
Number of shares retired during the year, ... 114
Highest premium received during the year, ... $0 25
Lowest premium received during the year, ... 05
Number of members withdrawn during the year, ... 93
Present number of members, ... 614
Present number of borrowers, ... 170
Present number of non-borrowers, ... 444
Number of loans secured by first mortgage of real estate, . . 148
Number of loans on shares, ... 74
Largest loan to any one member, ... 5,000 00
Smallest loan to any one member, ... 50 00
Amount of expenses of the corporation for the year ending Oct. 31, 1894, . 635 89
Date of examination by commissioner: April 27.

MANSFIELD CO-OPERATIVE BANK — MANSFIELD.

Incorporated March 10, 1883. Commenced business March 21, 1883.

DAVID E. HARDING, *President.* ALFRED B. DAY, *Secretary.*
ALFRED B. DAY, *Treasurer.*

Names of security committee :
SAMUEL C. LOVELL, JAMES A. WHEELER,
WILLIAM C. WINTER.

Regular meetings the third Wednesday of each month.

BALANCE SHEET OCTOBER 31, 1894.

ASSETS.		LIABILITIES.	
Loans on real estate, . .	$176,015 00	Dues capital, . . .	$180,563 00
Loans on shares, . . .	20,021 00	Profits capital (all series), .	41,175 73
Permanent expense account,.	75 00	Guaranty fund, . . .	667 51
Unpaid interest, . . .	1,147 86	Surplus, ...	257 41
Unpaid premiums, . .	34 30		
Unpaid fines, . . .	60 81		
Cash in hands of treasurer, .	25,309 68		
	$222,663 65		$222,663 65

Detailed Statement of Receipts and Disbursements for the Year ending Oct. 31, 1894.

RECEIPTS.		DISBURSEMENTS.	
From dues capital, . .	$44,526 00	For real estate loans, . .	$29,100 00
interest, . . .	11,855 87	share loans, . . .	14,795 00
premiums, . . .	328 34	dues capital (withdrawn), .	27,664 00
fines, ...	116 25	dues capital (forfeited), .	56 00
transfer fees, . .	5 86	dues capital (retired), .	1,950 00
real estate loans repaid,	23,550 00	profits capital (with-	
share loans repaid, .	14,845 00	drawn), . . .	4,764 38
withdrawal profits, .	476 64	profits capital (forfeited),	2 88
forfeited shares, . .	53 29	profits capital (retired), .	430 25
		temporary expenses, .	726 19
		forfeited shares, . .	53 29
Cash on hand Oct. 31, 1893, .	9,094 42	Cash on hand Oct. 31, 1894,.	25,309 68
	$104,851 67		$104,851 67

Reconciliation of Share Account with Dues and Profits Capital.

DATE OF ISSUE.	Series.	Value per Share.	Shares in Force.	Total Value.		
Mar., 1883, .	1	$201 60	81	$16,329 60	Dues capital, as per general ledger, . .	$180,563 00
Nov., 1883, .	2	186 02	64	11,905 28		
May, 1884, .	3	174 72	102	17,821 44	Profits capital, as per	
Nov., 1884, .	4	163 69	43	7,038 67	general ledger, . .	41,175 73
May, 1885, .	5	153 01	62	9,486 62	Unpaid dues, . . .	1,411 00
Nov., 1885, .	6	142 69	20	2,853 80		
May, 1886, .	7	132 64	59	7,825 76		
Nov., 1886, .	8	122 88	59	7,249 92		
May, 1887, .	9	113 37	145	16,438 65		
Nov., 1887, .	10	104 16	185	19,269 60		
May, 1888, .	11	95 22	96	9,141 12		
Nov., 1888, .	12	86 51	104	8,997 04		
May, 1889, .	13	78 07	210	16,394 70		
Nov., 1889, .	14	69 86	141	9,850 26		
May, 1890, .	15	61 90	197	12,194 30		
Nov., 1890, .	16	54 17	66	3,575 22		
May, 1891, .	17	46 68	236	11,016 48		
Nov., 1891, .	18	39 41	175	6,896 75		
May, 1892, .	19	32 34	322	10,413 48		
Nov., 1892, .	20	25 48	178	4,535 44		
May, 1893, .	21	18 83	423	7,965 09		
Nov., 1893, .	22	12 37	233	2,882 21		
May, 1894, .	23	6 10	503	3,068 30		
Total, ...				$223,149 73	Total, . . .	$223,149 73

Number of shares issued during the year, ...	872
Number of shares now in force, ...	3,704
Number of shares now borrowed upon, ...	1,589
Largest number of shares held by any one member, . . .	25
Number of shares withdrawn during the year, ...	775
Number of shares forfeited during the year, ...	8
Number of shares retired during the year, ...	25

Highest per centum of interest received during the year: $6\frac{1}{8}$.

Lowest per centum of interest received during the year: $6\frac{1}{8}$.

Number of members withdrawn during the year, ...	64
Present number of members, ...	482
Present number of borrowers, ...	219
Present number of non-borrowers, ...	263
Number of loans secured by first mortgage of real estate, . .	172
Number of loans on shares, ...	156
Largest loan to any one member, ...	$5,000 00
Smallest loan to any one member, ...	10 00
Amount of expenses of the corporation for the year ending Oct. 31, 1894, .	735 19

Date of examination by commissioner: June 26.

MARBLEHEAD CO-OPERATIVE BANK — MARBLEHEAD.

Incorporated May 5, 1886.   Commenced business May 6, 1886.

JOHN LANCY, *President.*   BENJAMIN COLE, Jr., *Secretary.*
BENJAMIN COLE, Jr., *Treasurer.*

Names of security committee:
JOHN LANCY,   M. V. B. MORSE,
FRANKLIN MILLETT.

Regular meetings the first Thursday of each month.

BALANCE SHEET OCTOBER 31, 1894.

ASSETS.		LIABILITIES.	
Loans on real estate,	$77,450 00	Dues capital,	$78,658 00
Loans on shares,	2,430 00	Profits capital (all series),	16,071 51
Permanent expense account,	100 00	Guaranty fund,	401 40
Real estate by foreclosure,	2,121 48	Surplus,	796 47
Unpaid interest,	286 65	Forfeited share account,	137 39
Unpaid premiums,	18 10		
Unpaid fines,	34 76		
Town of Beverly bonds,	2,098 21		
City of Waltham bonds,	1,015 02		
Cash in hands of treasurer,	10,513 55		
	$96,067 77		$96,067 77

Detailed Statement of Receipts and Disbursements for the Year ending Oct. 31, 1894.

RECEIPTS.		DISBURSEMENTS.	
From dues capital,	$20,029 00	For real estate loans,	$16,750 00
interest,	4,959 24	share loans,	2,080 00
premiums,	325 30	dues capital (withdrawn),	7,852 00
fines,	201 16	dues capital (forfeited),	1,088 00
transfer fees,	3 25	dues capital (retired),	4,985 00
real estate loans repaid,	14,950 00	profits capital (withdrawn),	1,080 00
share loans repaid,	1,660 00	profits capital (forfeited),	143 43
withdrawal profits,	269 89	profits capital (retired),	1,151 30
forfeiture profits,	72 98	temporary expenses,	409 91
forfeited shares,	115 05	forfeited shares,	31 37
profits account,	33	insurance,	5 00
Cash on hand Oct. 31, 1893,	3,503 36	Cash on hand Oct. 31, 1894,	10,513 55
	$46,089 56		$46,089 56

Reconciliation of Share Account with Dues and Profits Capital.

DATE OF ISSUE.	Series.	Value per Share.	Shares in Force.	Total Value.		
May, 1886, .	1	$133 04	113	$15,033 52	Dues capital, as per general ledger, . .	$78,658 00
Nov., 1886, .	2	123 22	119	14,663 18		
May, 1887, .	3	113 61	107	12,156 27	Profits capital as per general ledger, . .	16,071 51
Nov., 1887, .	4	104 33	53	5,529 49		
May, 1888, .	5	95 34	112	10,678 08	Unpaid dues, . .	554 00
Nov., 1888, .	6	86 62	46	3,984 52		
May, 1889, .	7	78 15	37	2,891 55		
Nov., 1889, .	8	69 94	54	3,776 76		
May, 1890, .	9	61 97	54	3,346 38		
Nov., 1890, .	10	54 23	59	3,199 57		
May, 1891, .	11	46 74	76	3,552 24		
Nov., 1891, .	12	39 47	72	2,841 84		
May, 1892, .	13	32 41	72	2,333 52		
Nov., 1892, .	14	25 54	219	5,593 26		
May, 1893, .	15	18 87	126	2,377 62		
Nov., 1893, .	16	12 39	199	2,465 61		
May, 1894, .	17	6 10	141	860 10		
Total, ...				$95,283 51	Total, . . .	$95,283 51

Number of shares issued during the year, ... 351
Number of shares now in force, ... 1,659
Number of shares now borrowed upon, ... 455
Largest number of shares held by any one member, . . . 25
Number of shares withdrawn during the year, ... 235
Number of shares forfeited during the year, ... 38
Number of shares retired during the year, ... 64
Highest per centum of interest received during the year : 6.
Lowest per centum of interest received during the year : 4.
Number of members withdrawn during the year, ... 65
Present number of members, ... 366
Present number of borrowers, ... 80
Present number of non-borrowers, ... 286
Number of loans secured by first mortgage of real estate, . . . 77
Number of loans on shares, ... 17
Largest loan to any one member, ... $5,000 00
Smallest loan to any one member, ... 30 00
Amount of expenses of the corporation for the year ending Oct. 31, 1894, . 409 91
Date of examination by commissioner : April 20.

MARLBOROUGH CO-OPERATIVE BANK — MARL-BOROUGH.

Incorporated April 16, 1890.   Commenced business May 1, 1890.

CHARLES F. ROBINSON, *President.*   C. B. RUSSELL, *Secretary.*
C. B. RUSSELL, *Treasurer.*

Names of security committee :

JOHN S. FAY,   E. O. BRIGHAM,
H. C. WRIGHT,   E. F. LONGLEY,
W. H. HILL.

Regular meetings the second Thursday of each month.

BALANCE SHEET OCTOBER 31, 1894.

ASSETS.		LIABILITIES.	
Loans on real estate, . .	$83,200 00	Dues capital, . . .	$88,137 00
Loans on shares, . . .	1,740 00	Profits capital (all series), .	10,452 00
Permanent expense account, .	94 21	Guaranty fund, . . .	262 90
Unpaid interest, . . .	365 02	Surplus, ...	689 14
Unpaid premiums, . .	13 56	Forfeited share account, .	100 60
Unpaid fines, . . .	56 46		
Cash in hands of treasurer, .	14,172 39		
	$99,641 64		$99,641 64

Detailed Statement of Receipts and Disbursements for the Year ending Oct. 31, 1894.

RECEIPTS.		DISBURSEMENTS.	
From dues capital, . .	$32,092 00	For real estate loans, . .	$32,150 00
interest, ' . .	5,637 29	share loans, . . .	2,800 00
premiums, . . .	303 49	dues capital (withdrawn),	8,232 00
fines, ...	284 61	dues capital (forfeited),	122 00
transfer fees, . .	4 00	dues capital (retired), .	7,200 00
real estate loans repaid,	12,850 00	profits capital (with-	
share loans repaid, .	4,625 00	drawn, . . .	668 22
withdrawal profits, .	168 93	profits capital (forfeited),	13 58
forfeiture profits, . .	3 44	profits capital (retired), .	943 50
forfeited shares, . .	127 10	temporary expenses, .	387 92
unpaid interest, . .	536 63	permanent expenses, .	28 00
city bonds and income,	5,275 00	forfeited shares, . .	678 70
mortgage foreclosures,	3,627 65	interest, ...	569 18
		mortgage foreclosures, .	3,627 65
		unpaid interest, premi-	
		ums and fines, . .	742 19
Cash on hand Oct. 31, 1893, .	6,800 19	Cash on hand Oct. 31, 1894,	14,172 39
	$72,335 33		$72,335 33

Reconciliation of Share Account with Dues and Profits Capital.

DATE OF ISSUE.	Series.	Value per Share.	Shares in Force.	Total Value.		
May, 1890, .	1	$62 02	806	$49,988 12	Dues capital, as per general ledger, . . .	$88,137 00
Nov., 1890, .	2	54 29	224	12,160 96		
May, 1891, .	3	46 78	181	8,467 18	Profits capital, as per general ledger, . .	10,452 00
Nov., 1891, .	4	39 49	172	6,792 28		
May, 1892, .	5	32 41	245	7,940 45	Unpaid dues, . .	715 00
Nov., 1892, .	6	25 54	71	1,813 34		
May, 1893, .	7	18 87	303	5,717 61		
Nov., 1893, .	8	12 39	244	3,023 16		
May, 1894, .	9	6 10	649	3,348 90		
Dues paid in advance, . . .				52 00		
Total, ...				$99,304 00	Total, . . .	$99,304 00

Number of shares issued during the year, ... ▶. . 846
Number of shares now in force, ... 2,795
Number of shares now borrowed upon, ... 502
Largest number of shares held by any one member, . . . 25
Number of shares withdrawn during the year, ... 384
Number of shares forfeited during the year, ... 12
Number of shares retired during the year, ... 150
Highest premium received during the year, ... $0 40
Lowest premium received during the year, ... 05
Number of members withdrawn during the year, ... 85
Present number of members, ... 469
Present number of borrowers, ... 69
Present number of non-borrowers, ... 400
Number of loans secured by first mortgage of real estate, . . . 67
Number of loans on shares, ... 21
Largest loan to any one member, ... 5,000 00
Smallest loan to any one member, ... 10 00
Amount of expenses of the corporation for the year ending Oct. 31, 1894, . 455 63
Date of examination by commissioner: May 10.

MECHANICS' CO-OPERATIVE BANK — TAUNTON.

Incorporated Sept. 14, 1877. Commenced business Sept. 17, 1877.

WILLIAM H. LEWIS, *President.*   EDW. S. HERSEY, *Secretary.*

EDWIN H. KNOWLES, *Treasurer.*

Names of security committee:

CYRUS SAVAGE,   JAMES P. WILLIAMS,

J. J. GREEN, Jr.

Regular meetings on the first Monday after the fifteenth of each month.

BALANCE SHEET OCTOBER 31, 1894.

ASSETS.		LIABILITIES.	
Loans on real estate, . .	$411,245 00	Dues capital, . . .	$364,092 00
Loans on shares, . . .	16,640 00	Profits capital (all series), .	59,200 67
Temporary expense account,	364 97	Interest, ...	8,087 42
Real estate by foreclosure, .	4,343 53	Premiums, ...	432 82
Unpaid interest, . . .	4,409 19	Fines, ...	368 22
Unpaid premiums, . .	237 10	Guaranty fund, . . .	1,604 13
Unpaid fines, ...	1,197 12	Surplus, ...	607 00
Unpaid dues, ...	4,455 00	Forfeited share account, .	15 98
Cash in hands of treasurer, .	3,933 70	Advance payments, . .	1,818 62
		Matured shares, . . .	10,598 75
	$446,825 61		$446,825 61

Detailed Statement of Receipts and Disbursements for the Year ending Oct. 31, 1894.

RECEIPTS.		DISBURSEMENTS.	
From dues capital, . .	$95,289 00	For real estate loans, . .	$86,350 00
interest, . . .	20,331 21	share loans, . . .	25,500 00
premiums, . . .	1,052 37	dues capital(withdrawn),	89,982 00
fines, ...	30 26	dues capital (forfeited),	510 00
real estate loans repaid,	92,290 00	dues capital (retired), .	3,838 00
share loans repaid, .	26,365 00	dues capital (matured),	12,259 00
forfeited shares, . .	574 70	profits capital (withdrawn), . . .	16,188 45
unpaid loans, . .	1,600 00	profits capital (forfeited),	64 70
advance payments, .	15,164 80	profits capital (retired),	1,085 28
rent, expense account, .	146 30	profits capital(matured),	5,177 13
real estate by foreclosure, . . .	1,397 00	temporary expenses, .	1,505 97
matured share account,	18,379 22	unpaid loans, . .	3,190 00
suspense account, .	16,545 57	forfeited shares, . .	574 70
		advance payments, .	15,638 90
		real estate by foreclosure,	1,307 29
		matured share account,	20,904 19
		guaranty fund, . .	300 00
		interest paid on matured shares, . . .	1,009 00
		interest paid on retired shares, . . .	96 52
Cash on hand Oct. 31, 1893, .	249 49	Cash on hand Oct. 31, 1894,	3,933 70
	$289,414 92		$289,414 92

Reconciliation of Share Account with Dues and Profits Capital.

DATE OF ISSUE.	Series.	Value per Share.	Shares in Force.	Total Value.		
Jan., 1884, .	8	$181 98	88	$16,014 24	Dues capital, as per gen-	
Jan., 1885, .	9	159 47	87	13,873 89	eral ledger, . .	$364,092 00
Jan., 1886, .	10	138 40	155	21,452 00	Profits capital, as per	
Jan., 1887, .	11	118 65	63	7,474 95	general ledger, . .	59,200 67
July, 1887, .	12	109 21	430	46,960 30		
Jan., 1888, .	13	100 05	312	31,215 60		
July, 1888, .	14	91 19	195	17,782 05		
Jan., 1889, .	15	82 60	596	49,229 60		
July, 1889, .	16	74 27	247	18,344 69		
Jan., 1890, .	17	66 21	581	38,468 01		
July, 1890, .	18	58 42	368	21,498 56		
Jan., 1891, .	19	50 88	900	45,792 00		
July, 1891, .	20	43 55	719	31,312 45		
Jan., 1892, .	21	36 45	185	6,743 25		
July, 1892, .	22	29 56	954	28,200 24		
Jan., 1893, .	23	22 88	289	6,612 32		
July, 1893, .	24	16 40	814	13,349 60		
Jan., 1894, .	25	10 11	772	7,804 92		
July, 1894, .	26	4 00	291	1,164 00		
Total, ...				$423,292 67	Total, . . .	$423,292 67

Number of shares issued during the year, ... 1,200
Number of shares now in force, ... 8,046
Number of shares now borrowed upon, ... 2,546
Largest number of shares held by any one member, ... 25
Number of shares withdrawn during the year, ... 1,987
Number of shares forfeited during the year, ... 10
Number of shares retired during the year, ... 38
Number of shares matured during the year, ... 89
Highest per centum of interest received during the year : $6\frac{3}{10}$.
Lowest per centum of interest received during the year : $6\frac{5}{10}$.
Number of members withdrawn during the year, ... 222
Present number of members, ... 1,096
Present number of borrowers, ... 377
Present number of non-borrowers, ... 719
Number of loans secured by first mortgage of real estate, .   .   . 313
Number of loans on shares, ... 67
Largest loan to any one member, ... $5,000 00
Smallest loan to any one member, ... 50 00
Amount of expenses of the corporation for the year ending Oct. 31, 1894, . 1,359 67
Date of examination by commissioner : November 1.

MEDFORD CO-OPERATIVE BANK—MEDFORD.

Incorporated June 21, 1886. Commenced business July 7, 1886.

DANA I. McINTIRE, *President.*   JAMES S. STURTEVANT, *Secretary.*

JAMES S. STURTEVANT, *Treasurer.*

Names of security committee :

CHARLES P. LAURIAT,   ELI AYERS,
WALTER F. CUSHING,   JOSEPH E. OBER,
LEWIS H. LOVERING.

Regular meetings the first Wednesday of each month.

BALANCE SHEET OCTOBER 31, 1894.

ASSETS.		LIABILITIES.	
Loans on real estate, . .	$196,200 00	Dues capital, . . .	$190,988 00
Loans on shares, . . .	14,200 00	Profits capital (all series), .	35,188 63
Permanent expense account,	600 00	Guaranty fund, . . .	916 91
Unpaid interest, . . .	579 50	Surplus, ...	1,440 71
Unpaid premiums, . . .	55 10	Forfeited share account, .	2 16
Unpaid fines, ...	77 38		
Cash in hands of treasurer, .	16,824 43		
	$228,536 41		$228,536 41

Detailed Statement of Receipts and Disbursements for the Year ending Oct. 31, 1894.

RECEIPTS.		DISBURSEMENTS.	
From dues capital, . .	$57,875 00	For real estate loans, . .	$56,900 00
interest, . .	12,481 91	share loans, . . .	12,550 00
premiums, . . .	1,253 56	dues capital (withdrawn),	24,582 00
fines, ...	317 49	dues capital (forfeited),	238 00
transfer fees, . .	4 50	dues capital (retired), .	13,815 00
real estate loans repaid,	42,450 00	profits capital (withdrawn), . . .	3,402 84
share loans repaid, .	15,600 00	profits capital (forfeited),	31 20
withdrawal profits, .	776 01	profits capital (retired),	3,256 47
forfeiture profits, .	15 52	temporary expenses, .	1,090 57
forfeited shares, . .	8 96	permanent expenses, .	614 43
		forfeited shares, . .	8 96
Cash on hand Oct. 31, 1893, .	2,530 95	Cash on hand Oct. 31, 1894,	16,824 43
	$133,313 90		$133,313 90

Reconciliation of Share Account with Dues and Profits Capital.

Date of Issue.	Series.	Value per Share.	Shares In Force.	Total Value.		
July, 1886, .	1	$132 34	170	$22,497 80	Dues capital as per general ledger, . .	$190,988 00
Nov., 1886, .	2	125 49	157	19,701 93		
May, 1887, .	3	115 79	140	16,210 60	Profits capital as per general ledger, . .	.
Nov., 1887, .	4	106 16	144	15,287 04		35,188 63
May, 1888, .	5	96 99	107	10,377 93	Unpaid dues, . .	916 00
Nov., 1888, .	6	88 02	121	10,650 42		
May, 1889, .	7	79 33	180	14,279 40		
Nov., 1889, .	8	70 90	210	14,889 00		
May, 1890, .	9	62 73	322	20,199 06		
Nov., 1890, .	10	54 82	254	13,924 28		
May, 1891, .	11	47 14	340	16,027 60		
Nov., 1891, .	12	39 72	300	11,916 00		
May, 1892, .	13	32 55	350	11,392 50		
Nov., 1892, .	14	25 61	387	9,911 07		
May, 1893, .	15	18 90	430	8,127 00		
Nov., 1893, .	16	12 40	521	6,460 40		
May, 1894, .	17	6 10	826	5,038 60		
Dues paid in advance, . .				202 00		
Total, ...				$227,092 63	Total, . . .	$227,092 63

Number of shares issued during the year, ... 1,449
Number of shares now in force, ... 4,959
Number of shares now borrowed upon, ... 1,375
Largest number of shares held by any one member, ... 25
Number of shares withdrawn during the year, ... 803
Number of shares forfeited during the year, ... 20
Number of shares retired during the year, ... 171
Highest premium received during the year, ... $0 25
Lowest premium received during the year, ... 05
Number of members withdrawn during the year, ... 107
Present number of members, ... 538
Present number of borrowers, ... 128
Present number of non-borrowers, ... 410
Number of loans secured by first mortgage of real estate, . . 120
Number of loans on shares, ... 49
Largest loan to any one member, ... 5,000 00
Smallest loan to any one member, ... 50 00
Amount of expenses of the corporation for the year ending Oct. 31, 1894, . 1,240 00
Date of examination by commissioner: November 2.

MELROSE CO-OPERATIVE BANK — MELROSE.

Incorporated April 4, 1890.   Commenced business April 20, 1890.

LEVI S. GOULD, *President.*   E. K. BORDMAN, *Secretary.*
CHAS. W. COOK, *Treasurer.*

Names of security committee:
CHAS. W. COOK,   S. E. BENSON,
CHAS. E. TODD.

Regular meetings the first Friday of each month.

BALANCE SHEET OCTOBER 31, 1894.

ASSETS.		LIABILITIES.	
Loans on real estate,	$17,600 00	Dues capital,	$19,527 00
Loans on shares,	630 00	Profits capital (all series),	2,195 21
Permanent expense account,	97 16	Interest,	83 33
Unpaid interest,	374 20	Premiums,	17 45
Unpaid premiums,	80 10	Fines,	40 14
Unpaid fines,	91 13	Withdrawal profits,	11 55
Cash in hands of secretary,	87 14	Guaranty fund,	52 94
Cash in hands of treasurer,	3,046 92	Surplus,	79 03
	$22,006 65		$22,006 65

Detailed Statement of Receipts and Disbursements for the Year ending Oct. 31, 1894.

RECEIPTS.		DISBURSEMENTS.	
From dues capital,	$9,260 00	For real estate loans,	$3,800 00
interest,	1,025 18	share loans,	952 00
premiums,	144 40	dues capital(withdrawn),	9,417 00
fines,	185 41	dues capital (forfeited),	787 00
real estate loans repaid,	7,700 00	profits capital (withdrawn),	937 89
share loans repaid,	2,157 00	profits capital (forfeited),	92 19
withdrawal profits,	205 09	temporary expenses,	534 35
forfeiture profits,	13 86	forfeited shares,	334 50
forfeited shares,	334 50	withdrawal share account,	2,812 46
real estate,	1,000 00	real estate,	15 00
Cash on hand Oct. 31, 1893,	791 01	Cash on hand Oct. 31, 1894,	3,134 06
	$22,816 45		$22,816 45

Reconciliation of Share Account with Dues and Profits Capital.

DATE OF ISSUE.	Series.	Value per Share.	Shares in Force.	Total Value.		
April, 1890, .	1	$64 15	89	$5,709 35	Dues capital, as per general ledger, . . .	$19,527 00
July, 1890, .	2	60 10	16	961 60		
Oct., 1890, .	3	56 12	48	2,693 76	Profits capital, as per general ledger, . .	2,195 21
Jan., 1891, .	4	52 22	42	2,193 24		
April, 1891, .	5	48 37	19	919 03	Unpaid dues, . .	666 00
July, 1891, .	6	44 59	6	267 54		
Oct., 1891, .	7	40 88	9	367 92		
Jan., 1892, .	8	37 24	21	782 04		
April, 1892, .	9	33 65	22	740 30		
July, 1892, .	10	30 13	47	1,416 11		
Oct., 1892, .	11	26 66	15	399 90		
Jan., 1893, .	12	23 27	58	1,349 66		
April, 1893, .	13	19 92	77	1,533 84		
July, 1893, .	14	16 63	95	1,579 85		
Oct., 1893, .	15	13 39	28	374 92		
Jan., 1894, .	16	10 23	49	501 27		
April, 1894, .	17	7 10	42	298 20		
July, 1894, .	18	4 03	56	225 68		
Oct., 1894, .	19	1 00	34	34 00		

Dues paid in advance, .   .   40 00

Total, ... $22,388 21   Total,   .   .   . $22,388 21

Number of shares issued during the year, ... 203
Number of shares now in force, ... 773
Number of shares now borrowed upon, ... 110
Largest number of shares held by any one member,   .   .   . 25
Number of shares withdrawn during the year, ... 385
Number of shares forfeited during the year, ... 61
Highest premium received during the year, ... $0 30
Lowest premium received during the year, ... 05
Number of members withdrawn during the year, ... 50
Present number of members, ... 111
Present number of borrowers, ... 17
Present number of non-borrowers, ... 94
Number of loans secured by first mortgage of real estate,   .   .   . 12
Number of loans on shares, ... 6
Largest loan to any one member, ... 3,200 00
Smallest loan to any one member, ... 60 00
Amount of expenses of the corporation for the year ending Oct. 31, 1894,   . 534 35
Date of examination by commissioner: March 26.

MERCHANTS' CO-OPERATIVE BANK — BOSTON.

Incorporated Dec. 21, 1881.   Commenced business February, 1882.

A. J. MERCER, *President.*   A. E. DUFFILL, *Secretary.*

A. E. DUFFILL, *Treasurer.*

Names of security committee:

GEO. T. BOSSON,   A. S. PARSONS,
C. E. FOLSOM,   E. C. SCATES.

Regular meetings the second Monday of each month.

BALANCE SHEET OCTOBER 31, 1894.

ASSETS.		LIABILITIES.	
Loans on real estate,	$721,891 00	Dues capital,	$685,309 00
Loans on shares,	24,350 00	Profits capital (all series),	106,667 85
Temporary expense account,	1,381 83	Interest,	15,878 74
Real estate by foreclosure,	2,134 04	Premiums,	1,237 72
Profit and loss account,	371 45	Fines,	509 33
Personal account,	2 00	Transfer fees,	7 50
Cash in hands of treasurer,	66,783 68	Withdrawal profits,	1,089 89
		Guaranty fund,	3,827 97
		Surplus,	2,111 33
		Forfeited share account,	112 78
		Suspense,	161 89
	$816,914 00		$816,914 00

Detailed Statement of Receipts and Disbursements for the Year ending Oct. 31, 1894.

RECEIPTS.		DISBURSEMENTS.	
From dues capital,	$236,595 00	For real estate loans,	$190,233 00
interest,	47,878 80	share loans,	24,860 00
premiums,	4,695 03	dues capital (withdrawn),	88,493 00
fines,	2,904 72	dues capital (forfeited),	4,830 00
transfer fees,	22 00	dues capital (retired),	60,066 00
real estate loans repaid,	149,529 00	dues capital (matured),	18,381 00
share loans repaid,	30,460 00	profits capital (withdrawn),	13,638 86
withdrawal profits,	2,188 71	profits capital (forfeited),	1,024 92
forfeiture profits,	201 91	profits capital (retired),	14,899 59
forfeited shares,	5,489 92	profits capital (matured),	9,173 47
expense refunded,	38 00	temporary expenses,	3,510 00
real estate account,	7 00	real estate by foreclosure,	22,600 62
real estate by foreclosure,	22,525 01	forfeited shares,	5,493 32
suspense,	190 64	matured shares,	2,000 00
rent,	10 00	interest paid on retired shares,	1,242 99
		interest paid on matured shares,	167 23
		interest returned,	30 80
		real estate account,	15 00
		sundries,	241 43
Cash on hand Oct. 31, 1893,	24,949 17	Cash on hand Oct. 31, 1894,	66,783 68
	$527,684 91		$527,684 91

Reconciliation of Share Account with Dues and Profits Capital.

Date of Issue.	Series.	Value per Share.	Shares in Force.	Total Value.		
Dec., 1883, .	5	$190 80	14	$2,671 20	Dues capital, as per general ledger, . .	$685,309 00
June, 1884, .	6	178 58	102	18,215 16		
Dec., 1884, .	7	166 75	77	12,839 75	Profits capital, as per general ledger, . .	106,667 85
June, 1885, .	8	155 30	108	16,772 40		
Dec., 1885, .	9	144 25	113	16,300 25	Unpaid dues, . .	7,090 00
June, 1886, .	10	133 85	183	24,445 14		
Dec., 1886, .	11	123 28	195	24,039 60		
June, 1887, .	12	113 32	215	24,363 80		
Dec., 1887, .	13	103 70	385	39,924 50		
June, 1888, .	14	94 42	481	45,416 02		
Dec., 1888, .	15	85 46	739	63,154 94		
June, 1889, .	16	76 82	678	52,083 96		
Dec., 1889, .	17	68 48	803	54,989 44		
June, 1890, .	18	60 42	820	49,544 40		
Dec., 1890, .	19	52 63	1,249	65,734 87		
June, 1891, .	20	45 10	1,306	58,900 60		
Dec., 1891, .	21	37 83	1,353	51,183 99		
June, 1892, .	22	30 80	1,728	53,222 40		
Dec., 1892, .	23	24 01	1,977	47,467 77		
June, 1893, .	24	17 45	1,770	30,886 50		
Dec., 1893, .	25	11 12	2,843	31,614 16		
June, 1894, .	26	5 00	2,873	14,365 00		
Dues paid in advance, . . .				931 00		
Total, ...				$799,066 85	Total, . . .	$799,066 85

Number of shares issued during the year, ...	6,432
Number of shares now in force, ...	20,012
Number of shares now borrowed upon, ...	4,642
Largest number of shares held by any one member, ...	25
Number of shares withdrawn during the year, . . .	3,466
Number of shares forfeited during the year, ...	116
Number of shares retired during the year, ...	780
Number of shares matured during the year, ...	138
Highest premium received during the year, ...	$0 35
Lowest premium received during the year, ...	05
Number of members withdrawn during the year, ...	347
Present number of members, ...	2,130
Present number of borrowers, ...	423
Present number of non-borrowers, ...	1,707
Number of loans secured by first mortgage of real estate, . .	342
Number of loans on shares, ...	81
Largest loan to any one member, ...	5,000 00
Smallest loan to any one member, ...	50 00
Amount of expenses of the corporation for the year ending Oct. 31, 1894, .	3,472 00

Date of examination by commissioner: November 16.

MERRIMAC CO-OPERATIVE BANK — LAWRENCE.

Incorporated April 2, 1892. Commenced business April 28, 1892.

JOHN BREEN, *President.*   C. J. CORCORAN, *Secretary.*
C. A. McCARTHY, *Treasurer.*

Names of security committee:

D. J. O'MAHONEY,   JOHN TOBIN,
DANIEL GALLAGHER.

Regular meetings thè first Friday of each month.

BALANCE SHEET OCTOBER 31, 1894.

ASSETS.		LIABILITIES.	
Loans on real estate, . .	$12,550 00	Dues capital, . . .	$13,545 00
Loans on shares, . . .	1,575 00	Profits capital (all series), .	928 99
Permanent expense account,	177 50	Guaranty fund, . . .	35 58
Unpaid interest, . .	215 38	Surplus, ...	262 82
Unpaid premiums, . .	11 20		
Unpaid fines, . . .	58 14		
Cash in hands of treasurer, .	185 17		
	$14,772 39		$14,772 39

Detailed Statement of Receipts and Disbursements for the Year ending Oct. 31, 1894.

RECEIPTS.		DISBURSEMENTS.	
From dues capital, . .	$7,227 00	For real estate loans, . .	$4,150 00
interest, . .	591 25	. share loans, . . .	1,090 00
premiums, . .	31 65	dues capital (withdrawn),	2,798 00
fines, . . .	113 69	dues capital (forfeited),	149 00
transfer fees, . .	25	profits capital (with-	
share loans repaid, .	595 00	drawn), . . .	141 02
withdrawal profits, .	35 75	profits capital (forfeited),	6 90
forfeiture profits, .	1 81	permanent expenses, .	59 55
forfeited shares, . .	121 53	forfeited shares, . .	184 29
Cash on hand Oct. 31, 1893, .	46 00	Cash on hand Oct. 31, 1894,	185 17
	$8,763 93		$8,763 93

Reconciliation of Share Account with Dues and Profits Capital.

DATE OF ISSUE.	Series.	Value per Share.	Shares in Force.	Total Value.		
May, 1892, .	1	$32 24	350	$11,284 00	Dues capital, as per general ledger, . .	$13,545 00
Nov., 1892, .	2	25 45	37	941 65		
May, 1893, .	3	18 83	77	1,449 91	Profits capital as per general ledger, . .	928 99
Nov., 1893, .	4	12 37	39	582 43		
May, 1894, .	5	6 10	130	793 00	Unpaid dues,. . .	577 00
Total, ...				$15,050 99	Total, . . .	$15,050 99

Number of shares issued during the year, ... 183
Number of shares now in force, ... 633
Number of shares now borrowed upon, ... 76
Largest number of shares held by any one member, . . . 25
Number of shares withdrawn during the year, ... 168
Number of shares forfeited during the year, ... 18
Highest premium received during the year, ... $ 05
Lowest premium received during the year, ... 05
Number of members withdrawn during the year, ... 20
Present number of members, ... 87
Present number of borrowers, ... 24
Present number of non-borrowers, ... 63
Number of loans secured by first mortgage of real estate, . . 14
Number of loans on shares, ... 13
Largest loan to any one member, ... 2,500 00
Smallest loan to any one member, ... 15 00
Amount of expenses of the corporation for the year ending Oct. 31, 1894, . 59 55
Date of examination by commissioner : October 29.

MIDDLEBOROUGH CO-OPERATIVE BANK — MIDDLE-BOROUGH.

Incorporated May 1, 1889.   Commenced business May 21, 1889.

SAMUEL S. BOURNE, *President.*   JOSEPH E. BEALS, *Secretary.*
JOSEPH E. BEALS, *Treasurer.*

Names of security committee :
WARREN H. SOUTHWORTH,   SAMUEL S. BOURNE,
HENRY W. SEARS.

Regular meetings the third Tuesday of each month.

BALANCE SHEET OCTOBER 31, 1894.

ASSETS.			LIABILITIES.		
Loans on real estate,	.	$90,050 00	Dues capital,	.	$83,301 00
Loans on shares,	.	2,475 00	Profits capital (all series),	.	11,502 77
Permanent expense account,		110 00	Interest,	.	30 00
Unpaid interest,	.	132 25	Premiums,	.	1 50
Unpaid premiums,	.	7 25	Guaranty fund,	.	175 00
Unpaid fines,	.	20 20	Surplus,	.	618 36
Cash in hands of treasurer,	.	2,833 93			
		$95,628 63			$95,628 63

Detailed Statement of Receipts and Disbursements for the Year ending Oct. 31, 1894.

RECEIPTS.			DISBURSEMENTS.		
From dues capital,	.	$25,658 00	For real estate loans,	.	$23,273 00
interest,	.	5,246 57	share loans.	.	3,750 00
premiums,	.	290 95	dues capital (withdrawn),		13,989 00
fines,	.	95 83	profits capital (withdrawn),	.	1,907 49
transfer fees,	.	6 00	temporary expenses,	.	362 93
real estate loans repaid,		11,000 00			
share loans repaid,		3,525 00			
withdrawal profits,	.	119 39			
Cash on hand Oct. 31, 1893,	.	174 61	Cash on hand Oct. 31, 1894,		2,833 93
		$46,116 35			$46,116 35

Reconciliation of Share Account with Dues and Profits Capital.

DATE OF ISSUE.	Series.	Value per Share.	Shares in Force.	Total Value.		
May, 1889, .	1	$78 10	478	$37,331 80	Dues capital, as per general ledger, . .	$83,301 00
Nov., 1889, .	2	69 91	120	8,389 20		
May, 1890, .	3	61 95	133	8,239 35	Profits capital, as per	
Nov., 1890, .	4	54 23	215	11,659 45	general ledger, . .	11,502 77
May, 1891, .	5	46 75	163	7,620 25	Unpaid dues, . . .	428 00
Nov., 1891, .	6	39 47	114	4,499 58		
May, 1892, .	7	32 39	214	6,931 46		
Nov., 1892, .	8	25 53	148	3,778 44		
May, 1893, .	9	18 86	172	3,243 92		
Nov., 1893, .	10	12 38	129	1,597 02		
May, 1894, .	11	6 10	283	1,726 30		
Dues paid in advance, . . .				215 00		
Total, ...				$95,231 77	Total, . . .	$95,231 77

Number of shares issued during the year, ...	422
Number of shares now in force, ...	2,169
Number of shares now borrowed upon, ...	550
Largest number of shares held by any one member, ...	25
Number of shares withdrawn during the year, ...	331
Highest premium received during the year, ...	$0 15
Lowest premium received during the year, ...	05
Number of members withdrawn during the year, ...	66
Present number of members, ...	436
Present number of borrowers, ...	83
Present number of non-borrowers, ...	353
Number of loans secured by first mortgage of real estate, . . .	97
Number of loans on shares, ...	19
Largest loan to any one member, ...	3,600 00
Smallest loan to any one member, ...	50 00
Amount of expenses of the corporation for the year ending Oct. 31, 1894, .	392 93

Date of examination by commissioner: May 21.

MIDDLESEX CO-OPERATIVE BANK — LOWELL.

Incorporated Nov. 2, 1892. Commenced business Nov. 3, 1892.

JESSE H. SHEPARD, *President.* WILLIAM D. BROWN, *Secretary.*
WILLIAM D. BROWN, *Treasurer.*

Names of security committee:

GEO. W. CHASE, JOHN M. KINGSBURY,
WM. M. SHERWELL.

Regular meetings the last Friday of each month.

BALANCE SHEET OCTOBER 31, 1894.

ASSETS.		LIABILITIES.	
Loans on real estate, . .	$17,650 00	Dues capital, . . .	$20,498 00
Loans on shares, . . .	1,150 00	Profits capital (all series, .	1,156 07
Permanent expense account,	179 23	Guaranty fund, . . .	13 33
Unpaid interest, . . .	14 75	Surplus, ...	19 90
Unpaid premiums, . .	1 00		
Unpaid fines, . . .	8 36		
Cash in hands of treasurer, ..	2,683 96		
	$21,687 30		$21,687 30

Detailed Statement of Receipts and Disbursements for the Year ending Oct. 31, 1894.

RECEIPTS.		DISBURSEMENTS.	
From dues capital, . .	$15,149 00	For real estate loans, . .	$11,175 00
interest, . . .	964 33	share loans, . . .	1,460 00
premiums, . . .	90 40	dues capital (withdrawn),	4,612 00
fines, ...	63 56	profits capital (with-	
transfer fees, . .	1 25	drawn), . . .	167 81
real estate loans repaid,	2,400 00	temporary expenses, .	130 15
share loans repaid, .	460 00		
withdrawal profits, .	41 86		
Cash on hand Oct. 31, 1893, .	1,058 52	Cash on hand Oct. 31, 1894,	2,683 96
	$20,228 92		$20,228 92

Reconciliation of Share Account with Dues and Profits Capital.

Date of Issue.	Series.	Value per Share.	Shares in Force.	Total Value.		
Nov., 1892, .	1	$25 66	504	$12,932 64	Dues capital as per general ledger, . . .	$20,498 00
May, 1893, .	2	18 92	202	3,821 84		
Nov., 1893, .	3	12 42	212	2,633 04	Profits capital as per general ledger, . .	1,156 07
May, 1894, .	4	6 11	405	2,474 55	Unpaid dues, . .	208 00
Total, ...				$21,862 07		$21,862 07

Number of shares issued during the year, ... 744
Number of shares now in force, ... 1,323
Number of shares now borrowed upon, ... 166
Largest number of shares held by any one member, . . . 25
Number of shares withdrawn during the year, ... 429
Highest per centum of interest received during the year: $8\frac{1}{10}$.
Lowest per centum of interest received during the year: $6\frac{8}{10}$.
Number of members withdrawn during the year, ... 53
Present number of members, ... 173
Present number of borrowers, ... 22
Present number of non-borrowers, ... 151
Number of loans secured by first mortgage of real estate, . . . 14
Number of loans on shares, . . . _. 8
Largest loan to any one member, ... $3,000 00
Smallest loan to any one member, ... 50 00
Amount of expenses of the corporation for the year ending Oct. 31, 1894, . 142 15
Date of examination by commissioner: July 24.

MILFORD CO-OPERATIVE BANK—MILFORD.

Incorporated March 31, 1887. Commenced business April 1, 1887.

R. C. ELDRIDGE, *President.*   W. S. V. COOKE, *Secretary.*
                    W. S. V. COOKE, *Treasurer.*

Names of security committee:

| P. P. FIELD, | W. B. HALE, |
| L. E. HEATH, | C. R. SCOTT. |

Regular meetings the first Monday of each month.

BALANCE SHEET OCT. 31, 1894.

ASSETS.		LIABILITIES.	
Loans on real estate, . .	$168,190 00	Dues capital, . . .	$149,203 00
Loans on shares, . . .	6,245 00	Profits capital (all series), .	24,628 03
Permanent expense account,	125 00	Interest, ...	921 38
Unpaid interest, . . .	1,224 43	Fines, ...	23 52
Unpaid fines, ...	90 53	Transfer fees, . . .	1 00
Insurance, ...	11 96	Withdrawal profits, . .	22 82
Cash in hands of treasurer, .	956 52	Guaranty fund, . . .	550 00
		Surplus, ...	1,446 36
		Forfeited share account, .	47 33
	$176,843 44		$176,843 44

Detailed Statement of Receipts and Disbursements for the Year ending Oct. 31, 1894.

RECEIPTS.		DISBURSEMENTS.	
From dues capital, . .	$45,912 00	For real estate loans, . .	$30,115 00
interest, . . .	10,646 24	share loans, . . .	4,415 00
fines, ...	279 64	dues capital (withdrawn), . . .	25,161 00
transfer fees, . .	5 00	dues capital (forfeited),	740 00
real estate loans repaid,	28,165 00	dues capital (retired), .	21,491 00
share loans repaid, .	6,175 00	profits capital (withdrawn), . . .	3,444 51
withdrawal profits, .	378 08	profits capital (forfeited),	115 75
forfeiture profits, .	14 05	profits capital (retired),	5,317 82
forfeited shares, .	47 33	temporary expenses, .	693 43
town note repaid, .	6,500 00	forfeited shares, . .	3 15
		insurance, . . .	11 96
		town note, . . .	6,500 00
		profit and loss to dues capital, . . .	10 00
Cash on hand Oct. 31, 1893, .	852 80	Cash on hand Oct. 31, 1894,	956 52
	$98,975 14		$98,975 14

Reconciliation of Share Account with Dues and Profits Capital.

DATE OF ISSUE.	Series.	Value per Share.	Shares in Force.	Total Value.		
April, 1887, .	1	$114 49	269	$30,797 81	Dues capital, as per general ledger, . .	$149,203 00
Oct., 1887, .	2	105 26	159	16,736 34		
April, 1888, .	3	96 30	223	21,474 90	Profits capital, as per general ledger, . .	24,628 03
Oct., 1888, .	4	87 60	126	11,037 60		
April, 1889, .	5	79 15	183	14,484 45	Unpaid dues, . .	1,687 00
Oct., 1889, .	6	70 95	194	13,764 30		
April, 1890, .	7	62 99	130	8,188 70		
Oct., 1890, .	8	55 26	156	8,620 56		
April, 1891, .	9	47 76	218	10,411 68		
Oct., 1891, .	10	40 47	165	6,677 55		
April, 1892, .	11	33 40	279	9,318 60		
Oct., 1892, .	12	26 53	240	6,367 20		
April, 1893, .	13	19 86	498	9,890 28		
Oct., 1893, .	14	13 39	224	2,999 36		
April, 1894, .	15	7 10	587	4,167 70		
Oct., 1894, .	16	1 00	310	310 00		
Dues paid in advance, . . .				271 00		
Total, ...				$175,518 03	Total, . . .	$175,518 03

Number of shares issued during the year, ... 962
Number of shares now in force, ... 3,961
Number of shares now borrowed upon, ... 1,112
Largest number of shares held by any one member, ... 25
Number of shares withdrawn during the year, ... 804
Number of shares forfeited during the year, ... 20
Number of shares retired during the year, ... 251
Highest per centum of interest received during the year : 6⅜.
Lowest per centum of interest received during the year : 6.
Number of members withdrawn during the year, ... 150
Present number of members, ... 591
Present number of borrowers, ... 166
Present number of non-borrowers, ... 425
Number of loans secured by first mortgage of real estate, . . . 176
Number of loans on shares, ... 44
Largest loan to any one member, ... $5,000 00
Smallest loan to any one member, ... 50 00
Amount of expenses of the corporation for the year ending Oct. 31, 1894, . 768 43
Date of examination by commissioner : May 4.

MT. WASHINGTON CO-OPERATIVE BANK — SOUTH BOSTON.

Incorporated June 20, 1893.   Commenced business June 21, 1893.

THOMAS J. GIBLIN, *President.*   CHAS. P. MOONEY, *Secretary.*

CHAS. P. MOONEY, *Treasurer.*

Names of security committee:

CHAS. M. BROMWICH,   JOHN H. GIBLIN,

ALFRED F. MACDONALD.

Regular meetings the third Wednesday of each month.

BALANCE SHEET OCTOBER 31, 1894.

ASSETS.			LIABILITIES.		
Loans on real estate, . .	$8,550	00	Dues capital, . . .	$11,131	00
Loans on shares, . . .	105	00	Profits capital (all series), .	203	13
Permanent expense account,	142	22	Interest, ...	205	40
Temporary expense account,	9	45	Premiums, ...	5	48
Suspense account, . . .	19	60	Fines, ...	38	08
Cash in hands of treasurer, .	2,793	79	Withdrawal profits, . .	6	80
			Forfeiture profits, . .		90
			Guaranty fund, . . .	2	86
			Surplus, ...	26	41
	$11,620	06		$11,620	06

Detailed Statement of Receipts and Disbursements for the Year ending Oct. 31, 1894.

RECEIPTS.			DISBURSEMENTS.		
From dues capital, . .	$9,469	00	For real estate loans, . .	$8,900	00
interest, . . .	414	77	share loans, . . .	155	00
premiums, . . .	11	72	dues capital (withdrawn),	1,897	00
fines, . . .	72	58	dues capital (forfeited),	10	00
real estate loans repaid,	350	00	profits capital (withdrawn), . . .	44	37
share loans repaid, .	50	00			
withdrawal profits, .	10	34	profits capital (forfeited),		90
forfeiture profits, .		90	temporary expenses, .	23	95
forfeited shares, .	5	80	permanent expenses, .	174	37
surplus, . . .	5	31	forfeited shares, . .	5	80
permanent expense, .	16	80	interest paid, . . .	6	26
profit and loss, . .		10			
Cash on hand Oct. 31, 1893, .	3,604	12	Cash on hand Oct. 31, 1894,	2,793	79
	$14,011	44		$14,011	44

Reconciliation of Share Account with Dues and Profits Capital.

DATE OF ISSUE.	Series.	Value per Share.	Shares in Force.	Total Value.		
June, 1893, .	1	$17 36	495	$8,593 20	Dues capital, as per general ledger, . .	$11,131 00
Dec., 1893, .	2	11 09	219	2,428 71		
June, 1894, .	3	5 00	153	765 00	Profits capital, as per general ledger, . .	203 13
					Unpaid dues, . .	458 00
Suspense profits, ...				5 22		
Total, ...				$11,792 13		$11,792 13

Number of shares issued during the year, ... 394
Number of shares now in force, ... 867
Number of shares now borrowed upon, ... 65
Largest number of shares held by any one member,   . . . 25
Number of shares withdrawn during the year, ... 264
Number of shares forfeited during the year, ... 10
Highest per centum of interest received during the year: 6¼.
Lowest per centum of interest received during the year: 6.
Number of members withdrawn during the year, ... 45
Present number of members, ... 107
Present number of borrowers, ... 7
Present number of non-borrowers, ... 100
Number of loans secured by first mortgage of real estate,   . . 4
Number of loans on shares,   . . . : 3
Largest loan to any one member, ... $3,500 00
Smallest loan to any one member, ... 35 00
Amount of expenses of the corporation for the year ending Oct. 31, 1894, . 39 30
Date of examination by commissioner: October 15.

NEEDHAM CO-OPERATIVE BANK — NEEDHAM.

Incorporated April 21, 1892. Commenced business May 9, 1892.

ALBERT E. MILLER, *President.*   W. G. MOSELEY, *Secretary.*
W. G. MOSELEY, *Treasurer.*

Names of security committee:

E. G. POND,   R. G. ROPER,
WM. CARTER,   F. G. TUTTLE,
JOHN MOSELEY.

Regular meetings the first Monday after the first Friday.

BALANCE SHEET OCTOBER 31, 1894.

ASSETS.		LIABILITIES.	
Loans on real estate,	$9,850 00	Dues capital,	$10,627 00
Loans on shares,	1,210 00	Profits capital (all series),	749 98
Permanent expense account,	115 00	Guaranty fund,	15 14
Cash in hands of treasurer,	256 83	Surplus,	39 71
	$11,431 83		$11,431 83

Detailed Statement of Receipts and Disbursements for the Year ending Oct. 31, 1894.

RECEIPTS.		DISBURSEMENTS.	
From dues capital,	$5,764 00	For real estate loans,	$4,416 67
interest,	579 53	share loans,	1,310 00
premiums,	35 35	dues capital (withdrawn),	2,285 00
fines,	31 30	profits capital (withdrawn,)	87 41
transfer fees,	25	temporary expenses,	95 00
real estate loans repaid,	1,000 00	permanent expenses,	3 50
share loans repaid,	315 00		
withdrawal profits,	49 58		
Cash on hand Oct. 31, 1893,	679 40	Cash on hand Oct. 31, 1894,	256 83
	$8,454 41		$8,454 41

Reconciliation of Share Account with Dues and Profits Capital.

DATE OF ISSUE.	Series.	Value per Share.	Shares in Force.	Total Value.		
May, 1892, .	1	$32 37	243	$7,865 91	Dues capital, as per general ledger, . .	$10,627 00
Nov., 1892, .	2	25 50	76	1,938 00		
May, 1893, .	3	18.85	55	1,036 75	Profits capital, as per general ledger, . .	749 98
Nov., 1893, .	4	12 38	19	235 22		
May, 1894, .	5	6 10	61	372 10	Unpaid dues, . .	75 00
Dues paid in advance, . . .				4 00		
Total, ...				$11,451 98	Total, . . .	$11,451 98

Number of shares issued during the year, ... 90
Number of shares now in force, ... 454
Number of shares now borrowed upon, ... 133
Largest number of shares held by any one member, . . . 15
Number of shares withdrawn during the year, ... 151
Highest per centum of interest received during the year: $6\frac{3}{5}$.
Lowest per centum of interest received during the year: $6\frac{3}{10}$.
Number of members withdrawn during the year, ... 32
Present number of members, ... 85
Present number of borrowers, ... 17
Present number of non-borrowers, ... 68
Number of loans secured by first mortgage of real estate, . . . 13
Number of loans on shares, ... 10
Largest loan to any one member, ... $2,000 00
Smallest loan to any one member, ... 30 00
Amount of expenses of the corporation for the year ending Oct. 31, 1894, . 118 50
Date of examination by commissioner: June 28.

NEW BEDFORD CO-OPERATIVE BANK — NEW BEDFORD.

Incorporated July 11, 1881.   Commenced business Aug. 19, 1881.

GEORGE R. STETSON, *President.*   GIDEON B. WRIGHT, *Secretary.*
CHARLES R. PRICE, *Treasurer.*

Names of security committee:
SAMUEL S. PAINE,   BENJ. F. BROWNELL,
JASPER W. BRALEY.

Regular meetings the third Friday of each month.

BALANCE SHEET OCTOBER 31, 1894.

ASSETS.			LIABILITIES.		
Loans on real estate, . .	$290,526	19	Dues capital, . . .	$257,583	00
Loans on shares, . .	16,223	00	Profits capital (all series), .	54,579	81
Permanent expense account,	54	45	Guaranty fund, . . .	2,999	09
Unpaid interest, . . .	1,156	68	Surplus, ...	2,493	02
Unpaid fines, . . .	119	06	Forfeited share account, .	121	16
Unpaid dues, ...	1,886	00	Personal accounts, . .	1,763	27
Personal accounts, . .	533	10			
Cash in hands of treasurer, .	9,040	87			
	$319,539	35		$319,539	35

Detailed Statement of Receipts and Disbursements for the Year ending Oct. 31, 1894.

RECEIPTS.			DISBURSEMENTS.		
From dues capital, . .	$66,680	00	For real estate loans, . .	$64,124	78
interest, . . .	19,345	48	share loans, . . .	15,000	00
fines, . . .	448	68	dues capital (withdrawn),	40,718	00
transfer fees, . .	2	75	dues capital (retired), .	16,740	00
real estate loans repaid,	63,988	62	dues capital (matured),	9,138	00
share loans repaid, .	14,722	00	profits capital (withdrawn), . . .	7,585	21
withdrawal profits, .	646	85	profits capital (retired), .	7,338	72
profit and loss, . .	47	59	profits capital (matured),	4,013	61
personal accounts, .	3,137	74	temporary expenses, .	1,892	63
			permanent expenses, .	41	00
			interest on matured shares, . . .	236	77
			interest on retired shares,	259	16
			personal accounts, .	1,272	18
Cash on hand Oct. 31, 1893, .	8,381	22	Cash on hand Oct. 31, 1894,	9,040	87
	$177,400	93		$177,400	93

Reconciliation of Share Account with Dues and Profits Capital.

Date of Issue.	Series.	Value per Share.	Shares in Force.	Total Value.		
Aug., 1883, .	5	$195 15	24	$4,683 60	Dues capital, as per general ledger, . . .	$257,583 00
Feb., 1884, .	6	183 16	56	10,256 96		
Aug., 1884, .	7	171 59	71	12,182 89	Profits capital, as per general ledger, . .	54,579 81
Feb., 1885, .	8	160 41	78	12,511 98		
May, 1885, .	9	154 95	44	6,817 80		
Nov., 1885, .	10	144 24	88	12,693 12		
May, 1886, .	11	133 95	174	23,307 30		
Nov., 1886, .	12	123 92	141	17,472 72		
May, 1887, .	13	114 22	175	19,988 50		
Nov., 1887, .	14	104 82	132	13,836 24		
May, 1888, .	15	95 72	273	26,131 56		
Nov., 1888, .	16	86 90	228	19,813 20		
May, 1889, .	17	78 36	229	17,944 44		
Nov., 1889, .	18	70 09	211	14,788 99		
May, 1890, .	19	62 06	291	18,059 46		
Nov., 1890, .	20	54 30	233	12,651 90		
May, 1891, .	21	46 79	299	13,990 21		
Nov., 1891, .	22	39 49	339	13,387 11		
May, 1892, .	23	32 41	371	12,024 11		
Nov., 1892, .	24	25 54	374	9,551 96		
May, 1893, .	25	18 86	484	9,128 24		
Nov., 1893, .	26	12 39	618	7,657 02		
May, 1894, .	27	6 10	435	2,653 50		
Dues paid in advance, . .				630 00		
Total, ...				$312,162 81	Total, . . .	$312,162 81

Number of shares issued during the year, ...	1,245	
Number of shares now in force, ...	5,368	
Number of shares now borrowed upon, ...	2,074	
Largest number of shares held by any one member, ...	25	
Number of shares withdrawn during the year, ...	1,041	
Number of shares retired during the year, ...	123	
Number of shares matured during the year, ...	66	
Highest premium received during the year, ...		$0 26
Lowest premium received during the year, ...		01
Number of members withdrawn during the year, ...	140	
Present number of members, ...	735	
Present number of borrowers, ...	250	
Present number of non-borrowers, ...	485	
Number of loans secured by first mortgage of real estate, . . .	185	
Number of loans on shares, ...	65	
Largest loan to any one member, ...		5,000 00
Smallest loan to any one member, ...		10 00
Amount of expenses of the corporation for the year ending Oct. 31, 1894, .		1,959 18
Date of examination by commissioner : October 1.		

NEWBURYPORT CO-OPERATIVE BANK—NEWBURYPORT.

Incorporated March 15, 1888.   Commenced business April 9, 1888.

LUTHER DAME, *President.*   GEORGE E. STICKNEY, *Secretary.*
GEORGE E. STICKNEY, *Treasurer.*

Names of security committee :
CHAS. H. GOODWIN,   LEONARD N. KENT,
W. HERBERT NOYES.

Regular meetings the second Monday of each month.

BALANCE SHEET OCTOBER 31, 1894.

ASSETS.		LIABILITIES.	
Loans on real estate, . .	$118,160 00	Dues capital, . . .	$114,513 00
Loans on shares, . . .	3,820 00	Profits capital (all series), .	15,711 14
Temporary expense account,	66 73	Interest, ...	593 34
Furniture and fixtures, . .	200 00	Premiums, ...	48 05
Cash in hands of treasurer, .	10,745 56	Fines, ...	19 82
		Transfer fees, . . .	25
		Withdrawal profits, . .	56 82
		Guaranty fund, . . .	750 00
		Surplus, ...	1,299 87
	$132,992 29		$132,992 29

Detailed Statement of Receipts and Disbursements for the Year ending Oct. 31, 1894.

RECEIPTS.		DISBURSEMENTS.	
From dues capital, . .	$36,659 00	For real estate loans, . .	$26,185 00
interest, . . .	7,235 97	share loans, . . .	2,710 00
premiums, . . .	605 11	dues capital (withdrawn),	18,958 00
fines, ...	284 12	dues capital (retired), .	5,760 00
transfer fees, . .	1 25	profits capital (withdrawn), .	2,074 04
real estate loans repaid,	20,775 00	profits capital (retired), .	1,070 14
share loans repaid, .	1,420 00	temporary expenses, .	928 05
withdrawal profits, .	494 31	Cash on hand Oct. 31, 1894,	10,745 56
Cash on hand Oct. 31, 1893, .	956 03		
	$68,430 79		$68,430 79

Reconciliation of Share Account with Dues and Profits Capital.

DATE OF ISSUE.	Series.	Value per Share.	Shares in Force.	Total Value.		
Apr., 1888, .	1	$95 43	246	$23,475 78	Dues capital, as per gen-	
Oct., 1888, .	2	87 04	128	11,141 12	eral ledger, . .	$114,513 00
Apr., 1889, .	3	78 81	166	13,082 46	Profits capital, as per	
Oct., 1889, .	4	70 76	162	11,463 12	general ledger, . .	15,711 14
Apr., 1890, .	5	62 91	217	13,651 47	Unpaid dues, . .	897 00
Oct., 1890, .	6	55 28	146	8,070 88		
Apr., 1891, .	7	47 79	280	13,381 20		
Oct., 1891, .	8	40 54	281	11,391 74		
Apr., 1892, .	9	33 47	273	9,137 31		
Oct., 1892, .	10	26 60	169	4,495 40		
Apr., 1893, .	11	19 91	337	6,709 67		
Oct., 1893, .	12	13 41	189	2,534 49		
Apr., 1894, .	13	7 10	325	2,307 50		
Oct., 1894, .	14	1 00	243	243 00		
Dues paid in advance, . . .				36 00		
Total, ...				$131,121 14	Total, . . .	$131,121 14

Number of shares issued during the year, ... 665	
Number of shares now in force, ... 3,162	
Number of shares now borrowed upon, ... 734	
Largest number of shares held by any one member, ... 25	
Number of shares withdrawn during the year, ... 636	
Number of shares retired during the year, ... 86	
Highest premium received during the year, ...	$0 05
Lowest premium received during the year, ...	05
Number of members withdrawn during the year, ... 126	
Present number of members, ... 461	
Present number of borrowers, ... 116	
Present number of non-borrowers, ... 345	
Number of loans secured by first mortgage of real estate, . . . 119	
Number of loans on shares, ... 22	
Largest loan to any one member, ...	3,200 00
Smallest loan to any one member, ...	50 00
Amount of expenses of the corporation for the year ending Oct. 31, 1894, .	928 05

Date of examination by commissioner : December 17.

NEWTON CO-OPERATIVE BANK — NEWTON.

Incorporated June 14, 1888.   Commenced business Sept. 4, 1888.

FRANCIS A. DEWSON, *President.*   J. CHEEVER FULLER, *Secretary.*

J. CHEEVER FULLER, *Treasurer.*

Names of security committee:

J. W. FRENCH,	F. J. HALE,
J. F. HECKMAN,	T. B. FITZPATRICK,
G. F. SIMPSON.	

Regular meetings the first Tuesday of each month.

BALANCE SHEET OCTOBER 31, 1894.

ASSETS.		LIABILITIES.	
Loans on real estate, . .	$272,000 00	Dues capital, . . .	$245,495 00
Loans on shares, . . .	7,275 00	Profits capital (all series), .	29,094 15
Suspense account, . . .	35 60	Interest, ...	2,588 50
Cash in hands of secretary, .	674 81	Premiums, ...	255 25
Cash in hands of treasurer, .	1,199 81	Fines, ...	44 30
		Withdrawal profits, . .	261 05
		Guaranty fund, . . .	1,480 54
		Surplus, ...	1,960 43
		Security committee, . .	6 00
	$281,185 22		$281,185 22

Detailed Statement of Receipts and Disbursements for the Year ending Oct. 31, 1894.

RECEIPTS.		DISBURSEMENTS.	
From dues capital, . .	$95,591 00	For real estate loans, . .	$100,700 00
interest, . . .	15,226 40	share loans, . . .	8,525 00
premiums, . . .	1,562 50	dues capital (withdrawn),	40,588 00
fines, ...	305 65	dues capital (retired), .	15,286 00
real estate loans repaid,	48,250 00	profits capital (with-	
share loans repaid, .	12,170 00	drawn), . . .	3,559 76
withdrawal profits, .	891 21	profits capital (retired), .	2,544 34
security committee, .	76 00	temporary expenses, .	2,028 54
		permanent expenses, .	400 00
		security committee, .	80 00
		interest paid on retired	
		shares, . . .	247 30
Cash on hand Oct. 31, 1893,	1,760 80	Cash on hand Oct. 31, 1894,	1,874 62
	$175,833 56		$175,833 56

Reconciliation of Share Account with Dues and Profits Capital.

DATE OF ISSUE.	Series.	Value per Share.	Shares In Force.	Total Value.		
Sept., 1888, .	1	$88 65	610	$54,076 50	Dues capital, as per general ledger, . .	$245,495 00
Mar., 1889, .	2	80 20	409	32,801 80		
Sept., 1889, .	3	71 09	158	11,374 42	Profits capital, as per general ledger, . .	29,094 15
Mar., 1890, .	4	64 02	427	27,336 54		
Sept., 1890, .	5	56 29	347	19,532 63	Unpaid dues, . .	1,482 00
Mar., 1891, .	6	48 78	546	26,633 88		
Sept., 1891, .	7	41 49	476	19,749 24		
Mar., 1892, .	8	34 41	629	21,643 89		
Sept., 1892, .	9	27 54	610	16,799 40		
Mar., 1893, .	10	20 87	936	19,534 32		
Sept., 1893, .	11	14 39	737	10,605 43		
Mar., 1894, .	12	8 10	1,541	12,482 10		
Sept., 1894, .	13	2 00	1,073	2,146 00		
Dues paid in advance, . . .				1,355 00		
Total, ...				$276,071 15	Total, . . .	$276,071 15

Number of shares issued during the year, ...	3,064	
Number of shares now in force, ...	8,499	
Number of shares now borrowed upon, ...	1,708	
Largest number of shares held by any one member, . . .	25	
Number of shares withdrawn during the year, . . .	1,886	
Number of shares retired during the year, ...	235	
Highest premium received during the year, ...		$0 15
Lowest premium received during the year, ...		05
Number of members withdrawn during the year, ...	169	
Present number of members, ...	977	
Present number of borrowers, ...	181	
Present number of non-borrowers, ...	796	
Number of loans secured by first mortgage of real estate, . .	175	
Number of loans on shares, ...	39	
Largest loan to any one member, ...	5,000 00	
Smallest loan to any one member, ...	50 00	
Amount of expenses of the corporation for the year ending Oct. 31, 1894, .	2,428 54	

Date of examination by commissioner : February 15.

NORTH ABINGTON CO-OPERATIVE BANK — NORTH ABINGTON.

Incorporated March 23, 1888. Commenced business April 4, 1888.

Moses N. Arnold, *President.*   Ernest W. Calkins, *Secretary.*
Edward P. Boynton, *Treasurer.*

Names of security committee :
Joseph L. Greenwood,   Eliphalet R. Bates,
Samuel N. Turner.

Regular meetings the first Wednesday of each month.

BALANCE SHEET OCTOBER 31, 1894.

ASSETS.		LIABILITIES.	
Loans on real estate, . .	$45,400 00	Dues capital, . . .	$40,115 00
Loans on shares, . . .	900 00	Profits capital (all series), .	6,207 82
Permanent expense account, .	90 00	Interest, ...	252 83
Temporary expense account,	12 50	Premiums, ...	12 90
Unpaid interest, . . .	269 50	Fines, ...	13 72
Unpaid premiums, . .	13 65	Withdrawal profits, . .	11 39
Unpaid fines, ...	39 16	Guaranty fund, . . .	127 00
Tax account, ...	56 12	Surplus, ...	604 47
Cash in hands of secretary, .	26 76	Forfeited share account, .	5 64
Cash in hands of treasurer, . .	543 08		
	$47,350 77		$47,350 77

Detailed Statement of Receipts and Disbursements for the Year ending Oct. 31, 1894.

RECEIPTS.		DISBURSEMENTS.	
From dues capital, . .	$11,913 00	For real estate loans, . .	$8,700 00
interest, . . .	2,620 10	share loans, . . .	650 00
premiums, . . .	134 05	dues capital(withdrawn),	4,917 00
fines, ...	149 24	dues capital (retired), .	5,717 00
transfer fees, . .	50	profits capital (with-	
real estate loans repaid,	5,850 00	drawn), . . .	573 82
share loans repaid, .	450 00	profits capital (retired),	1,136 02
withdrawal profits, .	143 14	temporary expenses, .	155 22
Cash on hand Oct. 31, 1893, . .	1,214 99	tax account, . . .	56 12
		Cash on hand Oct. 31, 1894,	569 84
	$22,475 02		$22,475 02

Reconciliation of Share Account with Dues and Profits Capital.

DATE OF ISSUE.	Series.	Value per Share.	Shares In Force.	Total Value.		
April, 1888, .	1	$96 06	168	$16,138 08	Dues capital, as per general ledger, . . .	$40,115 00
Oct., 1888, .	2	87 40	55	4,807 00		
April, 1889, .	3	79 04	56	4,426 24	Profits capital, as per general ledger, . .	6,207 82
Oct., 1889, .	4	70 81	36	2,549 16		
April, 1890, .	5	62 85	40	2,514 00	Unpaid dues, . . .	434 00
Oct., 1890, .	6	55 14	47	2,591 58		
April, 1891, .	7	47 65	100	4,765 00		
Oct., 1891, .	8	40 38	15	605 70		
April, 1892, .	9	33 32	49	1,632 68		
Oct., 1892, .	10	26 47	126	3,335 22		
April, 1893, .	11	19 82	94	1,863 08		
Oct., 1893, .	12	13 36	49	654 64		
April, 1894, .	13	7 09	116	822 44		
Oct., 1894, .	14	1 00	42	42 00		
Dues paid in advance, . .				10 00		
Total, ...				$46,756 82	Total, . . .	$46,756 82

Number of shares issued during the year, ...	176
Number of shares now in force, ...	993
Number of shares now borrowed upon, ...	254
Largest number of shares held by any one member, ...	25
Number of shares withdrawn during the year, ...	150
Number of shares retired during the year, ...	79
Highest premium received during the year, ...	$0 05
Lowest premium received during the year, ...	05
Number of members withdrawn during the year, ...	33
Present number of members, ...	199
Present number of borrowers, ...	47
Present number of non-borrowers, ...	152
Number of loans secured by first mortgage of real estate, . . .	52
Number of loans on shares, ...	5
Largest loan to any one member, ...	2,000 00
Smallest loan to any one member, ...	50 00
Amount of expenses of the corporation for the year ending Oct. 31, 1894,	215 22

Date of examination by commissioner : April 17.

NORTHAMPTON CO-OPERATIVE BANK — NORTH-AMPTON.

Incorporated May 21, 1889. Commenced business May 24, 1889.

E. C. DAVIS, *President.*   H. R. GRAVES, *Secretary.*
M. L. GRAVES, *Treasurer.*

Names of security committee:
C. S. CROUCH,   M. L. GRAVES,
S. R. COOLEY.

Regular meetings the first Monday of each month.

BALANCE SHEET OCTOBER 31, 1894.

ASSETS.		LIABILITIES.	
Loans on real estate,	$85,200 00	Dues capital,	$82,132 00
Loans on shares,	2,700 00	Profits capital (all series),	10,161 66
Permanent expense account,	139 40	Guaranty fund,	122 70
Unpaid interest,	427 50	Surplus,	513 35
Unpaid premiums,	72 40	Forfeited share account,	12 70
Unpaid fines,	72 15		
Unpaid dues,	912 00		
Cash in hands of treasurer,	3,418 96		
	$92,942 41		$92,942 41

Detailed Statement of Receipts and Disbursements for the Year ending Oct. 31, 1894.

RECEIPTS.		DISBURSEMENTS.	
From dues capital,	$30,813 00	For real estate loans,	$33,950 00
interest,	4,559 50	share loans,	2,850 00
premiums,	762 36	dues capital (withdrawn),	13,728 00
fines,	139 94	profits capital (with-	
transfer fees,	2 75	drawn),	1,379 22
real estate loans repaid,	15,300 00	temporary expenses,	641 54
share loans repaid,	1,850 00		
withdrawal profits,	143 42		
Cash on hand Oct. 31, 1893,	2,396 75	Cash on hand Oct. 31, 1894,	3,418 96
	$55,967 72		$55,967 72

Reconciliation of Share Account with Dues and Profits Capital.

DATE OF ISSUE.	Series.	Value per Share.	Shares in Force.	Total Value.		
June, 1889, .	1	$76 70	432	$33,134 40	Dues capital, as per general ledger, . .	$82,132 00
Dec., 1889, .	2	68 70	102	7,007 40		
June, 1890, .	3	60 83	82	4,988 06	Profits capital, as per general ledger, . .	10,161 66
Dec., 1890, .	4	53 14	99	5,260 86		
June, 1891, .	5	45 67	125	5,708 75		
Nov., 1891, .	6	39 44	266	10,491 04		
May, 1892, .	7	32 47	191	6,201 77		
Nov., 1892, .	8	25 57	276	7,057 32		
May, 1893, .	9	18 87	401	7,566 87		
Nov., 1893, .	10	12 39	201	2,490 39		
May, 1894, .	11	6 10	368	2,244 80		
Dues paid in advance, . . .				142 00		
Total, ...				$92,293 66	Total, . . .	$92,293 66

Number of shares issued during the year, ... 648
Number of shares now in force, ... 2,543
Number of shares now borrowed upon, ... 553
Largest number of shares held by any one member, . . . 25
Number of shares withdrawn during the year, ... 550
Highest premium received during the year, ... $1 00
Lowest premium received during the year, ... 05
Number of members withdrawn during the year, ... 92
Present number of members, ... 528
Present number of borrowers, ... 86
Present number of non-borrowers, ... 442
Number of loans secured by first mortgage of real estate, . . . 72
Number of loans on shares, ... 14
Largest loan to any one member, ... 3,700 00
Smallest loan to any one member, ... 50 00
Amount of expenses of the corporation for the year ending Oct. 31, 1894, . 674 14
Date of examination by commissioner: March 9.

NORTH DIGHTON CO-OPERATIVE BANK — NORTH DIGHTON.

Incorporated April 14, 1890. Commenced business April 21, 1890.

JOSEPH PHILBRICK, *President.*   NATHANIEL R. LINCOLN, *Secretary.*
EDWARD LINCOLN, *Treasurer.*

Names of security committee:
EDWARD ALMY,   JAMES M. LINCOLN,
WILLIAM T. PLACE.

Regular meetings the second Monday of each month.

BALANCE SHEET OCTOBER 31, 1894.

ASSETS.		LIABILITIES.	
Loans on real estate, . .	$25,200 00	Dues capital, . . .	$23,674 00
Loans on shares, . . .	585 00	Profits capital (all series), .	2,033 58
Permanent expense account,	30 00	Interest, ...	833 91
Temporary expense account,	57 75	Premiums, ...	44 75
Unpaid interest, . . .	10 75	Fines, ...	16 50
Unpaid premiums, . .	20	Guaranty fund, . . .	62 22
Pass-book account, . .	28 80	Surplus, ...	103 34
Town note, ...	600 00		
Cash in hands of treasurer, .	255 80		
	$26,768 30		$26,768 30

Detailed Statement of Receipts and Disbursements for the Year ending Oct. 31, 1894.

RECEIPTS.		DISBURSEMENTS.	
From dues capital, . .	$8,710 00	For real estate loans, . .	$4,750 00
interest, . . .	1,458 41	share loans, . . .	910 00
premiums, . . .	78 05	dues capital (withdrawn),	6,871 00
fines, ...	30 01	profits capital (withdrawn), . .	498 23
real estate loans repaid,	3,050 00	temporary expenses, .	142 35
share loans repaid, .	690 00	town note, . . .	600 00
pass-books, . . .	70	Cash on hand Oct. 31, 1894,	255 80
Cash on hand Oct. 31, 1893, .	10 21		
	$14,027 38		$14,027 38

Reconciliation of Share Account with Dues and Profits Capital.

Date of Issue.	Series.	Value per Share.	Shares in Force.	Total Value.		
April, 1890, .	1	$60 95	274	$16,700 30	Dues capital, as per general ledger, . .	$23,674 00
April, 1891, .	2	46 41	64	2,970 24	Profits capital, as per	
April, 1892, .	3	32 52	93	3,024 36	general ledger, . .	2,033 58
April, 1893, .	4	19 39	112	2,171 68	Unpaid dues, . .	62 00
April, 1894, .	5	7 00	129	903 00		
Total, ...				$25,769 58	Total, . . .	$25,769 58

Number of shares issued during the year, ... 168
Number of shares now in force, ... 672
Number of shares now borrowed upon, ... 181
Largest number of shares held by any one member, ... 25
Number of shares withdrawn during the year, ... 340
Highest premium received during the year, ... $0 05
Lowest premium received during the year, ... 05
Number of members withdrawn during the year, ... 33
Present number of members, ... 109
Present number of borrowers, ... 34
Present number of non-borrowers, ... 75
Number of loans secured by first mortgage of real estate, . . . 26
Number of loans on shares, ... 10
Largest loan to any one member, ... 1,800 00
Smallest loan to any one member, ... 25 00
Amount of expenses of the corporation for the year ending Oct. 31, 1894, . 152 35
Date of examination by commissioner: August 27.

NORTH EASTON CO-OPERATIVE BANK — NORTH EASTON.

Incorporated April 23, 1889.   Commenced business April 23, 1889.

L. B. CROCKETT, *President.*   WM. H. CLEMENTS, *Secretary.*

WM. H. CLEMENTS, *Treasurer.*

Names of security committeee :

EDW. R. HAYWARD,   HIRAM WILLIAMS,

L. L. BERRY.

Regular meetings the third Monday of each month.

BALANCE SHEET OCTOBER 31, 1894.

ASSETS.		LIABILITIES.	
Loans on real estate,	$64,500 00	Dues capital,	$59,231 00
Loans on shares,	1,180 00	Profits capital (all series),	8,071 60
Temporary expense account,	4 50	Interest,	295 90
Real estate by foreclosure,	1,362 40	Premiums,	44 65
Unpaid interest,	452 50	Fines,	8 44
Unpaid premiums,	75 45	Withdrawal profits,	25 76
Unpaid fines,	36 78	Guaranty fund,	613 61
Cash in hands of treasurer,	1,816 64	Surplus,	1,121 97
		Forfeited share account,	15 34
	$69,428 27		$69,428 27

Detailed Statement of Receipts and Disbursements for the Year ending Oct. 31, 1894.

RECEIPTS.		DISBURSEMENTS.	
From dues capital,	$23,997 00	For real estate loans,	$21,100 00
interest,	3,736 36	share loans,	510 00
premiums,	653 90	dues capital (withdrawn),	11,658 00
fines,	208 39	dues capital (forfeited),	230 00
transfer fees,	75	dues capital (retired),	3,806 00
real estate loans repaid,	12,000 00	profits capital (withdrawn),	1,132 31
share loans repaid,	780 00	profits capital (forfeited),	42 70
withdrawal profits,	266 32	profits capital (retired),	684 57
forfeiture profits,	28 86	temporary expenses,	233 17
forfeited shares,	243 00	permanent expenses,	58 25
		forfeited shares,	243 00
		interest on retired shares,	92 72
		real estate,	1,362 40
Cash on hand Oct. 31, 1893,	1,055 18	Cash on hand Oct. 31, 1894,	1,186 64
	$42,969 76		$42,969 76

Reconciliation of Share Account with Dues and Profits Capital.

DATE OF ISSUE.	Series.	Value per Share.	Shares in Force.	Total Value.		
April, 1889, .	1	$81 18	226	$18,346 68	Dues capital, as per general ledger, . . .	$59,231 00
Oct., 1889, .	2	72 66	79	5,740 14		
April, 1890, .	3	64 38	90	5,794 20	Profits capital, as per general ledger, . .	8,071 60
Oct., 1890, .	4	56 34	48	2,704 32		
April, 1891, .	5	48 56	180	8,740 80	Unpaid dues, . . .	686 00
Oct., 1891, .	6	41 06	110	4,516 60		
April, 1892, .	7	33 80	189	6,388 20		
Oct., 1892, .	8	26 80	266	7,128 80		
April, 1893, .	9	20 01	146	2,921 46		
Oct., 1893, .	10	13 45	240	3,228 00		
April, 1894, .	11	7 12	320	2,278 40		
Oct., 1894, .	12	1 00	171	171 00		
Dues paid in advance, . . .				30 00		
Total, ...				$67,988 60	Total, . . .	$67,988 60

Number of shares issued during the year, ... , .	561	
Number of shares now in force, ...	2,065	
Number of shares now borrowed upon, ...	372	
Largest number of shares held by any one member, ...	25	
Number of shares withdrawn during the year, ...	479	
Number of shares forfeited during the year, ...	8	
Number of shares retired during the year, ...	66	
Highest premium received during the year, ...		$0 50
Lowest premium received during the year, ...		0 05
Number of members withdrawn during the year, ...	75	
Present number of members, ...	310	
Present number of borrowers, ...	87	
Present number of non-borrowers, ...	223	
Number of loans secured by first mortgage of real estate, . . .	80	
Number of loans on shares, ...	12	
Largest loan to any one member, ...		3,000 00
Smallest loan to any one member, ...		25 00
Amount of expenses of the corporation for the year ending Oct. 31, 1894, .		291 42

Date of examination by commissioner: March 6.

NORWOOD CO-OPERATIVE BANK — NORWOOD.

Incorporated Sept. 20, 1889.   Commenced business Oct. 1, 1889.

FRANCIS O. WINSLOW, *President.*   IRVING S. FOGG, *Secretary.*
IRVING S. FOGG, *Treasurer.*

Names of security committee:

TYLER THAYER,   GEORGE W. GAY,
EDMUND J. SHATTUCK.

Regular meetings the first Tuesday of each month.

BALANCE SHEET OCTOBER 31, 1894.

ASSETS.		LIABILITIES.	
Loans on real estate,	$53,300 00	Dues capital,	$48,533 00
Loans on shares,	1,275 00	Profits capital (all series),	5,446 17
Unpaid fines,	17 87	Interest,	66 63
Cash in hands of treasurer,	30 18	Premiums,	3 50
		Transfer fees,	25
		Withdrawal profits,	19 92
		Guaranty fund,	70 93
		Surplus,	482 65
	$54,623 05		$54,623 05

Detailed Statement of Receipts and Disbursements for the Year ending Oct. 31, 1894.

RECEIPTS.		DISBURSEMENTS.	
From dues capital,	$19,210 00	For real estate loans,	$15,450 00
interest,	2,860 93	share loans,	1,125 00
premiums,	145 25	dues capital (withdrawn),	8,804 00
fines,	79 69	profits capital (withdrawn),	807 77
transfer fees,	50	temporary expenses,	231 97
real estate loans repaid,	2,850 00		
share loans repaid,	450 00		
withdrawal profits,	177 34		
Cash on hand Oct. 31, 1893,	675 21	Cash on hand Oct. 31, 1894,	30 18
	$26,448 92		$26,448 92

Reconciliation of Share Account with Dues and Profits Capital.

DATE OF ISSUE.	Series.	Value per Share.	Shares in Force.	Total Value.		
Oct., 1889, .	1	$70 85	276	$19,554 60	Dues capital, as per general ledger, . .	$48,533 00
April, 1890, .	2	62 95	101	6,357 95		
Oct., 1890, .	3	55 23	48	2,651 04	Profits capital, as per general ledger, . .	5,446 17
April, 1891, .	4	47 74	55	2,625 70		
Oct., 1891, .	5	40 45	188	7,604 60	Unpaid dues, . . .	431 00
April, 1892, .	6	33 37	105	3,503 85		
Oct., 1892, .	7	26 51	142	3,764 42		
April, 1893, .	8	19 85	201	3,989 85		
Oct., 1893, .	9	13 38	122	1,632 36		
April, 1894, .	10	7 10	358	2,541 80		
Oct., 1894, .	11	1 00	167	167 00		
Dues paid in advance, . . .				17 00		
Total, ...				$54,410 17	Total, . . .	$54,410 17

Number of shares issued during the year, ... 603
Number of shares now in force, ... 1,763
Number of shares now borrowed upon, ... 316
Largest number of shares held by any one member, . . . 25
Number of shares withdrawn during the year, ... 337
Highest premium received during the year, ... $0 05
Lowest premium received during the year, ... 05
Number of members withdrawn during the year, ... 27
Present number of members, ... 290
Present number of borrowers, ... 55
Present number of non-borrowers, ... 235
Number of loans secured by first mortgage of real estate, . . . 56
Number of loans on shares, ... 6
Largest loan to any one member, ... 5,000 00
Smallest loan to any one member, ... 50 00
Amount of expenses of the corporation for the year ending Oct. 31, 1894, . 261 97
Date of examination by commissioner : June 29.

ORANGE CO-OPERATIVE BANK—ORANGE.

Incorporated Jan. 8, 1889. Commenced business Jan. 23, 1889.

FRANK S. EWING, *President.*   ELISHA S. HALL, *Secretary.*
                    ELISHA S. HALL, *Treasurer.*

Names of security committee :

ADELBERT W. BALLOU,   WILLARD E. JOHNSON,
              JOHN L. WILLIAMS.

Regular meetings the fourth Wednesday of each month.

BALANCE SHEET OCTOBER 31, 1894.

ASSETS.		LIABILITIES.	
Loans on real estate, . .	$58,785 00	Dues capital, . . .	$56,619 00
Loans on shares, . . .	4,730 00	Profits capital (all series), .	7,042 93
Permanent expense account, .	80 50	Interest, ...	1,202 10
Temporary expense account,	4 50	Premiums, ...	40 85
Cash in hands of treasurer, .	1,936 21	Fines, ...	30 48
		Withdrawal profits, . .	68 94
		Guaranty fund, . . .	130 99
		Surplus, ...	394 92
		Forfeited share account, .	6 00
	$65,536 21		$65,536 21

Detailed Statement of Receipts and Disbursements for the Year ending Oct. 31, 1894.

RECEIPTS.		DISBURSEMENTS.	
From dues capital, .	$19,451 00	For real estate loans, . .	$19,320 00
interest, . . .	3,622 11	share loans, . . .	3,400 00
premiums, . . .	166 25	dues capital (withdrawn),	10,398 00
fines, ...	98 15	dues capital (retired), .	4,889 00
transfer fees, . .	25	profits capital (withdrawn), . . .	1,163 70
real estate loans repaid,	15,065 00	profits capital (retired),	848 68
share loans repaid, .	1,895 00	temporary expenses, .	246 43
withdrawal profits, .	230 84	Cash on hand Oct. 31, 1894, .	1,936 21
Cash on hand Oct. 31, 1893, .	1,673 42		
	$42,202 02		$42,202 02

Reconciliation of Share Account with Dues and Profits Capital.

DATE OF ISSUE.	Series.	Value per Share.	Shares in Force.	Total Value.		
Jan., 1889, .	1	$82 33	311	$25,604 63	Dues capital, as per general ledger, . .	$56,619 00
July, 1889, .	2	74 08	83	6,148 64		
Jan., 1890, .	3	66 08	65	4,295 20	Profits capital, as per general ledger, . .	7,042 93
July, 1890, .	4	58 32	55	3,207 60		
Jan., 1891, .	5	50 79	83	4,215 57	Unpaid dues, . .	905 00
July, 1891, .	6	43 50	98	4,263 00		
Jan., 1892, .	7	36 41	164	5,971 24		
July, 1892, .	8	29 55	123	3,634 65		
Jan., 1893, .	9	22 88	135	3,088 80		
July, 1893, .	10	16 40	90	1,476 00		
Jan., 1894, .	11	10 11	160	1,617 60		
July, 1894, .	12	4 00	253	1,012 00		
Dues paid in advance, . . .				32 00		
Total, ...				$64,566 93	Total, . . .	$64,566 93

Number of shares issued during the year, ... 477
Number of shares now in force, ... 1,620
Number of shares now borrowed upon, ... 502
Largest number of shares held by any one member, . . . 25
Number of shares withdrawn during the year, ... 382
Number of shares retired during the year, ... 76
Highest per centum of interest received during the year: $8\frac{7}{10}$.
Lowest per centum of interest received during the year: 6.
Number of members withdrawn during the year, ... 33
Present number of members, ... 243
Present number of borrowers, ... 81
Present number of non-borrowers, ... 162
Number of loans secured by first mortgage of real estate, . . . 75
Number of loans on shares, ... 38
Largest loan to any one member, ... $2,200 00
Smallest loan to any one member, ... 50 00
Amount of expenses of the corporation for the year ending Oct. 31, 1894, . 264 31
Date of examination by commissioner: February 19.

PEABODY CO-OPERATIVE BANK — PEABODY.

Incorporated May 28, 1888. Commenced business June 16, 1888.

GEO. F. SANGER, *President.*   HARRY F. WALKER, *Secretary.*
HARRY F. WALKER, *Treasurer.*

Names of security committee:

N. M. QUINT,   S. S. LITTLEFIELD,
W. B. RICHARDSON.

Regular meetings the third Saturday of each month.

BALANCE SHEET OCTOBER 31, 1894.

ASSETS.		LIABILITIES.	
Loans on real estate,	$128,750 00	Dues capital,	$114,178 00
Loans on shares,	1,600 00	Profits capital (all series),	13,676 06
Temporary expense account,	25 50	Interest,	2,763 51
Cash in hands of treasurer,	1,964 78	Premiums,	251 23
		Fines,	38 25
		Withdrawal profits,	35 59
		Guaranty fund,	213 56
		Surplus,	1,184 08
	$132,340 28		$132,340 28

Detailed Statement of Receipts and Disbursements for the Year ending Oct. 31, 1894.

RECEIPTS.		DISBURSEMENTS.	
From dues capital,	$39,010 00	For real estate loans,	$30,100 00
interest,	6,923 84	share loans,	1,200 00
premiums,	672 99	dues capital (withdrawn),	16,445 00
fines,	116 57	profits capital (withdrawn),	2,075 29
transfer fees,	75	temporary expenses,	396 48
real estate loans repaid,	4,850 00		
share loans repaid,	425 00		
withdrawal profits,	87 15		
Cash on hand Oct. 31, 1893,	95 25	Cash on hand Oct. 31, 1894,	1,964 78
	$52,181 55		$52,181 55

Reconciliation of Share Account with Dues and Profits Capital.

Date of Issue.	Series.	Value per Share.	Shares in Force.	Total Value.		
June, 1888, .	1	$91 56	417	$38,180 52	Dues capital, as per general ledger, . .	$114,178 00
Dec., 1888, .	2	83 15	109	9,063 35		
June, 1889, .	3	74 96	177	13,267 92	Profits capital, as per general ledger, . .	13,676 06
Dec., 1889, .	4	67 00	107	7,169 00		
June, 1890, .	5	59 27	173	10,253 71	Unpaid dues, . . .	802 00
Dec., 1890, .	6	51 76	145	7,505 20		
June, 1891, .	7	44 47	228	10,139 16		
Dec. 1891, .	8	37 40	238	5,161 20		
June, 1892, .	9	30 53	197	6,014 41		
Dec., 1892, .	10	23 86	228	5,440 08		
June, 1893, .	11	17 39	579	10,068 81		
Dec., 1893, .	12	11 10	407	4,517 70		
June, 1894, .	13	5 00	313	1,565 00		
Dues paid in advance, . . .				310 00		
Total, ...				$128,656 06	Total, . . .	$128,656 06

Number of shares issued during the year, ...	795
Number of shares now in force, ...	3,218
Number of shares now borrowed upon, ...	784
Largest number of shares held by any one member, . . .	25
Number of shares withdrawn during the year, ...	515
Highest premium received during the year, ...	$0 15
Lowest premium received during the year, ...	05
Number of members withdrawn during the year, ...	43
Present number of members, ...	487
Present number of borrowers, ...	118
Present number of non-borrowers, ...	369
Number of loans secured by first mortgage of real estate, . . .	183
Number of loans on shares, ...	15
Largest loan to any one member, . ·	4,000 00
Smallest loan to any one member, ...	50 00
Amount of expenses of the corporation for the year ending Oct. 31, 1894, .	503 12

Date of examination by commissioner: November 13.

PEOPLE'S CO-OPERATIVE BANK—FALL RIVER.

Incorporated Feb. 18, 1882. Commenced business March 15, 1882.

WILTON REED, *President.*   SAMUEL HADFIELD, *Secretary.*
SAMUEL HADFIELD, *Treasurer.*

Names of security committee:

JOHN H. ESTES,   SAMUEL HADFIELD,
PATRICK KIERAN,   CHAS. E. MILLS,
EDW. S. ADAMS.

Regular meetings third Wednesday of each month.

BALANCE SHEET OCTOBER 31, 1894.

ASSETS.		LIABILITIES.	
Loans on real estate,	$180,200 00	Dues capital,	$171,309 00
Loans on shares,	9,550 00	Profits capital (all series),	27,885 25
Unpaid interest,	1,150 25	Guaranty fund,	657 94
Unpaid premiums,	113 15	Surplus,	1,019 12
Unpaid fines,	121 22	Forfeited share account,	652 29
Cash in hands of treasurer,	10,388 98		
	$201,523 60		$201,523 60

Detailed Statement of Receipts and Disbursements for the Year ending Oct. 31, 1894.

RECEIPTS.		DISBURSEMENTS.	
From dues capital,	$58,140 00	For real estate loans,	$55,600 00
interest,	10,437 50	share loans,	11,950 00
premiums,	1,079 35	dues capital(withdrawn),	28,454 00
fines,	226 85	dues capital (forfeited),	459 00
real estate loans repaid,	49,050 00	dues capital (matured),	15,620 00
share loans repaid,	6,050 00	profits capital (with-	
forfeiture profits,	5 37	drawn),	2,888 23
forfeited shares,	500 88	profits capital (forfeited),	44 40
real estate,	360 80	profits capital (matured),	7,353 89
		temporary expenses,	1,087 01
		forfeited shares,	92 70
Cash on hand Oct. 31, 1893,	8,087 46	Cash on hand Oct. 31, 1894,	10,388 98
	$133,938 21		$133,938 21

Reconciliation of Share Account with Dues and Profits Capital.

DATE OF ISSUE.	Series.	Value per Share.	Shares in Force.	Total Value.		
July, 1883, .	4	$196 45	18	$3,536 10	Dues capital, as per general ledger, . .	$171,309 00
Jan., 1884, .	5	184 38	13	2,396 94		
July, 1884, .	6	172 68	6	1,036 08	Profits capital, as per general ledger, . .	27,885 25
Jan., 1885, .	7	161 43	19	3,067 17		
July, 1885, .	8	150 61	9	1,355 49	Unpaid dues, . .	1,916 00
Nov., 1885, .	9	143 56	45	6,460 20		
May, 1886, .	10	133 35	66	8,801 10		
Nov., 1886, .	11	123 45	33	4,073 85		
May, 1887, .	12	113 79	40	4,551 60		
Nov., 1887, .	13	104 49	117	12,225 33		
May, 1888, .	14	95 48	116	11,075 68		
Nov., 1888, .	15	86 71	215	18,642 65		
May, 1889, .	16	78 22	80	6,257 60		
Nov., 1889, .	17	70 03	151	10,574 53		
May, 1890, .	18	61 98	315	19,523 70		
Nov., 1890, .	19	54 21	240	13,010 40		
May, 1891, .	20	46 72	330	15,417 60		
Nov., 1891, .	21	39 41	297	11,704 77		
May, 1892, .	22	32 32	513	16,580 16		
Nov., 1892, .	23	25 47	350	8,914 50		
May, 1893, .	24	18 82	549	10,332 18		
Nov., 1893, .	25	12 36	678	8,380 08		
May, 1894, .	26	6 09	506	3,081 54		
Dues paid in advance, . . .				111 00		
Total, ...				$201,110 25	Total, . . .	$201,110 25

Number of shares issued during the year, ...	1,333
Number of shares now in force, ...	4,706
Number of shares now borrowed upon, ...	1,353
Largest number of shares held by any one member, . . .	25
Number of shares withdrawn during the year, . . .	1,235
Number of shares forfeited during the year, ...	21
Number of shares matured during the year, ...	111
Highest premium received during the year, ...	$0 10
Lowest premium received during the year, ...	05
Number of members withdrawn during the year, ...	177
Present number of members, ...	593
Present number of borrowers, ...	141
Present number of non-borrowers, ...	452
Number of loans secured by first mortgage of real estate, . .	118
Number of loans on shares, ...	49
Largest loan to any one member, ...	5,000 00
Smallest loan to any one member, ...	50 00
Amount of expenses of the corporation for the year ending Oct. 31, 1894, .	1,087 01

Date of examination by commissioners: September 13.

PIONEER CO-OPERATIVE BANK – BOSTON.

Incorporated July 26, 1877.   Commenced business August 6, 1877.

GAMALIEL BRADFORD, *President.*   DANIEL ELDREDGE, *Secretary.*
DANIEL ELDREDGE, *Treasurer.*

Names of security committee :

HIRAM AMES,   JOHN K. FELLOWS,
GAMALIEL BRADFORD,   WALTER H. ROBERTS.

Regular meetings the first Monday of each month.

BALANCE SHEET OCTOBER 31, 1894.

ASSETS.		LIABILITIES.	
Loans on real estate, . .	$326,750 00	Dues capital, . . .	$289,281 00
Loans on shares, . . .	12,450 00	Profits capital (all series), .	60,243 02
Temporary expense account,	275 00	Interest, ...	1,754 52
Real estate by foreclosure, .	3,056 55	Premiums, ...	135 65
Unpaid interest, . . .	2,304 50	Fines, ...	145 30
Unpaid premiums, . .	158 15	Transfer fees, . . .	50
Unpaid fines, . . .	218 40	Withdrawal profits, . .	127 93
Mortgages, ...	4,700 00	Guaranty fund, . . .	2,334 40
Cash in hands of treasurer; .	9,815 11	Surplus, ...	5,346 62
		Forfeited share account, .	326 25
		Matured shares, . .	32 52
	$359,727 71		$359,727 71

Detailed Statement of Receipts and Disbursements for the Year ending Oct. 31, 1894.

RECEIPTS.		DISBURSEMENTS.	
From dues capital, . .	$75,028 00	For real estate loans, . .	$55,850 00
interest, . . .	21,075 46	share loans, . . .	7,500 00
premiums, . . .	1,648 35	dues capital (withdrawn),	36,932 00
fines, . . .	1,075 66	dues capital (forfeited),	1,010 00
transfer fees, . .	7 25	dues capital (retired), .	46,974 00
real estate loans repaid,	78,200 00	dues capital (matured),	5,616 00
share loans repaid, .	15,900 00	profits capital (withdrawn), . . .	6,335 62
withdrawal profits, .	1,583 30	profits capital (forfeited),	166 82
forfeiture profits, .	56 70	profits capital (retired),	16,136 50
forfeited shares, . .	68 00	profits capital (matured),	2,734 20
mortgages, . . .	400 00	temporary expenses, .	2,177 32
surplus,' . . .	5 04	profits, ...	04
retired shares, . .	59,646 64	dues capital, . . .	5 00
taxes, ...	54 56	matured shares, . .	4,713 38
matured shares, . .	4,745 90	interest, ...	1,000 10
estates, ...	4,111 84	retired shares, . . .	59,646 64
		estates, ...	7,217 45
Cash on hand Oct. 31, 1893, .	223 48	Cash on hand Oct. 31, 1894,	9,815 11
	$263,830 18		$263,830 18

Reconciliation of Share Account with Dues and Profits Capital.

DATE OF ISSUE.	Series.	Value per Share.	Shares in Force.	Total Value.		
Oct., 1883, .	11	$193 19	16	$3,091 04	Dues capital, as per general ledger, . .	$289,281 00
April, 1884, .	12	181 04	48	8,689 92	Profits capital, as per general ledger, . .	
Oct., 1884, .	13	169 35	22	3,725 70		60,243 02
April, 1885, .	14	158 10	77	12,173 70	Unpaid dues, . . .	3,012 00
Oct., 1885, .	15	147 19	36	5,298 84		
April, 1886, .	16	136 63	279	38,119 77		
Oct., 1886, .	17	126 42	145	18,330 90		
April, 1887, .	18	116 55	137	15,967 35		
Oct., 1887, .	19	107 00	183	19,581 00		
April, 1888, .	20	97 74	370	36,163 80		
Oct., 1888, .	21	88 78	264	23,437 92		
April, 1889, .	22	80 11	368	29,480 48		
Oct., 1889, .	23	71 72	281	20,153 32		
April, 1890, .	24	63 59	378	24,037 02		
Oct., 1890, .	25	55 72	295	16,437 40		
April, 1891, .	26	48 09	400	19,236 00		
Oct., 1891, .	27	40 70	338	13,756 60		
April, 1892, .	28	33 54	409	13,717 86		
Oct., 1892, .	29	26 61	291	7,743 51		
April, 1893, .	30	19 89	617	12,272 13		
Oct., 1893, .	31	13 39	494	6,614 66		
April, 1894, .	32	7 10	521	3,699 10		
Oct., 1894, .	33	1 00	552	552 00		
Dues paid in advance, . . .				256 00		
Total, ...				$352,536 02	Total, . . .	$352,536 02

Number of shares issued during the year, ...	1,225	
Number of shares now in force, ...	6,521	
Number of shares now borrowed upon, ...	1,944	
Largest number of shares held by any one member, ...	25	
Number of shares withdrawn during the year, . . .	1,053	
Number of shares forfeited during the year, ...	43	
Number of shares retired during the year, ...	420	
Number of shares matured during the year, ...	41	
Highest premium received during the year, ...		$0 20
Lowest premium received during the year, ...		05
Number of members withdrawn during the year, ...	217	
Present number of members, ...	879	
Present number of borrowers, ...	197	
Present number of non-borrowers, ...	682	
Number of loans secured by first mortgage of real estate, . . .	197	
Number of loans on shares, ...	51	
Largest loan to any one member, ...		5,000 00
Smallest loan to any one member, ...		50 00
Amount of expenses of the corporation for the year ending Oct. 31, 1894, .		2,177 32

Date of examination by commissioner : April 27.

PITTSFIELD CO-OPERATIVE BANK — PITTSFIELD.

Incorporated Feb. 15, 1889.   Commenced business March 5, 1889.

F. W. HINSDALE, *President.*   HOMER B. NASH, *Secretary.*
HOMER B. NASH, *Treasurer.*

Names of security committee:
H. S. RUSSELL,   WM. W. GAMWELL,
MICHAEL CASEY.

Regular meetings the first Wednesday of each month.

BALANCE SHEET OCTOBER 31, 1894.

ASSETS.		LIABILITIES.	
Loans on real estate, . .	$165,125 00	Dues capital, . . .	$161,572 00
Loans on shares, . . .	18,234 00	Profits capital (all series), .	18,530 36
Cash in hands of treasurer, .	101 92	Guaranty fund, . . .	503 98
		Surplus, ...	692 08
		Forfeited share account, .	2,162 50
	$183,460 92		$183,460 92

Detailed Statement of Receipts and Disbursements for the Year ending Oct. 31, 1894.

RECEIPTS.		DISBURSEMENTS.	
From dues capital, . .	$56,374 00	For real estate loans, . .	$58,156 00
interest, . . .	9,771 32	share loans, . . .	20,780 00
fines, ...	227 58	dues capital (withdrawn),	28,274 00
transfer fees, . .	3 75	dues capital (forfeited),	1,994 00
real estate loans repaid,	26,185 00	profits capital (with-	
share loans repaid, .	20,367 00	drawn), . . .	2,634 38
forfeiture profits, . .	332 00	profits capital (forfeited),	500 50
forfeited shares, . .	2,162 50	temporary expenses, .	926 04
		interest returned (over	
		payment), . . .	8 43
		bills payable, . .	2,200 00
		interest, . . .	22 15
Cash on hand Oct. 31, 1893, .	174 87	Cash on hand Oct. 31, 1894,	101 92
	$115,598 02		$115,598 02

Reconciliation of Share Account with Dues and Profits Capital.

DATE OF ISSUE.	Series.	Value per Share.	Shares in Force.	Total Value.		
Mar., 1889, .	1	$79 26	525	$41,611 50	Dues capital, as per general ledger, . .	$161,572 00
Sept., 1889, .	2	71 40	311	22,205 40		
Mar., 1890, .	3	63 73	295	18,800 35	Profits capital, as per general ledger, . .	18,530 36
Sept., 1890, .	4	56 18	315	17,696 70		
Mar., 1891, .	5	48 80	342	16,689 60	Unpaid dues, . . .	651 00
Sept., 1891, .	6	41 58	304	12,640 32		
Mar., 1892, .	7	34 54	490	16,924 60		
Sept., 1892, .	8	27 67	426	11,787 42		
Mar., 1893, .	9	21 00	489	10,269 00		
Sept., 1893, .	10	14 50	344	4,988 00		
Mar., 1894, .	11	8 17	648	5,294 16		
Sept., 1894, .	12	2 03	377	765 31		
Dues paid in advance, . . .				1,081 00		
Total, ...				$180,753 36	Total, . . .	$180,753 36

Number of shares issued during the year, ... 1,167
Number of shares now in force, ... 4,866
Number of shares now borrowed upon, ... 1,715
Largest number of shares held by any one member, ... 25
Number of shares withdrawn during the year, ... 1,039
Number of shares forfeited during the year, ... 81
Highest per centum of interest received during the year: 6.
Lowest per centum of interest received during the year: 6.
Number of members withdrawn during the year, ... 125
Present number of members, ... 739
Present number of borrowers, ... 215
Present number of non-borrowers, ... 524
Number of loans secured by first mortgage of real estate, . . . 120
Number of loans on shares, ... 115
Largest loan to any one member, ... $5,000 00
Smallest loan to any one member, ... 10 00
Amount of expenses of the corporation for the year ending Oct. 31, 1894, . 926 64
Date of examination by commissioner: May 29.

PLYMOUTH CO-OPERATIVE BANK — PLYMOUTH.

Incorporated June 7, 1882. Commenced business June 20, 1882.

CHARLES E. BARNES, *President.* ELMER E. AVERY, *Secretary.*
ELMER E. AVERY, *Treasurer.*

Names of security committee:

PELEG S. BURGESS, SETH W. PATY,
JOSEPH BARNES.

Regular meetings the third Tuesday of each month.

BALANCE SHEET OCTOBER 31, 1894.

ASSETS.		LIABILITIES.	
Loans on real estate,	$30,150 00	Dues capital,	$32,745 22
Loans on shares,	4,060 00	Profits capital (all series),	5,073 98
Permanent expense account,	289 38	Interest,	857 55
Temporary expense account,	179 29	Premiums,	116 92
Real estate by foreclosure,	746 46	Fines,	46 04
Suspense account,	1,004 64	Transfer fees,	50
Cash in hands of treasurer,	2,675 31	Withdrawal profits,	78 69
		Guaranty fund,	94 62
		Surplus,	13 26
		Forfeited share account,	42 30
		Rents,	36 00
	$39,105 08		$39,105 08

Detailed Statement of Receipts and Disbursements for the Year ending Oct. 31, 1894.

RECEIPTS.		DISBURSEMENTS.	
From dues capital,	$9,930 40	For real estate loans,	$8,750 00
interest,	2,011 10	share loans,	1,590 00
premiums,	257 35	dues capital (withdrawn),	2,907 47
fines,	93 57	dues capital (forfeited),	4 00
transfer fees,	2 00	dues capital (matured),	3,310 00
real estate loans repaid,	6,600 00	profits capital (withdrawn),	379 63
share loans repaid,	570 00	profits capital (forfeited),	12
withdrawal profits,	95 26	profits capital (matured),	1,489 86
forfeiture profits,	12	temporary expenses,	461 20
forfeited shares,	3 16	permanent expenses,	111 97
rents,	110 00	interest on matured shares,	11 00
over cash,	11 31	Cash on hand Oct. 31, 1894,	2,675 31
profits (reimbursed),	40		
Cash on hand Oct. 31, 1893,	2,005 89		
	$21,690 56		$21,690 56

Reconciliation of Share Account with Dues and Profits Capital.

DATE OF ISSUE.	Series.	Value per Share.	Shares in Force.	Total Value.		
June, 1883, .	3	$193 03	8	$1,544 24	Dues capital, as per general ledger, . . .	$32,745 22
Dec., 1883, .	4	181 31	15	2,719 65	Profits capital, as per general ledger, . .	
June, 1884, .	5	169 94	20	3,398 80		5,073 98
Dec., 1884, .	6	158 92	3	476 76		
Dec., 1885, .	8	138 01	5	690 05		
June, 1886, .	9	128 09	5	640 45		
Dec., 1886, .	10	118 48	4	473 92		
June, 1887, .	11	109 21	17	1,856 57		
Dec., 1887, .	12	100 19	33	3,306 27		
Dec., 1888, .	14	83 03	4	332 12		
June, 1889, .	15	74 83	6	448 98		
Dec., 1889, .	16	66 86	48	3,209 28		
June, 1890, .	17	59 13	29	1,714 77		
Dec., 1890, .	18	51 66	71	3,667 86		
June, 1891, .	19	44 39	31	1,376 09		
Dec., 1891, .	20	37 34	83	3,099 22		
June, 1892, .	21	30 47	84	2,559 48		
Dec., 1892, .	22	23 82	116	2,763 12		
June, 1893, .	23	17 36	101	1,753 36		
Dec., 1893, .	24	11 09	111	1,230 99		
June, 1894, .	25	5 00	71	355 00		
Dues paid in advance, . . .				202 22		
Total, ...				$37,819 20	Total, . . .	$37,819 20

Number of shares issued during the year, ... 200
Number of shares now in force, ... 865
Number of shares now borrowed upon, ... 250
Largest number of shares held by any one member, . . . 25
Number of shares withdrawn during the year, ... 106
Number of shares forfeited during the year, ... 2
Number of shares matured during the year, ... 24
Highest per centum of interest received during the year: 6.
Lowest per centum of interest received during the year: 6.
Number of members withdrawn during the year, ... 38
Present number of members, ... 183
Present number of borrowers, ... 57
Present number of non-borrowers, ... 126
Number of loans secured by first mortgage of real estate, . . 61
Number of loans on shares, ... 26
Largest loan to any one member, ... $2,200 00
Smallest loan to any one member, ... 50 00
Amount of expenses of the corporation for the year ending Oct. 31, 1894, . 480 82
Date of examination by commissioner: May 22.

PROVIDENT CO-OPERATIVE BANK — CHELSEA.

Incorporated Sept. 25, 1885.   Commenced business Sept. 28, 1885.

THOMAS MARTIN, *President.*   C. WILLIS GOULD, *Secretary.*
C. WILLIS GOULD, *Treasurer.*

Names of security committee:
MILTON RAY,   HENRY C. STARKEY,
JOHN W. DORR.

Regular meetings the fourth Monday of each month.

BALANCE SHEET OCTOBER 31, 1894.

ASSETS.		LIABILITIES.	
Loans on real estate,	$325,950 00	Dues capital,	$275,431 00
Loans on shares,	7,850 00	Profits capital (all series),	56,965 68
Unpaid interest,	2,264 50	Guaranty fund,	3,723 15
Unpaid premiums,	160 60	Surplus,	1,295 56
Unpaid fines,	75 70	Forfeited share account,	436 46
Maverick National Bank,	26 40		
Cash in hands of treasurer,	1,524 65		
	$337,851 85		$337,851 85

Detailed Statement of Receipts and Disbursements for the Year ending Oct. 31, 1894.

RECEIPTS.		DISBURSEMENTS.	
From dues capital,	$83,588 00	For real estate loans,	$84,250 00
interest,	18,833 42	share loans,	5,950 00
premiums,	2,928 30	dues capital (withdrawn),	28,359 00
fines,	870 14	dues capital (retired),	24,652 00
transfer fees,	4 50	profits capital (withdrawn),	3,486 45
real estate loans repaid,	36,550 00	profits capital (retired),	8,396 23
share loans repaid,	8,150 00	temporary expenses,	1,476 96
withdrawal profits,	864 46	taxes and repairs,	306 48
Maverick National B'k dividend,	5 28	interest, to correct error,	11 85
rents,	38 63		
real estate,	2,800 00		
Cash on hand Oct. 31, 1893,	3,780 89	Cash on hand Oct. 31, 1894,	1,524 65
	$158,413 62		$158,413 62

Reconciliation of Share Account with Dues and Profits Capital.

Date of Issue.	Series.	Value per Share.	Shares in Force.	Total Value.		
Sept., 1885, .	1	$154 12	106	$16,336 72	Dues capital, as per general ledger, . .	$275,431 00
Mar., 1886, .	2	142 87	147	21,001 89		
Sept., 1886, .	3	132 02	125	16,502 50	Profits capital, as per general ledger, . .	56,965 68
Mar., 1887, .	4	121 52	124	15,068 48		
Sept., 1887, .	5	111 41	125	13,926 25	Unpaid dues, . .	3,726 00
Mar., 1888, .	6	101 65	385	39,135 25		
Sept., 1888, .	7	92 28	195	17,994 60		
Mar., 1889, .	8	83 25	362	30,136 50		
Sept., 1889, .	9	74 52	227	16,916 04		
Mar., 1890, .	10	66 10	407	26,902 70		
Sept., 1890, .	11	57 96	289	16,750 44		
Mar., 1891, .	12	50 10	515	25,801 50		
Sept., 1891, .	13	42 51	491	20,872 41		
May, 1892, .	14	32 76	497	16,281 72		
Nov., 1892, .	15	25 76	541	13,936 16		
May, 1893, .	16	18 98	742	14,083 16		
Nov., 1893, .	17	12 44	657	8,173 08		
May, 1894, .	18	6 12	969	5,930 28		
Dues paid in advance, . . .				373 00		
Total, ...				$336,122 68	Total, . . .	$336,122 68

Number of shares issued during the year, ... 1,881
Number of shares now in force, ... 6,904
Number of shares now borrowed upon, ... 1,910
Largest number of shares held by any one member, ... 25
Number of shares withdrawn during the year, ... 1,216
Number of shares retired during the year, ... 257
Highest premium received during the year, ... $0 35
Lowest premium received during the year, ... 05
Number of members withdrawn during the year, ... 192
Present number of members, ... 861
Present number of borrowers, ... 216
Present number of non-borrowers, ... 645
Number of loans secured by first mortgage of real estate, . . 246
Number of loans on shares, ... 42
Largest loan to any one member, ... 5,000 00
Smallest loan to any one member, ... 50 00
Amount of expenses of the corporation for the year ending Oct. 31, 1894, . 1,476 96
Date of examination by commissioner: April 12.

QUINCY CO-OPERATIVE BANK—QUINCY.

Incorporated April 17, 1889.   Commenced business May 7, 1889.

JOHN F. WELCH, *President.*   RICHARD D. CHASE, *Secretary.*
RICHARD D. CHASE, *Treasurer.*

Names of security committee :

GEORGE H. FIELD,   JOHN H. DINEGAN,
ALBERT KEATING.

Regular meetings the first Wednesday of each month.

BALANCE SHEET OCTOBER 31, 1894.

ASSETS.		LIABILITIES.	
Loans on real estate, . .	$83,000 00	Dues capital, . . .	$78,013 00
Loans on shares, . . .	2,190 00	Profits capital (all series), .	11,708 03
Permanent expense account,	124 13	Guaranty fund, . . .	203 00
Unpaid interest, . . .	356 40	Surplus, ...	325 36
Unpaid premiums, . .	38 00	Forfeited share account, .	368 60
Unpaid fines, ...	53 19		
Cash in hands of treasurer, .	4,856 27		
	$90,617 99		$90,617 99

Detailed Statement of Receipts and Disbursements for the Year ending Oct. 31, 1894.

RECEIPTS.		DISBURSEMENTS.	
From dues capital, . .	$25,207 00	For real estate loans, . .	$19,700 00
interest, . . .	4,906 98	share loans, . . .	2,035 00
premiums, . . .	536 29	dues capital(withdrawn),	9,620 00
fines, ...	209 99	dues capital (forfeited),	340 00
transfer fees, . .	1 25	dues capital (retired), .	3,077 00
real estate loans repaid,	6,080 00	profits capital (withdrawn), . . .	1,126 42
share loans repaid, .	3,065 00	profits capital (forfeited),	38 40
withdrawal profits, .	283 41	profits capital (retired),	529 11
forfeiture profits, .	9 60	temporary expenses, .	480 02
forfeited shares, .	364 60	Cash on hand Oct. 31, 1894,	4,856 27
Cash on hand Oct. 31, 1893, .	1,138 10		
	$41,802 22		$41,802 22

Reconciliation of Share Account with Dues and Profits Capital.

DATE OF ISSUE.	Series.	Value per Share.	Shares in Force.	Total Value.		
May, 1889, .	1	$79 27	414	$32,817 78	Dues capital, as per general ledger, . .	$78,013 00
Nov., 1889, .	2	70 97	147	10,432 59		
May, 1890, .	3	62 88	148	9,306 24	Profits capital, as per general ledger, . .	11,708 03
Nov., 1890, .	4	55 00	82	4,510 00		
May, 1891, .	5	47 34	185	8,757 90	Unpaid dues, . .	810 00
Nov., 1891, .	6	39 90	172	6,862 80		
May, 1892, .	7	32 68	156	5,098 08		
Nov., 1892, .	8	25 71	174	4,473 54		
May, 1893, .	9	18 96	269	5,100 24		
Nov., 1893, .	10	12 43	131	1,628 33		
May, 1894, .	11	6 11	223	1,362 53		
Dues paid in advance, . . .				181 00		
Total, ...				$90,531 03	Total, . . .	$90,531 03

Number of shares issued during the year, ... 390
Number of shares now in force, ... 2,101
Number of shares now borrowed upon, ... 512
Largest number of shares held by any one member, . . . 25
Number of shares withdrawn during the year, ... 305
Number of shares forfeited during the year, ... 10
Number of shares retired during the year, ... 47
Highest premium received during the year, ... $0 35
Lowest premium received during the year, ... 05
Number of members withdrawn during the year, ... 36
Present number of members, ... 330
Present number of borrowers, ... 69
Present number of non-borrowers, ... 261
Number of loans secured by first mortgage of real estate, . . . 68
Number of loans on shares, ... 22
Largest loan to any one member, ... 3,000 00
Smallest loan to any one member, ... 15 00
Amount of expenses of the corporation for the year ending Oct. 31, 1894, . 510 02
Date of examination by commissioner: February 5.

RANDOLPH CO-OPERATIVE BANK — RANDOLPH.

Incorporated January 29, 1889.   Commenced business February 7, 1889.

JOHN B. THAYER, *President.*   P. H. McLAUGHLIN, *Secretary.*
P. H. McLAUGHLIN, *Treasurer.*

Names of security committee :
CHAS. A. WALES,   THOMAS FARWELL,
HARVEY W. BOYD.

Regular meetings the first Thursday of each month.

BALANCE SHEET OCTOBER 31, 1894.

ASSETS.		LIABILITIES.	
Loans on real estate,	$45,050 00	Dues capital,	$43,583 00
Loans on shares,	1,050 00	Profits capital (all series),	6,107 99
Temporary expense account,	41 11	Interest,	391 54
Real estate by foreclosure,	3,030 45	Premiums,	25 16
Cash in hands of treasurer,	2,047 81	Fines,	12 43
		Withdrawal profits,	117 90
		Guaranty fund,	279 02
		Surplus,	702 33
	$51,219 37		$51,219 37

Detailed Statement of Receipts and Disbursements for the Year ending Oct. 31, 1894.

RECEIPTS.		DISBURSEMENTS.	
From dues capital,	$12,284 00	For real estate loans,	$3,400 00
interest,	2,633 97	share loans,	925 00
premiums,	198 96	dues capital (withdrawn),	10,073 00
fines,	186 40	profits capital (withdrawn),	1,266 16
transfer fees,	25	temporary expenses,	149 43
real estate loans repaid,	450 00	forfeited shares,	28 24
share loans repaid,	1,170 00	taxes and insurance,	82 54
withdrawal profits,	315 43	Cash on hand Oct. 31, 1894,	2,047 81
rents,	56 00		
Cash on hand Oct. 31, 1893,	677 17		
	$17,972 18		$17,972 18

Reconciliation of Share Account with Dues and Profits Capital.

DATE OF ISSUE.	Series.	Value per Share.	Shares in Force.	Total Value.		
Feb., 1889, .	1	$81 00	330	$26,730 00	Dues capital, as per general ledger, . .	$43,583 00
Aug., 1889, .	2	72 82	75	5,461 50	Profits capital, as per general ledger, . .	6,107 99
Feb., 1890, .	3	64 90	32	2,076 80	Unpaid dues, . .	562 00
Aug., 1890, .	4	57 17	29	1,657 93		
Feb., 1891, .	5	49 16	126	6,260 94		
Aug., 1891, .	6	42 42	33	1,399 86		
Feb., 1892, .	7	35 36	44	1,555 84		
Aug., 1892, .	8	28 50	64	1,824 64		
Feb., 1893, .	9	21 85	48	1,048 80		
Aug., 1893, .	10	15 38	66	1,015 08		
Feb., 1894, .	11	9 10	96	873 60		
Aug., 1894, .	12	3 00	72	216 00		
Dues paid in advance, . . .				132 00		
Total, ...				$50,252 99	Total, . . .	$50,252 99

Number of shares issued during the year, ... 185
Number of shares now in force, ... 1,015
Number of shares now borrowed upon, ... 265
Largest number of shares held by any one member, . . . 20
Number of shares withdrawn during the year, ... 273
Highest premium received during the year, ... $0 05
Lowest premium received during the year, ... 05
Number of members withdrawn during the year, ... 39
Present number of members, ... 220
Present number of borrowers, ... 55
Present number of non-borrowers, ... 165
Number of loans secured by first mortgage of real estate, . . . 58
Number of loans on shares, ... 6
Largest loan to any one member, ... 3,400 00
Smallest loan to any one member, ... 100 00
Amount of expenses of the corporation for the year ending Oct. 31, 1894, . 199 43
Date of examination by commissioner : March 12.

READING CO-OPERATIVE BANK — READING.

Incorporated Nov. 27, 1886. Commenced business Dec. 6, 1886.

WENDELL BANCROFT, *President.*   HARRY P. BOSSON, *Secretary.*
EDGAR N. HUNT, *Treasurer.*

Names of security committee:
WENDELL BANCROFT,   MOSES E. NICHOLS,
LEWIS M. BANCROFT.

Regular meetings the first Monday of each month.

BALANCE SHEET OCTOBER 31, 1894.

ASSETS.		LIABILITIES.	
Loans on real estate, . .	$142,235 00	Dues capital, . . .	$139,553 00
Loans on shares, . . .	9,960 00	Profits capital (all series), .	24,607 03
Unpaid interest, . . .	1,100 00	Guaranty fund, . . .	843 67
Insurance account, . .	52 50	Surplus, . . .	703 79
Cash in hands of secretary, .	1 00	Forfeited share account, .	49 50
Cash in hands of treasurer, .	12,808 49	Uncompleted loans, . .	2,400 00
	$168,156 99		$168,156 99

Detailed Statement of Receipts and Disbursements for the Year ending Oct. 31, 1894.

RECEIPTS.		DISBURSEMENTS.	
From dues capital, . .	$43,553 00	For real estate loans, . .	$44,210 00
interest, . . .	8,642 08	share loans, . . .	6,215 00
premiums, . . .	832 57	dues capital (withdrawn),	21,433 00
fines, ...	452 11	dues capital (forfeited), .	18 00
transfer fees, . .	4 50	dues capital (retired), .	4,056 00
real estate loans repaid,	26,785 00	profits capital (withdrawn), . . .	3,033 31
share loans repaid, .	5,850 00	drawn), . . .	3,033 31
withdrawal profits, .	244 15	profits capital (forfeited),	72
forfeited shares, . .	2 55	profits capital (retired), .	1,103 64
uncompleted loans, .	2,400 00	temporary expenses, .	249 99
		salaries, . . .	520 00
		insurance, . . .	52 50
Cash on hand Oct. 31, 1893, .	4,935 69	Cash on hand Oct. 31, 1894, .	12,809 49
	$93,701 65		$93,701 65

Reconciliation of Share Account with Dues and Profits Capital.

DATE OF ISSUE.	Series.	Value per Share.	Shares In Force.	Total Value.		
Dec., 1886, .	1	$123 32	278	$34,282 96	Dues capital as per general ledger, . .	$139,553 00
June, 1887, .	2	113 57	62	7,041 34		
Dec., 1887, .	3	104 16	83	8,645 28	Profits capital as per general ledger, . .	24,607 03
June, 1888, .	4	95 00	92	8,740 00		
Dec., 1888, .	5	86 14	102	8,786 28	Unpaid dues, . .	1,595 00
June, 1889, .	6	77 54	191	14,810 14		
Dec., 1889, .	7	69 24	136	9,416 64		
June, 1890, .	8	61 19	163	9,973 97		
Dec., 1890, .	9	53 39	193	10,304 27		
June, 1891, .	10	45 82	251	11,500 82		
Dec., 1891, .	11	38 52	212	8,166 24		
June, 1892, .	12	31 41	337	10,585 17		
Dec., 1892, .	13	24 51	492	12,058 92		
May, 1893, .	14	18 90	212	4,006 80		
Nov., 1893, .	15	12 40	383	4,749 20		
May, 1894, .	16	6 10	430	2,623 00		
Dues paid in advance, . . .				64 00		
Total, ...				$165,755 03	Total, . . .	$165,755 03

Number of shares issued during the year, ... 886
Number of shares now in force, ... 3,617
Number of shares now borrowed upon, ... 980
Largest number of shares held by any one member, ... 25
Number of shares withdrawn during the year, ... 714
Number of shares forfeited during the year, ... 2
Number of shares retired during the year, ... 48
Highest premium received during the year, ... $0 15
Lowest premium received during the year, ... 05
Number of members withdrawn during the year, ... 81
Present number of members, ... 528
Present number of borrowers, ... 154
Present number of non-borrowers, ... 374
Number of loans secured by first mortgage of real estate, . . . 126
Number of loans on shares, ... 35
Largest loan to any one member, ... 3,500 00
Smallest loan to any one member, ... 30 00
Amount of expenses of the corporation for the year ending Oct. 31, 1894, . 769 99
Date of examination by commissioner: November 2.

RELIANCE CO-OPERATIVE BANK — CAMBRIDGE.

Incorporated July 16, 1889.　Commenced business July 10, 1889.

JOSEPH G. THORP, Jr., *President.*　　　　　EDWARD W. WHITE, *Secretary.*
EDWARD W. WHITE, *Treasurer.*

Names of security committee :

GEO. H. STEARNS,　　　　　MARSHALL N. STEARNS,
HERMAN BIRD,　　　　　MICHAEL CORCORAN,
GEO. A. ALLISON.

Regular meetings the second Wednesday of each month.

BALANCE SHEET OCTOBER 31, 1894.

ASSETS.		LIABILITIES.	
Loans on real estate, . .	$78,235 00	Dues capital, . . .	$88,556 00
Loans on shares, . . .	4,268 00	Profits capital (all series), .	9,128 30
Permanent expense account,.	366 06	Interest, ...	2,209 80
Temporary expense account,	145 64	Premiums, ...	200 98
Real estate by foreclosure, .	4,021 01	Fines, ...	165 81
Unpaid interest, . . .	492 45	Transfer fees, . . .	1 25
Unpaid premiums, . .	52 51	Withdrawal profits, . .	137 15
Unpaid fines, ...	148 12	Forfeiture profits, . .	36 57
Rent, ...	40 00	Guaranty fund, . . .	607 48
Cash in hands of treasurer, .	13,868 85	Surplus, ...	516 40
		Forfeited share account, .	20 60
		Security committee, . .	57 30
	$101,637 64		$101,637 64

Detailed Statement of Receipts and Disbursements for the Year ending
Oct. 31, 1894.

RECEIPTS.		DISBURSEMENTS.	
From dues capital, . .	$34,161 00	For real estate loans, . .	$29,960 00
interest, . . .	5,490 98	share loans, . .	4,703 00
premiums, . . .	513 07	dues capital (withdrawn),	14,905 00
fines, ...	294 99	dues capital (forfeited),	546 00
transfer fees, . .	.2 25	dues capital (retired), .	5,183 00
real estate loans repaid,	28,350 00	profits capital (with-	
share loans repaid, .	3,085 00	drawn), . . .	1,367 15
withdrawal profits, .	345 49	profits capital (forfeited),	58 67
forfeiture profits, .	41 67	profits capital (retired), .	855 70
forfeited shares, . .	16 50	temporary expenses, .	677 88
rent of office, . .	121 50	permanent expenses, .	70 50
security committee, .	37 50	forfeited shares, . .	33 25
		real estate foreclosed, .	4,021 01
		security committee, .	35 20
		rent, ...	27 50
Cash on hand Oct. 31, 1893, .	3,852 76	Cash on hand Oct. 31, 1894,	13,868 85
	$76,312 71		$76,312 71

Reconciliation of Share Account with Dues and Profits Capital.

DATE OF ISSUE.	Series.	Value per Share.	Shares in Force.	Total Value.		
July, 1889, .	1	$73 95	413	$30,541 35	Dues capital, as per general ledger, . . .	$88,556 00
Jan., 1890, .	2	66 01	196	12,937 96		
July, 1890, .	3	58 28	112	6,527 36	Profits capital, as per general ledger, . .	9,128 30
Jan., 1891, .	4	50 79	141	7,161 39		
July, 1891, .	5	43 51	179	7,788 29	Unpaid dues, . .	1,078 00
Jan., 1892, .	6	36 42	307	11,180 94		
July, 1892, .	7	29 54	284	8,389 36		
Jan., 1893, .	8	22 86	141	3,223 26		
July, 1893, .	9	16 37	260	4,256 20		
Jan., 1894, .	10	10 09	491	4,954 19		
July, 1894, .	11	4 00	402	1,608 00		
Dues paid in advance, . . .				194 00		
Total, ...				$98,762 30	Total, . .	$98,762 30

Number of shares issued during the year, ... 956
Number of shares now in force, ... 2,926
Number of shares now borrowed upon, ... 652
Largest number of shares held by any one member, . . . 25
Number of shares withdrawn during the year, ... 607
Number of shares forfeited during the year, ... 31
Number of shares retired during the year, ... 86
Highest premium received during the year, ... $0 40
Lowest premium received during the year, ... 05
Number of members withdrawn during the year, ... 80
Present number of members, ... 387
Present number of borrowers, ... 61
Present number of non-borrowers, ... 326
Number of loans secured by first mortgage of real estate, . . . 41
Number of loans on shares, ... 20
Largest loan to any one member, ... 5,000 00
Smallest loan to any one member, ... 20 00
Amount of expenses of the corporation for the year ending Oct. 31, 1894, . 592 16
Date of examination by commissioner: March 29.

ROXBURY CO-OPERATIVE BANK — ROXBURY.

Incorporated Oct. 3, 1889.   Commenced business Nov. 1, 1889.

FRANK TUCKER, *President.*   T. J. SPROUL, *Secretary.*
JOSEPH ENGEL, *Treasurer.*

Names of security committee :

| JOSEPH ENGEL, | W. A. FOLSOM, |
| R. A. WATSON, | A. M. LEONARD. |

Regular meetings on the first business day of each month.

BALANCE SHEET OCTOBER 31, 1894.

ASSETS.		LIABILITIES.	
Loans on real estate, . .	$69,250 00	Dues capital, . . .	$75,350 00
Loans on shares, . . .	3,140 00	Profits capital (all series), .	7,423 87
Permanent expense account,	398 00	Guaranty fund, . . .	262 00
Unpaid interest, . . .	97 00	Surplus, ...	410 71
Unpaid premiums, . . .	6 75		
Unpaid fines, ...	19 38		
Cash in hands of treasurer, .	10,535 45		
	$83,446 58		$83,446 58

Detailed Statement of Receipts and Disbursements for the Year ending Oct. 31, 1894.

RECEIPTS.		DISBURSEMENTS.	
From dues capital, . .	$34,153 00	For real estate loans, . .	$28,800 00
interest, . . .	4,330 86	share loans, . . .	4,130 00
premiums, . . .	377 70	dues capital (withdrawn),	14,844 00
fines, ...	136 39	profits capital (with-	
transfer fees, . .	1 50	drawn), . . .	1,167 05
real estate loans repaid,	16,850 00	temporary expenses, .	765 40
share loans repaid, .	3,780 00	forfeited shares, . .	8 84
withdrawal profits, .	291 76		
rent, temporary expense,	105 00		
Cash on hand Oct. 31, 1893, .	224 53	Cash on hand Oct. 31, 1894,	10,535 45
	$60,250 74		$60,250 74

Reconciliation of Share Account with Dues and Profits Capital.

DATE OF ISSUE.	Series.	Value per Share.	Shares in Force.	Total Value.		
Nov., 1889, .	1	$69 84	156	$10,895 04	Dues capital, as per general ledger, . .	$75,350 00
May, 1890, .	2	61 88	66	4,084 08		
Nov., 1890, .	3	54 16	327	17,710 32	Profits capital as per general ledger, . .	7,423 87
May, 1891, .	4	46 67	227	10,594 09		
Nov., 1891, .	5	39 40	234	9,219 60	Unpaid dues, . .	584 00
May, 1892, .	6	32 34	302	9,766 68		
Nov., 1892, .	7	25 49	194	4,945 06		
May, 1893, .	8	18 84	370	6,970 80		
Nov., 1893, .	9	12 38	250	3,095 00		
May, 1894, .	10	6 10	972	5,929 20		
Dues paid in advance, . . .				148 00		
Total, ...				$83,357 87	Total, . . .	$83,357 87

Number of shares issued during the year, ... 1,304
Number of shares now in force, ... 3,098
Number of shares now borrowed upon, ... 575
Largest number of shares held by any one member, . . . 25
Number of shares withdrawn during the year, ... 644
Highest premium received during the year, ... $0 20
Lowest premium received during the year, ... 05
Number of members withdrawn during the year, ... 83
Present number of members, ... 368
Present number of borrowers, ... 39
Present number of non-borrowers, ... 329
Number of loans secured by first mortgage of real estate, . . . 24
Number of loans on shares, ... 15
Largest loan to any one member, ... 5,000 00
Smallest loan to any one member, ... 50 00
Amount of expenses of the corporation for the year ending Oct. 31, 1894, . 885 40
Date of examination by commissioner: June 21.

SALEM CO-OPERATIVE BANK — SALEM.

Incorporated April 7, 1888. Commenced business April 13, 1888.

JOHN M. RAYMOND, *President.* ALBERT C. MACKINTIRE, *Secretary.*
ALBERT C. MACKINTIRE, *Treasurer.*

Names of security committee:

| JOHN M. RAYMOND, | FRANK A. NEWELL, |
| GEO. W. PICKERING, | E. A. MACKINTIRE. |

Regular meetings the second Friday of each month.

BALANCE SHEET OCTOBER 31, 1894.

ASSETS.		LIABILITIES.	
Loans on real estate,	$182,590 00	Dues capital,	$167,363 00
Loans on shares,	4,065 00	Profits capital (all series),	23,375 44
Temporary expense account,	9 00	Interest,	981 68
Unpaid interest,	1,052 67	Premiums,	139 80
Unpaid premiums,	175 05	Fines,	34 06
Unpaid fines,	132 36	Transfer fees,	25
Cash in hands of treasurer,	10,531 19	Withdrawal profits,	28 76
		Guaranty fund,	1,765 97
		Surplus,	4,834 75
		Forfeited share account,	31 56
	$198,555 27		$198,555 27

Detailed Statement of Receipts and Disbursements for the Year ending Oct. 31, 1894.

RECEIPTS.		DISBURSEMENTS.	
From dues capital,	$59,743 00	For real estate loans,	$49,510 00
interest,	11,246 27	share loans,	4,165 00
premiums,	1,762 35	dues capital (withdrawn),	36,403 00
fines,	286 13	dues capital (forfeited),	36 00
transfer fees,	2 75	dues capital (retired),	15,560 00
real estate loans repaid,	41,675 00	profits capital (with-	
share loans repaid,	5,325 00	drawn),	4,289 55
withdrawal profits,	396 41	profits capital (forfeited),	3 34
forfeiture profits,	1 54	profits capital (retired),	2,824 88
forfeited shares,	15 87	temporary expenses,	1,182 73
		forfeited shares,	51 19
Cash on hand Oct. 31, 1893,	4,102 56	Cash on hand Oct. 31, 1894,	10,531 19
	$124,556 88		$124,556 88

Reconciliation of Share Account with Dues and Profits Capital.

DATE OF ISSUE.	Series.	Value per Share.	Shares in Force.	Total Value.		
April, 1888, .	1	$96 89	245	$23,738 05	Dues capital, as per general ledger, . . .	$167,363 00
Oct., 1888, .	2	88 13	220	19,388 60		
April, 1889, .	3	79 62	261	20,780 82	Profits capital, as per general ledger, . .	23,375 44
Oct., 1889, .	4	71 46	221	15,792 66		
April, 1890, .	5	63 33	274	17,352 42	Unpaid dues, . .	1,649 00
Oct., 1890, .	6	55 55	367	20,386 85		
April, 1891, .	7	47 99	429	20,587 71		
Oct., 1891, .	8	40 65	330	13,414 50		
April, 1892, .	9	33 53	367	12,305 51		
Oct., 1892, .	10	26 61	316	8,408 76		
April, 1893, .	11	19 89	356	7,080 84		
Oct., 1893, .	12	13 38	550	7,359 00		
April, 1894, .	13	7 09	708	5,019 72		
Oct., 1894, .	14	1 00	657	657 00		
Dues paid in advance, . . .				115 00		
Total, ...				$192,387 44	Total, . . .	$192,387 44

Number of shares issued during the year, ...	1,497	
Number of shares now in force, ...	5,301	
Number of shares now borrowed upon, ...	1,113	
Largest number of shares held by any one member, . . .	25	
Number of shares withdrawn during the year, ...	1,108	
Number of shares forfeited during the year, ...	2	
Number of shares retired during the year, ...	250	
Highest premium received during the year, ...		$0 35
Lowest premium received during the year, ...		05
Number of members withdrawn during the year, ...	153	
Present number of members, ...	885	
Present number of borrowers, ...	186	
Present number of non-borrowers, ...	699	
Number of loans secured by first mortgage of real estate, . . .	202	
Number of loans on shares, ...	35	
Largest loan to any one member, ...		5,000 00
Smallest loan to any one member, ...		100 00
Amount of expenses of the corporation for the year ending Oct. 31, 1894, .		1,182 73

Date of examination by commissioner: February 26.

SANDWICH CO-OPERATIVE BANK — SANDWICH.

Incorporated Oct. 1, 1885. Commenced business Dec. 15, 1885.

JOHN E. PRATT, *President.*   W. II. HEALD, *Secretary.*
W. II. HEALD, *Treasurer.*

Names of security committee:

LEVI S. NYE,   E. B. HOWLAND,
W. E. BOYDEN.

Regular meetings the third Tuesday of each month.

BALANCE SHEET OCTOBER 31, 1894.

ASSETS.		LIABILITIES.	
Loans on real estate,	$11,250 00	Dues capital,	$12,138 00
Loans on shares,	1,450 00	Profits capital (all series),	1,798 80
Permanent expense account,	134 28	Interest,	237 78
Temporary expense account,	71 98	Fines,	15 07
Suspense account,	46 42	Withdrawal profits,	2 93
Cash in hands of treasurer,	1,271 92	Guaranty fund,	26 16
		Surplus,	5 86
	$14,224 60		$14,224 60

Detailed Statement of Receipts and Disbursements for the Year ending Oct. 31, 1894.

RECEIPTS.		DISBURSEMENTS.	
From dues capital,	$2,713 00	For real estate loans,	$2,100 00
interest,	633 02	share loans,	300 00
fines,	34 41	dues capital (withdrawn),	696 00
transfer fees,	75	profits capital (withdrawn),	53 19
share loans repaid,	50 00	temporary expenses,	118 44
withdrawal profits,	13 29	Cash on hand Oct. 31, 1894,	1,271 92
Cash on hand Oct. 31, 1893,	1,095 08		
	$4,539 55		$4,539 55

Reconciliation of Share Account with Dues and Profits Capital.

Date of Issue.	Series.	Value per Share.	Shares in Force.	Total Value.		
Dec., 1885, .	1	$128 92	33	$4,254 36	Dues capital, as per general ledger, . .	$12,138 00
June, 1886, .	2	120 47	1	120 47		
Dec., 1886, .	3	112 12	34	3,812 08	Profits capital, as per general ledger, . .	1,798 80
June, 1887, .	4	104 02	2	208 04		
Dec., 1887, .	5	95 95	3	287 85	Unpaid dues, . .	209 00
June, 1888, .	6	87 98	5	439 90		
Dec., 1888, .	7	80 15	12	961 80		
June, 1889, .	8	72 52	6	435 12		
Dec., 1889, .	9	65 08	9	585 72		
June, 1890, .	10	57 83	4	231 32		
Dec., 1890, .	11	50 70	12	608 40		
June, 1891, .	12	43 76	3	131 28		
Dec., 1891, .	13	36 95	14	517 30		
June, 1892, .	14	30 25	23	695 75		
Dec., 1892, .	15	23 70	10	237 00		
June, 1893, .	16	17 31	11	190 41		
Dec., 1893, .	17	11 08	25	277 00		
June, 1894, .	18	5 00	28	140 00		
Dues paid in advance, . . .				12 00		
Total, ...				$14,145 80	Total, . . .	$14,145 80

Number of shares issued during the year, ... 61
Number of shares now in force, ... 235
Number of shares now borrowed upon, ... 81
Largest number of shares held by any one member, . . . 12
Number of shares withdrawn during the year, ... 30
Highest per centum of interest received during the year: 8¼.
Lowest per centum of interest received during the year: 5.
Number of members withdrawn during the year, ... 4
Present number of members, ... 82
Present number of borrowers, ... 35
Present number of non-borrowers, ... 47
Number of loans secured by first mortgage of real estate, . . . 25
Number of loans on shares, ... 14
Largest loan to any one member, ... $1,000 00
Smallest loan to any one member, ... 50 00
Amount of expenses of the corporation for the year ending Oct. 31, 1894, . 118 44
Date of examination by commissioner: July 31.

SECURITY CO-OPERATIVE BANK — BROCKTON.

Incorporated Dec. 17, 1877.' Commenced business Dec. 20, 1877.

B. E. JONES, *President.*   HENRY C. GURNEY, *Secretary.*
FRED B. HOWARD, *Treasurer.*

Names of security committee:

L. F. SEVERANCE,   T. E. GIFFORD,
W. H. SAVAGE.

Regular meetings the third Thursday of each month.

BALANCE SHEET OCTOBER 31, 1894.

ASSETS.			LIABILITIES.		
Loans on real estate,	. .	$208,050 00	Dues capital,	. . .	$192,950 00
Loans on shares,	. .	7,816 00	Profits capital (all series),	.	30,436 47
Permanent expense account,	.	275 00	Interest,	. . . .	5,352 25
Temporary expense account,		438 86	Premiums,	. . . .	573 45
Real estate by foreclosure,	.	3,086 83	Fines,	. . . . .	132 81
Unpaid interest,	. .	2,463 04	Transfer fees,	. . .	1 25
Unpaid premiums,	. .	274 36	Withdrawal profits,	. .	279 74
Unpaid fines,	. . .	205 30	Forfeiture profits,	. .	6 79
Mortgages,	. . . .	6,000 00	Guaranty fund,	. .	1,162 10
Insurance paid,	. . .	11 25	Surplus,	. . . .	9 33
Cash in hands of secretary,	.	105 44	Forfeited share account,	.	53 00
Cash in hands of treasurer,	.	2,231 11			
		$230,957 19			$230,957 19

Detailed Statement of Receipts and Disbursements for the Year ending Oct. 31, 1894.

RECEIPTS.			DISBURSEMENTS.		
From dues capital,	. .	$63,011 00	For real estate loans,	. .	$35,450 00
interest,	. . .	15,052 95	share loans,	. . .	10,566 00
premiums,	. . .	1,519 57	dues capital (withdrawn),		34,904 00
fines,	. . . .	452 57	dues capital (forfeited),		343 00
transfer fees,	. .	3 75	dues capital (retired),	.	44,574 00
real estate loans repaid,	.	69,464 80	dues capital (matured),		13,215 00
share loans repaid,	.	14,665 00	profits capital (with-		
withdrawal profits,	.	1,135 14	drawn),	. . .	4,556 96
forfeiture profits,	.	26 33	profits capital (forfeited),		105 54
forfeited shares,	. .	42 50	profits capital (retired),		11,771 19
insurance,	. . .	44 28	profits capital (matured),		6,040 19
real estate by fore-			temporary expenses,	.	1,543 06
closure,	. . .	2,738 00	interest on retired shares,		1,108 12
			legal expenses,	. .	23 26
			insurance,	. . .	40 95
			real estate by foreclosure,		3,458 18
Cash on hand Oct. 31, 1893,	.	1,880 11	Cash on hand Oct. 31, 1894,		2,336 55
		$170,036 00			$170,036 00

Reconciliation of Share Account with Dues and Profits Capital.

DATE OF ISSUE.	Series.	Value per Share.	Shares In Force.	Total Value.		
Dec., 1883, .	7	$186 53	66	$12,310 98	Dues capital, as per general ledger, . .	$192,950 00
Dec., 1884, .	8	163 20	36	5,875 20		
Dec., 1885, .	9	141 40	81	11,453 40	Profits capital, as per general ledger, . .	30,436 47
Dec., 1886, .	10	121 06	91	11,016 46		
Dec., 1887, .	11	102 03	208	21,222 24	Unpaid dues, . . .	3,013 00
Dec., 1888, .	12	84 26	383	32,271 58		
Dec., 1889, .	13	67 66	606	41,001 96		
Dec., 1890, .	14	52 11	570	29,702 70		
Dec., 1891, .	15	37 55	739	27,749 45		
Dec., 1892, .	16	23 90	883	21,103 70		
June, 1893, .	17	17 40	242	4,210 80		
Dec., 1893, .	18	11 10	490	5,439 00		
June, 1894, .	19	5 00	531	2,655 00		
Dues paid in advance, . . .				387 00		
Total, ...				$226,309 47	Total, . . .	$226,399 47

Number of shares issued during the year, ...	1,105
Number of shares now in force, ...	4,926
Number of shares now borrowed upon, ...	1,354
Largest number of shares held by any one member, ...	25
Number of shares withdrawn during the year, ...	1,158
Number of shares forfeited during the year, ...	24
Number of shares retired during the year, ...	550
Number of shares matured during the year, ...	97
Highest premium received during the year, ...	$0 15
Lowest premium received during the year, ...	10
Number of members withdrawn during the year, ...	150
Present number of members, ...	679
Present number of borrowers, ...	171
Present number of non-borrowers, ...	508
Number of loans secured by first mortgage of real estate, . . .	190
Number of loans on shares, ...	43
Largest loan to any one member, ...	3,000 00
Smallest loan to any one member, ...	25 00
Amount of expenses of the corporation for the year ending Oct. 31, 1894, .	1,593 06

Date of examination by commissioner : February 26.

SOMERVILLE CO-OPERATIVE BANK — SOMERVILLE.

Incorporated May 4, 1880.   Commenced business June 7, 1880.

J. FRANK WELLINGTON, *President.*   FRANKLIN J. HAMBLIN, *Secretary.*
FRANKLIN J. HAMBLIN, *Treasurer.*

Names of security committee:

B. F. THOMPSON,   M. H. LOCKE,
N. H. REED.

Regular meetings the first Monday of each month.

BALANCE SHEET OCTOBER 31, 1894.

ASSETS.		LIABILITIES.	
Loans on real estate,	$396,150 00	Dues capital,	$360,261 00
Loans on shares,	16,500 00	Profits capital (all series),	59,520 81
Permanent expense account,	500 00	Interest,	2,491 12
Temporary expense account,	105 11	Premiums,	131 89
Insurance,	7 50	Fines,	112 75
Cash in hands of treasurer,	11,824 95	Withdrawal profits,	123 98
		Forfeiture profits,	33 67
		Guaranty fund,	1,575 00
		Surplus,	198 57
		Forfeited share account,	638 77
	$425,087 56		$425,087 56

Detailed Statement of Receipts and Disbursements for the Year ending Oct. 31, 1894.

RECEIPTS.		DISBURSEMENTS.	
From dues capital,	$120,416 00	For real estate loans,	$141,950 00
interest,	24,819 46	share loans,	10,975 00
premiums,	1,287 16	dues capital (withdrawn),	49,052 00
fines,	977 05	dues capital (forfeited),	1,841 00
transfer fees,	3 50	dues capital (retired),	19,809 00
real estate loans repaid,	87,000 00	dues capital (matured),	16,386 00
share loans repaid,	11,750 00	profits capital (withdrawn),	6,578 23
withdrawal profits,	682 96	profits capital (forfeited),	422 22
forfeiture profits,	91 51	profits capital (retired),	7,362 26
forfeited shares,	1,889 36	profits capital (matured),	7,693 03
insurance,	518 25	temporary expenses,	1,489 62
loans on city bonds,	27,500 00	permanent expenses,	40 11
suspense,	1 50	forfeited shares,	1,395 40
		security committee,	285 00
		finance committee,	96 00
		insurance,	518 25
Cash on hand Oct. 31, 1893,	781 32	Cash on hand Oct. 31, 1894,	11,824 95
	$277,718 07		$277,718 07

Reconciliation of Share Account with Dues and Profits Capital.

DATE OF ISSUE.	Series.	Value per Share.	Shares in Force.	Total Value.		
Oct., 1883, .	8	$191 33	27	$5,165 91	Dues capital, as per general ledger, . .	$360,261 00
April, 1884, .	9	179 47	68	12,203 96		
Oct., 1884, .	10	168 08	44	7,395 52	Profits capital, as per	
April, 1885, .	11	157 04	29	4,554 16	general ledger, . .	59,520 81
Oct., 1885, .	12	146 35	60	8,781 00	Unpaid dues, . .	2,569 00
April, 1886, .	13	135 98	79	10,742 42		
Oct., 1886, .	14	125 86	62	7,803 32		
April, 1887, .	15	116 07	219	25,419 33		
Oct., 1887, .	16	106 60	132	14,071 20		
April, 1888, .	17	97 44	283	27,575 52		
Oct., 1888, .	18	88 52	172	15,225 44		
April, 1889, .	19	79 87	331	26,436 97		
Oct., 1889, .	20	71 53	416	29,756 48		
April, 1890, .	21	63 43	651	41,292 93		
Oct., 1890, .	22	55 62	421	23,416 02		
April, 1891, .	23	48 03	755	36,262 65		
Oct., 1891, .	24	40 65	556	22,601 40		
April, 1892, .	25	33 51	1,078	36,123 78		
Oct., 1892, .	26	26 60	793	21,093 80		
April, 1893, .	27	19 90	1,061	21,113 90		
Oct., 1893, .	28	13 40	1,049	14,056 60		
April, 1894, .	29	7 10	1,305	9,265 50		
Oct., 1894, .	30	1 00	1,274	1,274 00		
Dues paid in advance, . . .				719 00		
Total, ...				$422,350 81	Total, . . .	$422,350 81

Number of shares issued during the year, ...	3,204	
Number of shares now in force, ...	10,865	
Number of shares now borrowed upon, ...	2,723	
Largest number of shares held by any one member, ...	25	
Number of shares withdrawn during the year, ...	1,664	
Number of shares forfeited during the year, ...	79	
Number of shares retired during the year, ...	175	
Number of shares matured during the year, ...	119	
Highest premium received during the year, ...		$0 10
Lowest premium received during the year, ...		05
Number of members withdrawn during the year, ...	214	
Present number of members, ...	1,196	
Present number of borrowers, ...	293	
Present number of non-borrowers, ...	903	
Number of loans secured by first mortgage of real estate, . . .	222	
Number of loans on shares, ...	71	
Largest loan to any one member, ...		5,000 00
Smallest loan to any one member, ...		50 00
Amount of expenses of the corporation for the year ending Oct. 31, 1894, .		1,629 73
Date of examination by commissioner: June 28.		

SOUTH FRAMINGHAM CO-OPERATIVE BANK — SOUTH FRAMINGHAM.

Incorporated April 16, 1889.   Commenced business May 6, 1889.

ALFRED M. EAMES, *President.*   HARRIE L. DAVENPORT, *Secretary.*
HARRIE L. DAVENPORT, *Treasurer.*

Names of security committee:

FRANK H. FALES,   ELEAZER GOULDING,
CHAS. H. FULLER.

Regular meetings the first Monday of each month.

BALANCE SHEET OCTOBER 31, 1894.

ASSETS.			LIABILITIES.		
Loans on real estate,	$92,350	00	Dues capital,	$88,445	00
Loans on shares,	3,865	00	Profits capital (all series),	11,812	83
Permanent expense account,	108	97	Guaranty fund,	489	97
Real estate by foreclosure,	1,150	00	Surplus,	399	43
Unpaid interest,	333	82	Forfeited share account,	464	21
Unpaid premiums,	15	30			
Unpaid fines,	54	76			
Rent,	5	50			
Note of town of Framingham,	1,000	00			
Cash in hands of treasurer,	2,728	09			
	$101,611	44		$101,611	44

Detailed Statement of Receipts and Disbursements for the Year ending Oct. 31, 1894.

RECEIPTS.			DISBURSEMENTS.		
From dues capital,	$29,968	00	For real estate loans,	$26,925	00
interest,	5,498	48	share loans,	2,580	00
premiums,	276	32	dues capital (withdrawn),	12,642	00
fines,	289	90	dues capital (forfeited),	300	00
real estate loans repaid,	8,950	00	dues capital (retired),	3,737	00
share loans repaid,	3,976	00	profits capital (withdrawn),	1,295	93
withdrawal profits,	178	02	profits capital (forfeited),	106	37
forfeiture profits,	11	70	profits capital (retired),	580	20
forfeited shares,	254	72	temporary expenses,	704	89
town note,	3,000	00	forfeited shares,	216	97
real estate by foreclosure,	93	18	real estate by foreclosure,	1,247	57
rent,	33	00			
temporary expense,		05			
Cash on hand Oct. 31, 1893,	535	65	Cash on hand Oct. 31, 1894,	2,728	09
	$53,064	02		$53,064	02

Reconciliation of Share Account with Dues and Profits Capital.

Date of Issue.	Series.	Value per Share.	Shares in Force.	Total Value.		
May, 1889, .	1	$77 86	442	$34,414 12	Dues capital, as per general ledger, . .	$88,445 00
Nov., 1889, .	2	69 77	200	13,954 00		
May, 1890, .	3	61 89	196	12,130 44	Profits capital, as per general ledger, . .	11,812 83
Nov., 1890, .	4	54 22	143	7,753 46		
May, 1891, .	5	46 75	103	4,815 25	Unpaid dues, . .	873 00
Nov., 1891, .	6	39 47	192	7,578 24		
May, 1892, .	7	32 40	184	5,961 60		
Nov., 1892, .	8	25 53	120	3,063 60		
May, 1893, .	9	18 86	281	5,299 66		
Nov., 1893, .	10	12 39	324	4,014 36		
May, 1894, .	11	6 10	321	1,958 10		
Dues paid in advance, . . .				188 00		
Total, ...				$101,130 83	Total, . . .	$101,130 83

Number of shares issued during the year, ... 702
Number of shares now in force, ... 2,506
Number of shares now borrowed upon, ... 681
Largest number of shares held by any one member, ... 25
Number of shares withdrawn during the year, ... 437
Number of shares forfeited during the year, ... 16
Number of shares retired during the year, ... 60
Highest per centum of interest received during the year : 7⅝.
Lowest per centum of interest received during the year : 6.
Number of members withdrawn during the year, ... 92
Present number of members, ... 389
Present number of borrowers, ... 85
Present number of non-borrowers, ... 304
Number of loans secured by first mortgage of real estate, . . . 83
Number of loans on shares, ... 22
Largest loan to any one member, ... $4,000 00
Smallest loan to any one member, ... 25 00
Amount of expenses of the corporation for the year ending Oct. 31, 1894, . 723 00
Date of examination by commissioner : February 15.

SOUTH SHORE CO-OPERATIVE BANK — WEYMOUTH.

Incorporated April 19, 1890.   Commenced business May 5, 1890.

FRANCIS AMBLER, *President.*   CHAS. G. SHEPPARD, *Secretary.*
CHAS. G. SHEPPARD, *Treasurer.*

Names of security committee:

GEORGE W. WHITE,   JOHN B. RHINES,
DAVID J. PIERCE.

Regular meetings the first Monday of each month.

BALANCE SHEET OCT. 31, 1894.

ASSETS.		LIABILITIES.	
Loans on real estate,	$37,250 00	Dues capital,	$38,545 00
Loans on shares,	3,620 00	Profits capital (all series),	4,852 50
Permanent expense account,	185 00	Guaranty fund,	65 00
Unpaid interest,	82 50	Surplus,	66 18
Unpaid premiums,	7 45	Forfeited share account,	4 00
Unpaid fines,	9 24	Security committee,	20 00
Cash in hands of treasurer,	2,398 49		
	$43,552 68		$43,552 68

Detailed Statement of Receipts and Disbursements for the Year ending Oct. 31, 1894.

RECEIPTS.		DISBURSEMENTS.	
From dues capital,	$14,587 00	For real estate loans,	$9,300 00
interest,	2,289 73	share loans,	1,845 00
premiums,	195 90	dues capital (withdrawn),	5,447 00
fines,	58 42	dues capital (forfeited),	4 00
transfer fees,	25	dues capital (retired),	2,000 00
real estate loans repaid,	2,200 00	profits capital (withdrawn),	421 98
share loans repaid,	1,290 00	profits capital (retired),	263 60
withdrawal profits,	105 71	temporary expenses,	198 93
forfeited shares,	4 00	permanent expenses,	78 99
security committee,	20 00	Cash on hand Oct. 31, 1894,	2,398 49
expense account,	5 00		
Cash on hand Oct. 31, 1893,	1,201 98		
	$21,957 99		$21,957 99

Reconciliation of Share Account with Dues and Profits Capital.

DATE OF ISSUE.	Series.	Value per Share.	Shares in Force.	Total Value.		
May, 1890, .	1	$62 61	338	$21,162 18	Dues capital as per general ledger, . . .	$38,515 00
Nov., 1890, .	2	54 79	88	4,821 52		
May, 1891, .	3	47 18	83	3,915 94	Profits capital as per general ledger, . .	4,852 50
Nov., 1891, .	4	39 78	75	2,983 50		
May, 1892, .	5	32 61	141	4,598 01	Unpaid dues, . .	174 00
Nov., 1892, .	6	25 67	58	1,488 86		
May, 1893, .	7	18 94	101	1,912 94		
Nov., 1893, .	8	12 42	124	1,540 08		
May, 1894, .	9	6 11	177	1,081 47		
Dues paid in advance, . . .				67 00		
Total, ...				$43,571 50		$43,571 50

Number of shares issued during the year, ...	385
Number of shares now in force, ...	1,185
Number of shares now borrowed upon, ...	304
Largest number of shares held by any one member, . . .	25
Number of shares withdrawn during the year, ...	282
Number of shares forfeited during the year, ...	4
Number of shares retired during the year, ...	40
Highest premium received during the year, ...	$0 15
Lowest premium received during the year, ...	05
Number of members withdrawn during the year, ...	55
Present number of members, ...	216
Present number of borrowers, ...	41
Present number of non-borrowers, ...	175
Number of loans secured by first mortgage of real estate, . . .	35
Number of loans on shares, ...	12
Largest loan to any one member, ...	3,000 00
Smallest loan to any one member, ...	50 00
Amount of expenses of the corporation for the year ending Oct. 31, 1894, .	224 42

Date of examination by commissioner: April 23.

SOUTH WEYMOUTH CO-OPERATIVE BANK — SOUTH WEYMOUTH.

Incorporated Feb. 28, 1889.   Commenced business March 9, 1889.

A. FENTON BULLOCK, *President.*   F. W. HOWE, *Secretary.*
ELLIS J. PITCHER, *Treasurer.*

Names of security committee:

LOUIS A. COOK,   JOHN H. STETSON,
FRANCIS F. BULLOCK,   CHAS. H. CLAPP,
JAS. F. FRAWLEY.

Regular meetings the second Saturday of each month.

BALANCE SHEET OCTOBER 31, 1894.

ASSETS.		LIABILITIES.	
Loans on real estate, . .	$35,000 00	Dues capital, . . .	$35,116 00
Loans on shares, . . .	4,825 00	Profits capital (all series), .	4,932 09
Permanent expense account,	118 00	Interest, ...	74 55
Temporary expense account,	3 00	Premiums, ...	5 15
Unpaid fines, ...	23 98	Withdrawal profits, . .	28 39
Cash in hands of treasurer, .	327 12	Guaranty fund, . . .	133 00
		Surplus, ...	7 92
	$40,297 10		$40,297 10

Detailed Statement of Receipts and Disbursements for the Year ending Oct. 31, 1894.

RECEIPTS.		DISBURSEMENTS.	
From dues capital, . .	$10,960 00	For real estate loans, . .	$6,200 00
interest, . . .	2,033 41	share loans, . . .	3,075 00
premiums, . . .	102 45	dues capital (withdrawn),	7,203 00
fines, ...	164 32	profits capital (with-	
transfer fees, . .	1 50	drawn), . . .	830 91
real estate loans repaid,	2,450 00	temporary expenses, .	178 70
share loans repaid, .	1,550 00		
withdrawal profits, .	207 98		
Cash on hand Oct. 31, 1893, .	345 07	Cash on hand Oct. 31, 1894,	327 12
	$17,814 73		$17,814 73

Reconciliation of Share Account with Dues and Profits Capital.

DATE OF ISSUE.	Series.	Value per Share.	Shares in Force.	Total Value.		
Mar., 1889, .	1	$80 29	207	$16,620 03	Dues capital, as per general ledger. . .	$35,116 00
Sept., 1889, .	2	72 17	50	3,608 50		
Mar., 1890, .	3	64 21	89	5,714 69	Profits capital, as per general ledger, . .	4,932 09
Sept., 1890, .	4	56 48	52	2,936 96		
Mar., 1891, .	5	48 92	59	2,886 28	Unpaid dues, . .	1,275 00
Sept., 1891, .	6	41 60	20	832 00		
Mar., 1892, .	7	34 50	56	1,932 00		
Sept., 1892, .	8	27 60	121	3,339 60		
Mar., 1893, .	9	20 89	109	2,277 01		
Sept., 1893, .	10	14 39	28	402 92		
Mar., 1894, .	11	8 10	81	656 10		
Sept., 1894, .	12	2 00	50	100 00		
Dues paid in advance, . . .				17 00		
Total, ...				$41,323 09	Total, . . .	$41,323 09

Number of shares issued during the year, ... 141
Number of shares now in force, ... 922
Number of shares now borrowed upon, ... 315
Largest number of shares held by any one member, . . . 25
Number of shares withdrawn during the year, ... 238
Highest premium received during the year, ... $0 20
Lowest premium received during the year, ... 05
Number of members withdrawn during the year, ... 32
Present number of members, ... 185
Present number of borrowers, ... 60
Present number of non-borrowers, ... 125
Number of loans secured by first mortgage of real estate, . . . 52
Number of loans on shares, ... 34
Largest loan to any one member, ... 3,050 00
Smallest loan to any one member, ... 25 00
Amount of expenses of the corporation for the year ending Oct. 31, 1894, . 206 50
Date of examination by commissioner : March 20.

SPRINGFIELD CO-OPERATIVE BANK — SPRINGFIELD.

Incorporated April 13, 1882. Commenced business May 9, 1882.

O. S. Greenleaf, *President.*   E. S. Batchelder, *Secretary.*
C. H. Churchill, *Treasurer.*

Names of security committee:
C. L. Shaw,   C. H. Churchill,
S. D. Sherwood.

Regular meetings the second Tuesday of each month.

BALANCE SHEET OCTOBER 31, 1894.

ASSETS.		LIABILITIES.	
Loans on real estate, . .	$292,361 84	Dues capital, . . .	$279,899 00
Loans on shares, . .	18,125 00	Profits capital (all series), .	46,016 48
Permanent expense account,	500 00	Guaranty fund, . . .	1,713 27
Real estate by foreclosure, .	2,412 00	Surplus, ...	1,503 53
Unpaid interest, . . .	1,511 80	Forfeited share account, .	192 73
Unpaid premiums, . .	34 65	Suspense account, . .	35 15
Unpaid fines, ...	223 76		
Cash in hands of treasurer, .	14,191 11		
	$329,360 16		$329,360 16

Detailed Statement of Receipts and Disbursements for the Year ending Oct. 31, 1894.

RECEIPTS.		DISBURSEMENTS.	
From dues capital, . .	$102,998 00	For real estate loans, . .	$121,575 00
interest, . . .	18,499 96	share loans, . . .	10,475 00
premiums, . . .	418 74	dues capital (withdrawn),	60,937 00
fines, ...	1,049 33	dues capital (forfeited),	199 00
transfer fees, . .	9 00	dues capital (retired), .	4,140 00
real estate loans repaid,	88,233 16	dues capital (matured),	4,657 00
share loans repaid, .	13,045 00	profits capital (withdrawn), . . .	10,042 64
withdrawal profits, .	1,094 12	profits capital (forfeited),	13 97
forfeiture profits, . .	4 52	profits capital (retired), .	1,768 45
forfeited shares, . .	14 90	profits capital (matured),	2,030 16
Damon property, . .	200 84	temporary expenses, .	1,340 35
		permanent expenses, .	76 62
		interest, ...	26 35
		Damon property, . .	157 48
Cash on hand Oct. 31, 1893, .	6,062 56	Cash on hand Oct. 31, 1894,	14,191 11
	$231,630 13		$231,630 13

Reconciliation of Share Account with Dues and Profits Capital.

DATE OF ISSUE.	Series.	Value per Share.	Shares in Force.	Total Value.		
May, 1883, .	3	$198 31	37	$7,337 47	Dues capital, as per general ledger, . .	$279,899 00
Nov., 1883, .	4	186 87	33	6,166 71		
May, 1884, .	5	175 72	55	9,664 60	Profits capital as per general ledger, . .	46,016 48
Nov., 1884, .	6	164 70	33	5,435 10		
May, 1885, .	7	154 15	90	13,873 50	Unpaid dues, . . .	2,713 00
Nov., 1885, .	8	143 92	65	9,354 80		
May, 1886, .	9	133 87	56	7,496 72		
Nov., 1886, .	10	124 14	54	6,703 56		
May, 1887, .	11	114 61	49	5,615 89		
Nov., 1887, .	12	105 47	111	11,707 17		
May, 1888, .	13	96 38	116	11,180 08		
Nov., 1888, .	14	87 65	83	7,274 95		
May, 1889, .	15	78 95	68	5,368 60		
Nov., 1889, .	16	70 69	198	13,996 62		
Feb., 1890, .	17	66 57	141	9,356 37		
May, 1890, .	18	62 57	190	11,888 30		
Aug., 1890, .	19	58 60	247	14,474 20		
Nov., 1890, .	20	54 70	137	7,493 90		
Feb., 1891, .	21	50 87	447	22,738 89		
May, 1891, .	22	47 12	284	13,382 08		
Aug., 1891, .	23	43 37	253	10,972 61		
Nov., 1891, .	24	39 74	350	13,909 00		
Feb., 1892, .	25	36 13	480	17,342 40		
May, 1892, .	26	32 57	522	17,001 54		
Aug., 1892, .	27	29 08	398	11,573 84		
Nov., 1892, .	28	25 62	534	13,681 08		
Feb., 1893, .	29	22 24	488	10,853 12		
May, 1893, .	30	18 91	454	8,585 14		
Aug., 1893, .	31	15 64	365	5,708 60		
Nov., 1893, .	32	12 41	443	5,497 63		
Feb., 1894, .	33	9 23	772	7,125 56		
May, 1894, .	34	6 10	639	3,897 90		
Aug., 1894, .	35	3 03	585	1,772 55		
Advance dues, . . .				168 00		
Total, ...				$328,628 48	Total, . . .	$328,628 48

Number of shares issued during the year, ... 2,713
Number of shares now in force, ... 8,777
Number of shares now borrowed upon, ... 2,103
Largest number of shares held by any one member, . . . 25
Number of shares withdrawn during the year, . . . 2,198
Number of shares forfeited during the year, ... 21
Number of shares retired during the year, ... 30
Number of shares matured during the year, ... 33
Highest premium received during the year, ... $0 25
Lowest premium received during the year, ... 05
Number of members withdrawn during the year, ... 266
Present number of members, ... 1,060
Present number of borrowers, ... 211
Present number of non-borrowers, ... 849
Number of loans secured by first mortgage of real estate, . . . 169
Number of loans on shares, ... 68
Largest loan to any one member, ... 5,000 00
Smallest loan to any one member, ... 25 00
Amount of expenses of the corporation for the year ending Oct. 31, 1894, . 1,532 17
Date of examination by commissioner : October 22.

STONEHAM CO-OPERATIVE BANK -- STONEHAM.

Incorporated Jan. 10, 1887. Commenced business Feb. 1, 1887.

JASON B. SANBORN, *President.* W. B. SNOW, *Secretary.*
W. B. SNOW, *Treasurer.*

Names of security committee:

LYMAN DIKE, A. H. COWDREY,
O. H. MARSTON.

Regular meetings the first Tuesday of each month.

BALANCE SHEET OCTOBER 31, 1894.

ASSETS.		LIABILITIES.	
Loans on real estate,	$115,650 00	Dues capital,	$106,176 00
Loans on shares,	4,850 00	Profits capital (all series),	18,437 20
Unpaid interest,	387 50	Guaranty fund,	825 00
Unpaid premiums,	40 25	Surplus,	250 30
Unpaid fines,	68 88	Forfeited share account,	38 58
Cash in hands of treasurer,	4,730 45		
	$125,727 08		$125,727 08

Detailed Statement of Receipts and Disbursements for the Year ending Oct. 31, 1894.

RECEIPTS.		DISBURSEMENTS.	
From dues capital,	$33,098 00	For real estate loans,	$27,300 00
interest,	6,899 27	share loans,	3,450 00
premiums,	611 10	dues capital (withdrawn),	20,435 00
fines,	226 87	dues capital (forfeited),	12 00
transfer fees,	1 75	dues capital (retired),	1,755 00
real estate loans repaid,	14,350 00	profits capital (withdrawn,)	3,262 11
share loans repaid,	4,100 00	profits capital (forfeited),	1 08
withdrawal profits,	318 61	profits capital (retired),	464 80
forfeiture profits,	1 08	temporary expenses,	533 26
forfeited shares,	10 32	interest,	89 35
Cash on hand Oct. 31, 1893,	2,416 05	Cash on hand Oct. 31, 1894,	4,730 45
	$62,033 05		$62,033 05

Reconciliation of Share Account with Dues and Profits Capital.

DATE OF ISSUE.	Series.	Value per Share.	Shares in Force.	Total Value.		
Feb., 1887, .	1	$119 94	162	$19,430 28	Dues capital, as per general ledger, . . .	$106,176 00
Aug., 1887, .	2	110 47	46	5,081 62	Profits capital, as per	
Feb., 1888, .	3	101 23	150	15,184 50	general ledger, . .	18,437 20
Aug., 1888, .	4	92 26	32	2,952 32	Unpaid dues, . . .	754 00
Feb., 1889, .	5	83 51	86	7,181 86		
May, 1889, .	6	79 23	73	5,783 79		
Nov., 1889, .	7	70 84	109	7,721 56		
May, 1890, .	8	62 72	154	9,658 88		
Nov., 1890, .	9	54 83	249	13,652 67		
May, 1891, .	10	47 19	185	8,730 15		
Nov., 1891, .	11	39 79	184	7,321 36		
May, 1892, .	12	32 63	229	7,472 27		
Nov., 1892, .	13	25 68	208	5,341 44		
May, 1893, .	14	18 94	189	3,579 66		
Nov., 1893, .	15	12 42	352	4,371 84		
May, 1894, .	16	6 11	300	1,833 00		
Dues paid in advance, . . .				70 00		
Total, ...				$125,367 20	Total, . . .	$125,367 20

Number of shares issued during the year, ...	741
Number of shares now in force, ...	2,708
Number of shares now borrowed upon, ...	722
Largest number of shares held by any one member, ...	25
Number of shares withdrawn during the year, ...	601
Number of shares forfeited during the year, ...	4
Number of shares retired during the year, ...	20
Highest premium received during the year, ...	$0 25
Lowest premium received during the year, ...	05
Number of members withdrawn during the year, ...	86
Present number of members, ...	395
Present number of borrowers, ...	103
Present number of non-borrowers, ...	292
Number of loans secured by first mortgage of real estate, . . .	109
Number of loans on shares, ...	26
Largest loan to any one member, ...	5,000 00
Smallest loan to any one member, ...	50 00
Amount of expenses of the corporation for the year ending Oct. 31, 1894, .	533 26
Date of examination by commissioner: June 29.	

STOUGHTON CO-OPERATIVE BANK — STOUGHTON.

Incorporated March 23, 1886. Commenced business April 10, 1886.

HENRI L. JOHNSON, *President.*   HENRY W. BRITTON, *Secretary.*
HENRY W. BRITTON, *Treasurer.*

Names of security committee:
RICHARD B. WARD,   GEORGE F. WALKER,
CHRISTOPHER FARRELL.

Regular meetings the second Saturday of each month.

BALANCE SHEET OCTOBER 31, 1894.

ASSETS.		LIABILITIES.	
Loans on real estate, . .	$148,275 00	Dues capital, . . .	$136,643 00
Loans on shares, . . .	13,975 00	Profits capital (all series), .	23,730 51
Permanent expense account,	50 00	Interest, ...	723 30
Temporary expense account,	6 00	Premiums, ...	68 50
Cash in hands of treasurer, .	2,299 55	Fines, ...	42 00
		Transfer fees, . . .	75
		Withdrawal profits, . .	131 52
		Forfeiture profits, . .	13 12
		Guaranty fund, . . .	1,279 00
		Surplus, ...	1,697 96
		Forfeited share account, .	275 89
	$164,605 55		$164,605 55

*Detailed Statement of Receipts and Disbursements for the Year ending
Oct. 31, 1894.*

RECEIPTS.		DISBURSEMENTS.	
From dues capital, . .	$40,224 00	For real estate loans, . .	$30,500 00
interest, . . .	8,969 36	share loans, . . .	10,245 00
premiums, . . .	734 60	dues capital (withdrawn),	25,353 00
fines, ...	517 03	dues capital (forfeited),	320 00
transfer fees, . .	8 75	profits capital (with-	
real estate loans repaid,	16,400 00	drawn), . . .	3,268 30
share loans repaid, .	3,105 00	profits capital (forfeited),	53 16
withdrawal profits, .	830 55	temporary expenses, .	647 69
forfeiture profits, . .	13 12	forfeited shares, . .	7 16
forfeited shares, . .	274 15		
Cash on hand Oct. 31, 1893, .	1,617 30	Cash on hand Oct. 31, 1894,	2,299 55
	$72,693 86		$72,693 86

Reconciliation of Share Account with Dues and Profits Capital.

DATE OF ISSUE.	Series.	Value per Share.	Shares in Force.	Total Value.		
April, 1886, .	1	$135 39	223	$30,191 97	Dues capital, as per general ledger, . .	$136,643 00
Mar., 1887, .	2	117 36	65	7,628 40		
Mar., 1888, .	3	98 65	177	17,461 05	Profits capital, as per general ledger, . .	23,730 51
Mar., 1889, .	4	81 08	255	20,675 40		
Sept., 1889, .	5	72 72	146	10,617 12	Unpaid dues, . .	1,440 00
Mar., 1890, .	6	64 60	209	13,501 40		
Sept., 1890, .	7	56 72	218	12,364 96		
Mar., 1891, .	8	49 09	220	10,799 80		
Sept., 1891, .	9	41 70	188	7,839 60		
Mar., 1892, .	10	34 54	290	10,016 60		
Sept., 1892, .	11	27 61	231	6,377 91		
Mar., 1893, .	12	20 90	400	8,360 00		
Sept., 1893, .	13	14 40	205	2,952 00		
Mar., 1894, .	14	8 10	293	2,373 30		
Sept., 1894, .	15	2 00	239	478 00		
Dues paid in advance, . . .				176 00		
Total, ...				$161,813 51	Total, . . .	$161,813 51

Number of shares issued during the year, ... 619
Number of shares now in force, ... 3,359
Number of shares now borrowed upon, ... 1,058
Largest number of shares held by any one member, . . . 25
Number of shares withdrawn during the year, ... 862
Number of shares forfeited during the year, ... 9
Highest premium received during the year, ... $0 40
Lowest premium received during the year, ... 05
Number of members withdrawn during the year, ... 119
Present number of members, ... 483
Present number of borrowers, ... 225
Present number of non-borrowers, ... 258
Number of loans secured by first mortgage of real estate, . . 164
Number of loans on shares, ... 61
Largest loan to any one member, ... 2,000 00
Smallest loan to any one member, ... 35 00
Amount of expenses of the corporation for the year ending Oct. 31, 1894, . 647 69
Date of examination by commissioner: June 7.

SUFFOLK CO-OPERATIVE BANK — BOSTON.

Incorporated Dec. 11, 1885.   Commenced business Jan. 1, 1886.

CHAS. A. POTTER, *President.*   CHAS. J. PAGE, *Secretary.*

CHAS. J. PAGE, *Treasurer.*

Names of security committee:

A. H. HOLWAY,   ALFRED FOSTER,

JOHN A. POTTER.

Regular meetings the first Wednesday of each month.

BALANCE SHEET OCTOBER 31, 1894.

ASSETS.		LIABILITIES.	
Loans on real estate, . .	$27,770 00	Dues capital, . . .	$28,473 00
Loans on shares, . .	2,210 00	Profits capital (all series), .	4,775 65
Unpaid interest, . . .	326 31	Guaranty fund, . . .	120 00
Unpaid premiums, . .	55 36	Surplus, ...	117 27
Unpaid fines, . . .	45 98	Forfeited share account, .	106 17
Suspense account, . . .	126 00		
Cash in hands of treasurer, .	3,058 44		
	$33,592 09		$33,592 09

Detailed Statement of Receipts and Disbursements for the Year ending Oct. 31, 1894.

RECEIPTS.		DISBURSEMENTS.	
From dues capital, .	$8,270 00	For real estate loans, . .	$7,875 00
interest, . . .	1,694 59	share loans, . . .	1,060 00
premiums, . .	319 33	dues capital(withdrawn),	5,873 00
fines, . . .	113 97	dues capital (forfeited),	555 00
real estate loans repaid,	6,950 00	profits capital (withdrawn), . . .	833 56
share loans repaid, .	1,100 00		
withdrawal profits, .	224 43	profits capital (forfeited),	97 83
forfeiture profits, .	36 70	temporary expenses, .	332 59
forfeited shares, .	88 90	Cash on hand Oct. 31, 1894,	3,058 44
Cash on hand Oct. 31, 1893, .	887 50		
	$19,685 42		$19,685 42

Reconciliation of Share Account with Dues and Profits Capital.

DATE OF ISSUE.	Series.	Value per Share.	Shares in Force.	Total Value.	,	
Jan., 1886, .	1	$140 03	16	$2,240 48	Dues capital, as per general ledger, . .	$28,473 00
July, 1886, .	2	130 53	6	783 18		
Jan., 1887, .	3	120 65	12	1,447 80	Profits capital, as per general ledger, . .	4,775 65
July, 1887, .	4	111 03	21	2,331 63		
Jan., 1888, .	5	101 71	25	2,542 75	Unpaid dues, . .	709 00
July, 1888, .	6	92 67	32	2,965 44		
Nov., 1888, .	7	86 85	3	260 55		
May, 1889, .	8	78 31	22	1,722 82		
Nov., 1889, .	9	70 07	45.	3,153 15		
May, 1890, .	10	62 12	30	1,863 60		
Nov., 1890, .	11	54 41	49	2,666 09		
May, 1891, .	12	46 94	24	1,126 56		
Nov., 1891, .	13	39 64	85	3,369 40		
May, 1892, .	14	32 53	115	3,740 95		
Nov., 1892, .	15	25 63	49	1,255 87		
May, 1893, .	16	18 93	79	1,495 47		
Nov., 1893, .	17	12 43	17	211 31		
May, 1894, .	18	6 12	105	642 60		
Dues paid in advance, . . .				138 00		
Total, ...				$33,957 65	Total, . . .	$33,957 65

Number of shares issued during the year, ... 132
Number of shares now in force, ... 735
Number of shares now borrowed upon, ... 229
Largest number of shares held by any one member,   .   .   . 25
Number of shares withdrawn during the year, ... 179
Number of shares forfeited during the year, ... 13
Highest premium received during the year, ... $0 25
Lowest premium received during the year, ... 05
Number of members withdrawn during the year, ... 27
Present number of members, ... 124
Present number of borrowers, ... 38
Present number of non-borrowers, ... 86
Number of loans secured by first mortgage of real estate,   .   .   . 31
Number of loans on shares, ... 12
Largest loan to any one member, ... 2,000 00
Smallest loan to any one member, ... 50 00
Amount of expenses of the corporation for the year ending Oct. 31, 1894,   . 482 59
Date of examination by commissioner : April 16.

TAUNTON CO-OPERATIVE BANK — TAUNTON.

Incorporated March 2, 1880. Commenced business March 17, 1880.

HENRY W. COLBY, *President.*   H. O. MORSE, *Secretary.*

GEO. E. DEAN, *Treasurer.*

Names of security committee:

DANIEL CAREY,   THOMAS BAKER,

JOHN H. DALGLISH.

Regular meetings the first Tuesday after the fifteenth of each month.

BALANCE SHEET OCTOBER 31, 1894.

ASSETS.		LIABILITIES.	
Loans on real estate,	$269,900 00	Dues capital,	$241,233 00
Loans on shares,	10,000 00	Profits capital (all series),	30,687 31
Permanent expense account,	319 08	Interest, }	
Temporary expense account,	598 11	Premiums, }	9,161 81
Suspense account,	2,362 99	Fines, }	
Cash in hands of treasurer,	171 06	Transfer fees, }	239 98
		Guaranty fund,	1,447 22
		Surplus,	498 08
		Forfeited share account,	83 84
	$283,351 24		$283,351 24

Detailed Statement of Receipts and Disbursements for the Year ending Oct. 31, 1894.

RECEIPTS.		DISBURSEMENTS.	
From dues capital,	$78,416 00	For real estate loans,	$86,250 00
interest, }		share loans,	12,850 00
premiums, }	19,587 07	dues capital (withdrawn),	40,805 00
fines, }		dues capital (retired),	53,082 00
transfer fees, }	488 16	profits capital (withdrawn),	6,557 88
real estate loans repaid,	88,250 00	profits capital (retired),	13,166 37
share loans repaid,	16,750 00	temporary expenses,	1,204 08
advance payments,	185 00	permanent expenses,	112 39
		advance payments,	185 00
		interest on retired shares,	2,384 40
Cash on hand Oct. 31, 1893,	13,091 95	Cash on hand Oct. 31, 1894,	171 06
	$216,768 18		$216,768 18

Reconciliation of Share Account with Dues and Profits Capital.

DATE OF ISSUE.	Series.	Value per Share.	Shares in Force.	Total Value.		
May, 1883, .	1	$192 31	15	$2,884 65	Dues capital, as per general ledger, . . .	$241,233 00
May, 1884, .	2	169 82	12	2,037 84	Profits capital, as per	
May, 1885, .	3	148 69	32	4,758 08	general ledger, . .	30,687 31
May, 1886, .	4	128 80	62	7,985 60	Unpaid dues, . . .	5,067 00
May, 1887, .	5	110 11	182	20,040 02	Suspense, . . .	05
May, 1888, .	6	92 45	327	30,231 15		
May, 1889, .	7	75 85	789	59,845 65		
May, 1890, .	8	60 19	885	53,268 15		
May, 1891, .	9	45 44	1,008	45,803 52		
May, 1892, .	10	31 52	642	20,235 84		
May, 1893, .	11	18 39	1,274	23,428 86		
May, 1894, .	12	6 00	1,078	6,468 00		
Total, ...				$276,987 36	Total, . . .	$276,987 36

Number of shares issued during the year, ... 1,373
Number of shares now in force, ... 6,306
Number of shares now borrowed upon, ... 2,758
Largest number of shares held by any one member, ... 25
Number of shares withdrawn during the year, ... 1,041
Number of shares retired during the year, ... 550
Highest premium received during the year, ... $0 05
Lowest premium received during the year, ... 05
Number of members withdrawn during the year, ... 178
Present number of members, ... 750
Present number of borrowers, ... 250
Present number of non-borrowers, ... 500
Number of loans secured by first mortgage of real estate, . . . 169
Number of loans on shares, ... 121
Largest loan to any one member, ... 5,000 00
Smallest loan to any one member, ... 50 00
Amount of expenses of the corporation for the year ending Oct. 31, 1894, 1,235 78
Date of examination by commissioner : November 5.

TROY CO-OPERATIVE BANK—FALL RIVER.

Incorporated July 18, 1880.   Commenced business July 20, 1880.

JEROME C. BORDEN, *President.*   GEO. H. EDDY, Jr., *Secretary.*
GEO. H. EDDY, Jr., *Treasurer.*

Names of security committee:

A. HOMER SKINNER,   JOHN M. YOUNG,
THOMAS D. COVELL.

Regular meetings the third Tuesday of each month.

BALANCE SHEET OCTOBER 31, 1894.

ASSETS.		LIABILITIES.	
Loans on real estate, . .	$319,550 00	Dues capital, . . .	$294,628 00
Loans on shares, . . .	11,350 00	Profits capital (all series), .	50,827 77
Unpaid interest, . .	947 75	Guaranty fund, . . .	1,216 69
Unpaid premiums, . .	72 48	Surplus, ...	3,082 10
Unpaid fines, ...	82 10	Forfeited share account, .	30 26
Unpaid dues, ...	1,624 00	Advance payments, . .	477 00
Cash in hands of treasurer, .	16,647 37	Unknown account, . .	11 88
	$350,273 70		$350,273 70

Detailed Statement of Receipts and Disbursements for the Year ending Oct. 31, 1894.

RECEIPTS.		DISBURSEMENTS.	
From dues capital, . .	$96,075 00	For real estate loans, . .	$117,593 00
interest, . .	18,929 03	share loans, . . .	12,850 00
premiums, . . .	1,486 50	dues capital (withdrawn), .	58,847 00
fines, ...	351 63	dues capital (forfeited), .	1,086 00
real estate loans repaid,	105,783 00	dues capital (retired), . .	8,748 00
share loans repaid, .	12,050 00	dues capital (matured), .	11,135 00
forfeited shares, . .	1,594 72	profits capital (withdrawn), .	9,120 83
unknown account, .	22 40	profits capital (forfeited), .	513 34
advance payments, .	1,689 20	profits capital (retired), .	1,643 40
real estate, . . .	1,500 00	profits capital (matured), .	5,116 87
		temporary expenses, .	1,546 78
		forfeited shares, . .	1,601 72
		unknown account, . .	10 52
		advance payments, .	1,342 20
		real estate, . . .	1,500 00
		loss on foreclosed real estate, . . .	387 67
Cash on hand Oct. 31, 1893, .	10,208 22	Cash on hand Oct. 31, 1894,	16,647 37
	$249,689 70		$249,689 70

Reconciliation of Share Account with Dues and Profits Capital.

DATE OF ISSUE.	Series.	Value per Share.	Shares In Force.	Total Value.		
April, 1883, .	7	$201 99	51	$10,301 49	Dues capital, as per general ledger, . .	$294,628 00
Oct., 1883, .	8	189 65	31	5,879 15	eral ledger, . .	
April, 1884, .	9	177 77	34	6,044 18	Profits capital, as per	
Oct., 1884, .	10	166 39	37	6,156 43	general ledger, . .	50,827 77
April, 1885, .	11	155 35	61	9,476 35		
Oct., 1885, .	12	144 75	86	12,448 50		
April, 1886, .	13	134 50	99	13,315 50		
Oct., 1886, .	14	124 58	114	14,202 12		
April, 1887, .	15	114 99	64	7,359 36		
Oct., 1887, .	16	105 68	178	18,811 04		
April, 1888, .	17	96 63	184	17,779 92		
Oct., 1888, .	18	87 88	143	12,566 84		
April, 1889, .	19	79 39	290	23,023 10		
Oct., 1889, .	20	71 14	269	19,136 66		
April, 1890, .	21	63 15	444	28,038 60		
Oct., 1890, .	22	55 40	306	16,952 40		
April, 1891, .	23	47 87	521	24,940 27		
Oct., 1891, .	24	40 56	390	15,818 40		
April, 1892, .	25	33 47	770	25,771 90		
Oct., 1892, .	26	26 58	613	16,293 54		
April, 1893, .	27	19 89	1,008	20,049 12		
Oct., 1893, .	28	13 40	902	12,086 80		
April, 1894, .	29	7 10	1,151	8,172 10		
Oct., 1894, .	30	1 00	832	832 00		
Total, ...				$345,455 77	Total, . . .	$345,455 77

Number of shares issued during the year, ...	2,334
Number of shares now in force, ...	8,578
Number of shares now borrowed upon, ...	2,088
Largest number of shares held by any one member, . . .	25
Number of shares withdrawn during the year, ...	1,790
Number of shares forfeited during the year, ...	19
Number of shares retired during the year, ...	129
Number of shares matured during the year, ...	80
Highest premium received during the year, ...	$0 15
Lowest premium received during the year, ...	05
Number of members withdrawn during the year, ...	270
Present number of members, ...	1,252
Present number of borrowers, ...	196
Present number of non-borrowers, ...	1,056
Number of loans secured by first mortgage of real estate, . .	177
Number of loans on shares, ...	79
Largest loan to any one member, ...	5,000 00
Smallest loan to any one member, ...	50 00
Amount of expenses of the corporation for the year ending Oct. 31, 1894, .	1,546 78

Date of examination by commissioner: July 30.

VOLUNTEER CO-OPERATIVE BANK — BOSTON.

Incorporated Nov. 16, 1887. Commenced business Jan. 1, 1888.

WALTER C. SHAPLEIGH, *President.* FRANK E. BURBANK, *Secretary.*

FRANK E. BURBANK, *Treasurer.*

Names of security committeee:

JOHN A. REED,	M. J. GILLESPIE,
JAMES A. COOK,	THOS. C. RILEY.

Regular meetings the third Wednesday of each month.

BALANCE SHEET OCTOBER 31, 1894.

ASSETS.		LIABILITIES.	
Loans on real estate, . .	$192,850 00	Dues capital, . . .	$182,102 00
Loans on shares, . . .	2,200 00	Profits capital (all series), . .	27,284 25
Temporary expense account, .	84 80	Interest, ...	219 47
Real estate by foreclosure, .	2,446 30	Withdrawal profits, . .	87 41
Unpaid premiums, . .	1 75	Guaranty fund, . . .	767 00
Unpaid fines, ...	37 88	Surplus, ...	352 12
Bond for deed of real estate, .	1,772 19	Forfeited share account, .	133 90
Cash in hands of secretary, .	30 06		
Cash in hands of treasurer, .	11,523 17		
	$210,946 15		$210,946 15

Detailed Statement of Receipts and Disbursements for the Year ending Oct. 31, 1894.

RECEIPTS.		DISBURSEMENTS.	
From dues capital, . .	$63,589 00	For real estate loans, . .	$63,900 00
,, interest, . . .	12,303 31	share loans, . . .	2,900 00
premiums, . . .	629 00	dues capital (withdrawn), .	28,599 00
fines, ...	628 17	dues capital (forfeited), .	2,294 00
transfer fees, . .	2 25	dues capital (retired), .	19,155 00
real estate loans repaid,	52,150 00	interest, ...	57 08
share loans repaid, .	4,650 00	profits capital (withdrawn),	3,209 15
withdrawal profits, .	889 51	profits capital (forfeited),	381 72
forfeiture profits, .	64 04	profits capital (retired),	3,858 94
forfeited shares, . .	219 22	retired shares, . .	23,027 00
real estate by foreclosure,	9,765 10	temporary expenses, .	1,351 90
retired shares, . .	23,027 00	fines, ...	1 50
profits, ...	23	forfeited shares, . .	145 72
		mortgages foreclosed, .	13,733 64
		surplus, ...	500 00
		cash short, . . .	12 69
		taxes, insurance, etc., .	249 95
Cash on hand Oct. 31, 1893, .	7,013 69	Cash on hand Oct. 31, 1894, .	11,553 23
	$174,930 52		$174,930 52

Reconciliation of Share Account with Dues and Profits Capital.

DATE OF ISSUE.	Series.	Value per Share.	Shares in Force.	Total Value.		
Jan., 1888, .	1	$102 62	280	$28,733 60	Dues capital, as per general ledger, .	$182,102 00
July, 1888, .	2	93 40	191	17,839 40		
Jan., 1889, .	3	84 55	259	21,898 45	Profits capital, as per general ledger, .	27,284 25
July, 1889, .	4	75 93	324	24,601 32		
Jan., 1890, .	5	67 64	248	16,774 72	Unpaid dues, .	1,797 00
July, 1890, .	6	59 62	252	15,024 24		
Jan., 1891, .	7	51 87	300	15,561 00		
July, 1891, .	8	44 34	220	9,754 80		
Jan., 1892, .	9	37 07	481	17,830 67		
July, 1892, .	10	30 05	434	13,041 70		
Jan., 1893, .	11	23 22	552	12,817 44		
April, 1893, .	12	19 90	223	4,437 70		
July, 1893, .	13	16 63	137	2,278 31		
Oct., 1893, .	14	13 40	174	2,331 60		
Jan., 1894, .	15	10 23	369	3,774 87		
April, 1894, .	16	7 11	326	2,317 86		
July, 1894, .	17	4 03	319	1,285 57		
Oct., 1894, .	18	1 00	360	360 00		
Dues paid in advance, . . .				520 00		
Total, ...				$211,183 25	Total, . . .	$211,183 25

Number of shares issued during the year, ... 1,669
Number of shares now in force, ... 5,449
Number of shares now borrowed upon, ... 1,112
Largest number of shares held by any one member, ... 25
Number of shares withdrawn during the year, ... 1,362
Number of shares forfeited during the year, ... 99
Number of shares retired during the year, ... 287
Highest per centum of interest received during the year : $6\frac{1}{2}$.
Lowest per centum of interest received during the year : 6.
Number of members withdrawn during the year, ... 201
Present number of members, ... 665
Present number of borrowers, ... 105
Present number of non-borrowers, ... 560
Number of loans secured by first mortgage of real estate, . . . 105
Number of loans on shares, ... 21
Largest loan to any one member, ... $5,000 00
Smallest loan to any one member, ... 50 00
Amount of expenses of the corporation for the year ending Oct. 31, 1894, . 1,351 90
Date of examination by commissioner : March 27.

WAKEFIELD CO-OPERATIVE BANK — WAKEFIELD.

Incorporated Jan. 31, 1887. Commenced business March 5, 1887.

ARLON S. ATHERTON, *President.*   HARRY FOSTER, *Secretary.*
HARRY FOSTER, *Treasurer.*

Names of security committee:

RICHARD S. STOUT,   JOHN LEMMAN,
ROGER HOWARD,   EVERETT W. EATON,
OLIVER WALTON.

Regular meetings the first Saturday of each month.

BALANCE SHEET OCTOBER 31, 1894.

ASSETS.		LIABILITIES.	
Loans on real estate, . .	$147,400 00	Dues capital, . . .	$141,016 00
Loans on shares, . . .	5,600 00	Profits capital (all series), .	23,846 10
Permanent expense account,	70 00	Guaranty fund, . . .	460 00
Unpaid interest, . .	545 25	Surplus, ...	852 73
Unpaid premiums, . .	46 30		
Unpaid fines, . . .	58 98		
Cash in hands of treasurer, .	12,454 30		
	$166,174 83		$166,174 83

Detailed Statement of Receipts and Disbursements for the Year ending Oct. 31, 1894.

RECEIPTS.		DISBURSEMENTS.	
From dues capital, . .	$48,613 00	For real estate loans, . .	$40,400 00
interest, . .	9,387 45	share loans, . . .	11,300 00
premiums, . . .	802 30	dues capital (withdrawn),	21,432 00
fines, ...	249 80	dues capital (retired), .	26,547 00
transfer fees, . .	5 25	profits capital (with-	
real estate loans repaid,	35,000 00	drawn), . . .	2,355 23
share loans repaid, .	15,950 00	profits capital (retired),	5,439 98
withdrawal profits, .	589 48	temporary expenses, .	527 70
		interest on retired shares,	430 06
Cash on hand Oct. 31, 1893, .	10,288 99	Cash on hand Oct. 31, 1894,	12,454 30
	$120,886 27		$120,886 27

Reconciliation of Share Account with Dues and Profits Capital.

DATE OF ISSUE.	Series.	Value per Share.	Shares in Force.	Total Value.		
Mar., 1887, .	1	$120 58	80	$2,286 40	Dues capital, as per general ledger, .	$141,016 00
May, 1887, .	2	117 28	72	1,964 16	eral ledger, .	
Nov., 1887, .	3	107 51	106	2,492 06	Profits capital, as per	
May, 1888, .	4	98 00	151	3,020 00	general ledger, .	23,846 10
Nov., 1888, .	5	88 76	99	1,659 24	Unpaid dues, .	1,231 00
May, 1889, .	6	79 95	110	1,534 50		
Nov., 1889, .	7	71 36	157	1,783 52		
May, 1890, .	8	63 05	218	1,972 90		
Nov., 1890, .	9	55 06	290	2,047 40		
May, 1891, .	10	47 34	391	2,087 94		
Nov., 1891, .	11	39 87	316	1,222 92		
May, 1892, .	12	32 63	313	823 19		
Nov., 1892, .	13	25 66	255	423 30		
May, 1893, .	14	18 91	287	261 17		
Nov., 1893, .	15	12 40	539	215 60		
May, 1894, .	16	6 10	518	51 80		
Dues paid in advance, . . .				175 00		
Total, ...				$166,093 10	Total, . . .	$166,093 10

Number of shares issued during the year, ...	1,171
Number of shares now in force, ...	3,902
Number of shares now borrowed upon, ...	928
Largest number of shares held by any one member, ...	25
Number of shares withdrawn during the year, ...	840
Number of shares retired during the year, ...	407
Highest premium received during the year, ...	$0 10
Lowest premium received during the year, ...	05
Number of members withdrawn during the year, ...	126
Present number of members, ...	590
Present number of borrowers, ...	139
Present number of non-borrowers, ...	451
Number of loans secured by first mortgage of real estate, . .	133
Number of loans on shares, ...	31
Largest loan to any one member, ...	4,600 00
Smallest loan to any one member, ...	50 00
Amount of expenses of the corporation for the year ending Oct. 31, 1894, .	545 70

Date of examination by commissioner : June 26.

WALTHAM CO-OPERATIVE BANK—WALTHAM.

Incorporated Oct. 13, 1880. Commenced business Oct. 20, 1880.

EDW. P. SMITH, *Vice-President.*   DANIEL F. VILES, *Secretary.*
              DANIEL F. VILES, *Treasurer.*

Names of security committee:
EDW. P. SMITH,   M. T. CONNELLY.

Regular meetings the third Thursday of each month.

BALANCE SHEET OCTOBER 31, 1894.

ASSETS.		LIABILITIES.	
Loans on real estate,	$607,050 00	Dues capital,	$506,025 00
Loans on shares,	7,700 00	Profits capital (all series),	101,735 37
Real estate account,	68 65	Interest,	3,229 50
Unpaid interest,	4,774 25	Premiums,	345 89
Unpaid premiums,	562 90	Fines,	168 89
Unpaid fines,	520 30	Transfer fees,	25
Cash in hands of treasurer,	2,404 71	Guaranty fund,	6,500 00
		Surplus,	4,840 87
		Outstanding bills,	235 04
	$623,080 81		$623,080 81

Detailed Statement of Receipts and Disbursements for the Year ending Oct. 31, 1894.

RECEIPTS.		DISBURSEMENTS.	
From dues capital,	$169,883 00	For real estate loans,	$149,650 00
interest,	39,686 55	share loans,	7,050 00
premiums,	4,460 26	dues capital (withdrawn),	252,718 00
fines,	1,968 12	dues capital (forfeited),	438 00
transfer fees,	14 75	dues capital (matured),	15,276 00
real estate loans repaid,	252,200 00	profits capital (withdrawn),	60,514 57
share loans repaid,	18,450 00	profits capital (forfeited),	52 14
withdrawal profits,	2,988 37	profits capital (matured),	7,809 33
forfeiture profits,	4 02	temporary expenses,	3,476 34
forfeited shares,	490 14	real estate account,	806 84
real estate account,	1,600 00	real estate by foreclosure,	2,300 00
rents,	140 02	Cash on hand Oct. 31, 1894,	2,404 71
Cash on hand Oct. 31, 1893,	10,610 70		
	$502,495 93		$502,495 93

Reconciliation of Share Account with Dues and Profits Capital.

DATE OF ISSUE.	Series.	Value per Share.	Shares in Force.	Total Value.		
April, 1884, .	8	$185 71	92	$17,103 72	Dues capital, as per general ledger, . .	$506,025 00
Oct., 1884, .	9	173 71	125	21,713 75		
April, 1885, .	10	161 92	116	18,782 72	Profits capital, as per	
Oct., 1885, .	11	150 57	138	20,778 66	general ledger, . .	101,735 37
April, 1886, .	12	139 62	173	24,154 26	Unpaid dues, . .	7,562 00
Oct., 1886, .	13	129 02	160	20,643 20		
Apr., 1887, .	14	118 79	218	25,896 22		
Oct., 1887, .	15	108 91	183	19,930 53		
April, 1888, .	16	99 36	377	37,458 72		
Oct., 1888, .	17	90 13	439	39,567 07		
April, 1889, .	18	81 21	507	41,173 47		
Oct., 1889, .	19	72 61	499	36,239 39		
Jan., 1890, .	20	68 39	307	20,995 73		
April, 1890, .	21	64 27	331	21,273 37		
July, 1890, .	22	60 21	381	22,940 01		
Oct., 1890, .	23	56 23	455	25,584 65		
Jan., 1891, .	24	52 32	378	19,776 96		
April, 1891, .	25	48 47	459	22,247 73		
July, 1891, .	26	44 69	382	17,071 58		
Oct., 1891, .	27	40 97	466	19,092 02		
Jan., 1892, .	28	37 31	441	16,453 71		
April, 1892, .	29	33 72	577	19,456 44		
July, 1892, .	30	30 19	572	17,268 68		
Oct., 1892, .	31	26 71	400	10,684 00		
Jan., 1893, .	32	23 30	561	13,071 30		
April, 1893, .	33	19 95	870	17,356 50		
July, 1893, .	34	16 65	571	9,507 15		
Oct., 1893, .	35	13 41	416	5,578 56		
Jan., 1894, .	36	10 22	433	4,425 26		
April, 1894, .	37	7 11	642	4,564 62		
July, 1894, .	38	4 03	513	2,067 39		
Oct., 1894, .	39	1 00	757	757 00		
Dues paid in advance, . . .				1,715 00		
Total, ...				$615,322 37	Total, . . .	$615,322 37

Number of shares issued during the year, ... 2,604
Number of shares now in force, ... 12,939
Number of shares now borrowed upon, ... 3,368
Largest number of shares held by any one member, ... 25
Number of shares withdrawn during the year, ... 5,464
Number of shares forfeited during the year, ... 12
Number of shares matured during the year, ... 114
Highest per centum of interest received during the year: 7½.
Lowest per centum of interest received during the year: 6.
Number of members withdrawn during the year, ... 875
Present number of members, ... 1,911
Present number of borrowers, ... 474
Present number of non-borrowers, ... 1,437
Number of loans secured by first mortgage of real estate, . . . 432
Number of loans on shares, ... 42
Largest loan to any one member, ... $5,000 00
Smallest loan to any one member, ... 50 00
Amount of expenses of the corporation for the year ending Oct. 31, 1894, . 3,476 34
Date of examination by commissioner: June 11.

WATERTOWN CO-OPERATIVE BANK—WATERTOWN.

Incorporated June 5, 1888. Commenced business June 28, 1888.

CHARLES BRIGHAM, *President.*   SAMUEL S. GLEASON, *Secretary.*
SAMUEL S. GLEASON, *Treasurer.*

Names of security committee:

JAMES H. NORCROSS,   HORACE W. OTIS,
SAMUEL S. GLEASON.

Regular meetings the fourth Thursday of each month.

BALANCE SHEET OCTOBER 31, 1894.

ASSETS.		LIABILITIES.	
Loans on real estate, . .	$141,979 00	Dues capital, . . .	$133,953 00
Loans on shares, . . .	7,405 00	Profits capital (all series), .	15,567 81
Temporary expense account,	356 39	Interest, ...	3,811 52
Unpaid interest, . . .	210 25	Premiums, ...	343 80
Unpaid premiums, . .	20 75	Fines, ...	90 41
Unpaid fines, . . .	11 58	Transfer fees, . . .	1 50
Office furniture, . . .	400 00	Withdrawal profits, . .	182 41
Cash in hands of treasurer, .	4,712 31	Guaranty fund, . . .	274 69
		Surplus, ...	870 14
	$155,095 28		$155,095 28

Detailed Statement of Receipts and Disbursements for the Year ending Oct. 31, 1894.

RECEIPTS.		DISBURSEMENTS.	
From dues capital, . .	$43,525 00	For real estate loans, . .	$50,669 00
interest, . . .	8,447 85	share loans, . . .	5,180 00
premiums, . . .	791 22	dues capital (withdrawn),	13,327 00
fines, ...	196 25	dues capital (retired), .	5,351 00
transfer fees, . .	2 50	profits capital (withdrawn), . . .	1,364 24
real estate loans repaid,	17,450 00		
share loans repaid, .	4,354 00	profits capital (retired),	796 50
withdrawal profits, .	339 73	temporary expenses, .	1,292 24
town note, . . .	5,000 00	office furniture, . .	300 00
Cash on hand Oct. 31, 1893, .	2,885 74	Cash on hand Oct. 31, 1894,	4,712 31
	$82,992 29		$82,992 29

Reconciliation of Share Account with Dues and Profits Capital.

DATE OF ISSUE.	Series.	Value per Share.	Shares in Force.	Total Value.		
June, 1888, .	1	$91 93	315	$28,957 95	Dues capital as per general ledger, .	$133,953 00
Dec., 1888, .	2	83 45	153	12,767 85	eral ledger, .	
June, 1889, .	3	75 18	128	9,623 04	Profits capital as per	
Dec., 1889, .	4	67 17	186	12,493 62	general ledger, . .	15,567 81
June, 1890, .	5	59 40	398	23,641 20	Unpaid dues, . .	818 00
Dec., 1890, .	6	51 84	156	8,087 04		
June, 1891, .	7	44 51	317	14,109 67		
Dec., 1891, .	8	37 41	442	16,535 22		
June, 1892, .	9	30 53	186	5,678 58		
Dec., 1892, .	10	23 85	258	6,153 30		
June, 1893, .	11	17 38	288	5,005 44		
Dec., 1893, .	12	11 10	439	4,872 90		
June, 1894, .	13	5 00	429	2,145 00		
Dues paid in advance, . . .				268 00		
Total, ...				$150,338 81	Total, . . .	$150,338 81

Number of shares issued during the year, ... 938
Number of shares now in force, ... 3,695
Number of shares now borrowed upon, ... 1,086
Largest number of shares held by any one member, . . . 25
Number of shares withdrawn during the year, ... 500
Number of shares retired during the year, ... 67
Highest per centum of interest received during the year: $7\frac{3}{10}$.
Lowest per centum of interest received during the year: $6\frac{3}{10}$.
Number of members withdrawn during the year, ... 71
Present number of members, ... 404
Present number of borrowers, ... 111
Present number of non-borrowers, ... 293
Number of loans secured by first mortgage of real estate, . . 82
Number of loans on shares, ... 29
Largest loan to any one member, ... $3,000 00
Smallest loan to any one member, ... 30 00
Amount of expenses of the corporation for the year ending Oct. 31, 1894, . 1,392 24
Date of examination by commissioner: February 19.

WEBSTER CO-OPERATIVE BANK — WEBSTER.

Incorporated Aug. 2, 1889.   Commenced business Aug. 8, 1889.

LOUIS E. PATTISON, *President.*   C. M. NASH, *Secretary.*

C. M. NASH, *Treasurer.*

Names of security committee:

LOUIS E. PATTISON,   JOHN J. LOVE,

MOSES MOREAU.

Regular meetings the second Thursday of each month.

BALANCE SHEET OCTOBER 31, 1894.

ASSETS.		LIABILITIES.	
Loans on real estate, . .	$34,700 00	Dues capital, . . .	$32,324 00
Loans on shares, . . .	900 00	Profits capital (all series), .	3,127 46
Temporary expense account,	60 24	Interest, ...	529 90
Unpaid interest, . . .	4 88	Premiums, ...	29 94
Unpaid premiums, . . .	40	Fines, ...	12 10
Unpaid fines, ...	7 52	Withdrawal profits, . .	26 82
Cash in hands of treasurer, .	801 80	Guaranty fund, . . .	237 00
		Surplus, ...	187 62
	$36,474 84		$36,474 84

Detailed Statement of Receipts and Disbursements for the Year ending Oct. 31, 1894.

RECEIPTS.		DISBURSEMENTS.	
From dues capital, . .	$12,159 00	For real estate loans, . .	$14,100 00
interest, . . .	1,923 93	share loans, . . .	800 00
premiums, . . .	114 16	dues capital (withdrawn),	6,598 00
fines, ...	40 58	profits capital (withdrawn), . . .	509 48
real estate loans repaid,	7,200 00		
share loans repaid, .	800 00	temporary expenses, .	195 79
withdrawal profits, .	123 12		
Cash on hand Oct. 31, 1893, .	644 28	Cash on hand Oct. 31, 1894,	801 80
	$23,005 07		$23,005 07

Reconciliation of Share Account with Dues and Profits Capital.

DATE OF ISSUE.	Series.	Value per Share.	Shares in Force.	Total Value.		
Aug., 1889, .	1	$71 56	207	$14,812 92	Dues capital, as per general ledger, . . .	$32,324 00
Feb., 1890, .	2	64 02	17	1,088 34		
Aug., 1890, .	3	56 62	100	5,662 00	Profits capital, as per general ledger, . .	3,127 46
Feb., 1891, .	4	49 35	10	493 50		
Aug., 1891, .	5	42 24	52	2,196 48	Unpaid dues, . .	87 00
Feb., 1892, .	6	35 27	74	2,609 98		
Aug., 1892, .	7	28 48	98	2,791 04		
Feb., 1893, .	8	21 84	136	2,970 24		
Aug., 1893, .	9	15 38	47	722 86		
Feb., 1894, .	10	9 10	171	1,556 10		
Aug., 1894, .	11	3 00	177	531 00		
Dues paid in advance, . . .				104 00		
Total, ...				$35,538 46	Total, . . .	$35,538 46

Number of shares issued during the year, ... 353
Number of shares now in force, ... 1,089
Number of shares now borrowed upon, ... 230
Largest number of shares held by any one member, . . . 25
Number of shares withdrawn during the year, ... 219
Highest per centum of interest received during the year: $6\frac{3}{10}$.
Lowest per centum of interest received during the year: $6\frac{3}{10}$.
Number of members withdrawn during the year, ... 28
Present number of members, ... 154
Present number of borrowers, ... 37
Present number of non-borrowers, ... 117
Number of loans secured by first mortgage of real estate, . . 38
Number of loans on shares, ... 8
Largest loan to any one member, ... $4,700 00
Smallest loan to any one member, ... 40 00
Amount of expenses of the corporation for the year ending Oct. 31, 1894, . 275 79
Date of examination by commissioner: April 23.

WEIR CO-OPERATIVE BANK — TAUNTON.

Incorporated July 11, 1884. Commenced business July 16, 1884.

WM. F. BODFISH, *President.*   ALBERT H. TETLOW, *Secretary.*

T. PRESTON. BURT, *Treasurer.*

Names of security committee :

CHAS. H. PAULL,   H. M. STAPLES,

HORATIO H. HALL.

Regular meetings the sixteenth day of each month.

BALANCE SHEET OCTOBER 31, 1894.

ASSETS.		LIABILITIES.	
Loans on real estate, .	$177,300 00	Dues capital, . . .	$162,492 00
Loans on shares. . .	9,550 00	Profits capital (all series), .	28,788 34
Temporary expense account,	156 61	Interest, ...	3,876 52
Real estate by foreclosure, .	1,450 96	Premiums, ...	210 25
Unpaid interest, . . .	715 00	Fines, ...	114 18
Unpaid premiums, . .	37 10	Transfer fees, . . .	1 25
Unpaid fines, ...	77 76	Guaranty fund, . . .	740 00
Cash in hands of treasurer, .	8,389 84	Surplus, ...	1,421 43
		Advance payments, . .	33 30
	$197,677 27		$197,677 27

Detailed Statement of Receipts and Disbursements for the Year ending Oct. 31, 1894.

RECEIPTS.		DISBURSEMENTS.	
From dues capital, . .	$42,992 00	For real estate loans, . .	$51,800 00
interest, . . .	11,379 25	share loans, . . .	7,800 00
premiums, . . .	604 05	dues capital (withdrawn),	24,431 00
fines, ...	305 08	dues capital (retired), .	13,146 00
transfer fees, . .	3 75	profits capital (with-	
real estate loans repaid,	55,500 00	drawn), . . .	4,080 74
share loans repaid, .	3,500 00	profits capital (retired),	4,357 08
Maverick Nat'l Bank,	253 25	temporary expenses, .	573 33
advance payments, .	147 25	taxes, ...	19 10
		interest on retired shares,	90 48
Cash on hand Oct. 31, 1893, .	2 94	Cash on hand Oct. 31, 1894,	8,389 84
	$114,687 57		$114,687 57

Reconciliation of Share Account with Dues and Profits Capital.

DATE OF ISSUE.	Series.	Value per Share.	Shares in Force.	Total Value.		
July, 1884, .	1	$166 59	16	$2,665 44	Dues capital, as per general ledger, .	$162,492 00
Jan., 1885, .	2	156 22	7	1,093 54		
July, 1885, .	3	145 93	25	3,648 25	Profits capital as per	
Jan., 1886, .	4	135 96	127	17,266 92	general ledger, . .	28,788 34
July, 1886, .	5	126 26	168	21,211 68	Unpaid dues, . .	790 00
Jan., 1887, .	6	116 85	137	16,008 45		
July, 1887, .	7	107 71	126	13,571 46		
Jan., 1888, .	8	98 82	237	23,420 34		
July, 1888, .	9	90 22	190	17,141 80		
Jan., 1889, .	10	81 83	59	4,827 97		
July, 1889, .	11	73 71	200	14,742 00		
Jan., 1890, .	12	65 83	35	2,304 05		
July, 1890, .	13	58 15	151	8,780 65		
Jan., 1891, .	14	50 73	283	14,356 59		
July, 1891, .	15	43 52	150	6,528 00		
Jan., 1892, .	16	36 42	99	3,605 58		
July, 1892, .	17	29 55	100	2,955 00		
Jan., 1893, .	18	22 88	221	5,056 48		
July, 1893, .	19	16 40	239	3,919 60		
Jan., 1894, .	20	10 11	714	7,218 54		
July, 1894, .	21	4 00	437	1,748 00		
Total, ...				$192,070 34	Total, . . .	$192,070 34

Number of shares issued during the year, ... 1,167
Number of shares now in force, ... 3,721
Number of shares now borrowed upon, ... 1,169
Largest number of shares held by any one member, ... 25
Number of shares withdrawn during the year, ... 572
Number of shares retired during the year, ... 114
Highest premium received during the year, ... $0 05
Lowest premium received during the year, ... 05
Number of members withdrawn during the year, ... 49
Present number of members, ... 484
Present number of borrowers, ... 165
Present number of non-borrowers, ... 319
Number of loans secured by first mortgage of real estate, . . . 145
Number of loans on shares, ... 23
Largest loan to any one member, ... 4,500 00
Smallest loan to any one member, ... 50 00
Amount of expenses of the corporation for the year ending Oct. 31, 1894, . 573 33
Date of examination by commissioner : November 5.

WESTFIELD CO-OPERATIVE BANK—WESTFIELD.

Incorporated Dec. 13, 1881.   Commenced business Dec. 19, 1881.

MOSES P. BRECKINRIDGE, *President.*   OLIN C. TOWLE, *Secretary.*
                            OLIN C. TOWLE, *Treasurer.*

Names of security committee:

AUGUSTUS W. HOLTON,   SUMNER B. CAMPBELL,
                    EDWIN D. AVERY.

Regular meetings the third Monday of each month.

BALANCE SHEET OCTOBER 31, 1894.

ASSETS.		LIABILITIES.	
Loans on real estate, . .	$155,154 57	Dues capital, . . .	$144,513 64
Loans on shares, . . .	13,908 06	Profits capital (all series), .	25,156 82
Permanent expense account,	70 00	Interest, ...	610 43
Temporary expense account,	13 75	Fines, ...	55 29
Cash in hands of treasurer, .	11,245 45	Salary account, . . .	50 00
		Guaranty fund, . . .	1,375 71
		Surplus, ...	55 77
		Forfeited share account, .	1,720 13
		Withdrawal share account, .	554 32
		Matured shares, . . .	6,299 72
	$180,391 83		$180,391 83

Detailed Statement of Receipts and Disbursements for the Year ending Oct. 31, 1894.

RECEIPTS.		DISBURSEMENTS.	
From dues capital, . .	$42,675 28	For real estate loans, . .	$14,167 93
interest, . . .	10,755 90	share loans, . . .	10,206 17
fines, ...	116 79	dues capital (withdrawn),	38,448 00
real estate loans repaid,	27,595 72	dues capital (forfeited),	910 00
share loans repaid, .	9,757 00	dues capital (matured),	11,232 00
withdrawal profits, .	177 12	profits capital (with-	
forfeiture profits, .	4 20	drawn), . . .	6,687 46
forfeited shares, . .	1,153 00	profits capital (forfeited),	247 20
salary account, . .	50 00	profits capital (matured),	4,700 28
matured share account,	15,932 28	temporary expenses, .	411 40
		withdrawal share account,	737 22
		matured share account,	9,632 56
Cash on hand Oct. 31, 1893, .	408 38	Cash on hand Oct. 31, 1894,	11,245 45
	$108,625 67		$108,625 67

Reconciliation of Share Account with Dues and Profits Capital.

DATE OF ISSUE.	Series.	Value per Share.	Shares in Force.	Total Value.		
Dec., 1882, .	2	$197 71	59	$11,664 89	Dues capital, as per gen-	
June, 1883, .	3	186 57	34	6,343 38	eral ledger, . .	$144,513 64
Dec., 1883, .	4	175 63	47	8,254 61	Profits capital, as per	
June, 1884, .	5	165 15	11	1,816 65	general ledger, . .	25,156 82
Dec., 1884, .	6	154 72	65	10,056 80	Unpaid dues, . .	3,405 36
June, 1885, .	7	144 88	29	4,201 52		
Dec., 1885, .	8	135 19	35	4,731 65		
June, 1886, .	9	125 72	9	1,131 48		
Dec., 1886, .	10	116 46	122	14,208 12		
June, 1887, .	11	107 58	41	4,410 78		
Dec., 1887, .	12	98 92	119	11,771 48		
June, 1888, .	13	90 42	63	5,696 46		
Dec., 1888, .	14	82 18	196	16,107 28		
June, 1889, .	15	74 16	98	7,267 68		
Dec., 1889, .	16	66 37	85	5,641 45		
June, 1890, .	17	58 71	76	4,461 96		
Dec., 1890, .	18	51 32	191	9,802 12		
June, 1891, .	19	44 18	233	10,293 94		
Dec., 1891, .	20	37 19	342	12,718 98		
June, 1892, .	21	30 37	230	6,985 10		
Dec , 1892, .	22	23 80	295	7,021 00		
June, 1893, .	23	17 36	241	4,183 76		
Dec., 1893, .	24	11 09	297	3,293 73		
June, 1894, .	25	5 00	201	1,005 00		
Dues paid in advance, . . .				6 00		
Total, ...				$173,075 82	Total, . . .	$173,075 82

Number of shares issued during the year, ... 553
Number of shares now in force, ... 3,119
Number of shares now borrowed upon, ... 1,403
Largest number of shares held by any one member, ... 25
Number of shares withdrawn during the year, ... 961
Number of shares forfeited during the year, ... 10
Number of shares matured during the year, ... 78
Highest per centum of interest received during the year: 6.
Lowest per centum of interest received during the year: 6.
Number of members withdrawn during the year, ... 85
Present number of members, ... 452
Present number of borrowers, ... 214
Present number of non-borrowers, ... 238
Number of loans secured by first mortgage of real estate, . . . 136
Number of loans on shares, ... 103
Largest loan to any one member, ... $4,000 00
Smallest loan to any one member, ... 5 00
Amount of expenses of the corporation for the year ending Oct. 31, 1894, . 451 40
Date of examination by commissioner: October 22.

WEST NEWTON CO-OPERATIVE BANK — WEST NEWTON.

Incorporated June 16, 1892.   Commenced business June 22, 1892.

MARCUS MORTON, *President.*   ARTHUR CARROLL, *Secretary.*
ARTHUR CARROLL, *Treasurer.*

Names of security committee:
C. M. WHITTLESEY,   HENRY H. HUNT,
HERBERT S. WARE.

Regular meetings the fourth Wednesday of each month.

BALANCE SHEET OCTOBER 31, 1894.

ASSETS.		LIABILITIES.	
Loans on real estate,	$13,500 00	Dues capital,	$14,708 00
Loans on shares,	1,160 00	Profits capital (all series),	572 58
Expense account,	107 00	Interest,	349 76
Unpaid interest,	19 00	Premiums,	37 35
Unpaid premiums,	2 20	Fines,	24 99
Unpaid fines,	8 30	Withdrawal profits,	15 06
Cash in hands of treasurer,	1,040 12	Guaranty fund,	13 65
		Surplus,	36 57
		Forfeited share account,	78 66
	$15,836 62		$15,836 62

Detailed Statement of Receipts and Disbursements for the Year ending Oct. 31, 1894.

RECEIPTS.		DISBURSEMENTS.	
From dues capital,	$9,040 00	For real estate loans,	$9,400 00
interest,	726 53	share loans,	1,370 00
premiums,	75 55	dues capital (withdrawn),	1,931 00
fines,	57 89	dues capital (forfeited),	161 00
transfer fees,	25	profits capital (withdrawn),	75 24
real estate loans repaid,	2,000 00	profits capital (forfeited),	24 40
share loans repaid,	360 00	temporary expenses,	37 75
withdrawal profits,	19 27	forfeited shares,	77 48
forfeiture profits,	20 38		
forfeited shares,	156 14		
Cash on hand Oct. 31, 1893,	1,660 98	Cash on hand Oct. 31, 1894,	1,040 12
	$14,116 99		$14,116 99

Reconciliation of Share Account with Dues and Profits Capital.

DATE OF ISSUE.	Series.	Value per Share.	Shares in Force.	Total Value.		
June, 1892, .	1	$30 54	255	$7,787 70	Dues capital, as per general ledger, . .	$14,708 00
Dec., 1892, .	2	23 87	149	3,556 63	Profits capital, as per	
June, 1893, .	3	17 39	85	1,478 15	general ledger, . .	572 58
Dec., 1893, .	4	11 10	171	1,898 10	Unpaid dues, . . .	220 00
June, 1894, .	5	5 00	145	725 00		
Dues paid in advance, . . .				55 00		
Total, ...				$15,500 58	Total, . . .	$15,500 58

Number of shares issued during the year, ... 352
Number of shares now in force, ... 805
Number of shares now borrowed upon, ... 142
Largest number of shares held by any one member, . . . 25
Number of shares withdrawn during the year, ... 145
Number of shares forfeited during the year, ... 29
Highest premium received during the year, ... $0 15
Lowest premium received during the year, ... 05
Number of members withdrawn during the year, ... 27
Present number of members, ... 114
Present number of borrowers, ... 15
Present number of non-borrowers, ... 99
Number of loans secured by first mortgage of real estate, . . . 11
Number of loans on shares, ... 4
Largest loan to any one member, ... 1,750 00
Smallest loan to any one member, ... 50 00
Amount of expenses of the corporation for the year ending Oct. 31, 1894, . 100 00
Date of examination by commissioner: May 28.

WEST ROXBURY CO-OPERATIVE BANK—BOSTON.

Incorporated Feb. 1, 1881. Commenced business March 3, 1881.

JOHN PEARCE, *President.*   BENJ. H. JONES, *Secretary*
                    EDWARD M. BREWER, *Treasurer.*

Names of security committee:

EDW. M. BREWER,   HENRY A. WOOD,
                    R. S. BARROWS.

Regular meetings the first Thursday of each month.

BALANCE SHEET OCTOBER 31, 1894.

ASSETS.		LIABILITIES.	
Loans on real estate, . .	$194,350 00	Dues capital, . . .	$208,473 00
Loans on shares, . . .	27,750 00	Profits capital (all series), .	40,447 88
Unpaid interest, . . .	342 59	Guaranty fund, . . .	1,523 20
Unpaid fines, ...	48 24	Surplus, ...	1,437 24
Bonds of city of Cleveland,		Forfeited share account, .	39 82
Ohio, 7 per cent., . .	1,000 00		
Bonds of city of Malden,			
Mass , 4 per cent., . .	1,600 00		
Bonds of city of Pittsfield,			
Mass., 4½ per cent , . .	5,000 00		
Bonds of town of Everett,			
Mass., 4 per cent., . .	3,800 00		
Accrued interest on same, .	200 75		
Rent account, . . .	85 00		
Cash in hands of treasurer, .	17,744 56		
	$251,921 14		$251,921 14

Detailed Statement of Receipts and Disbursements for the Year ending Oct. 31, 1894.

RECEIPTS.		DISBURSEMENTS.	
From dues capital, . .	$58,552 00	For real estate loans, . .	$49,300 00
interest, . . .	13,324 49	share loans, . . .	19,900 00
premiums, . .	49 20	dues capital (withdrawn),	18,800 00
fines, ...	316 41	dues capital (retired), .	6,562 00
transfer fees, . .	6 75	dues capital (matured),	4,480 00
real estate loans repaid,	23,450 00	profits capital (with-	
share loans repaid, .	19,450 00	drawn), . . .	2,466 42
withdrawal profits, .	616 68	profits capital (retired),	1,377 36
city and town bonds, .	15,000 00	profits capital (matured),	2,034 76
		temporary expenses, .	1,039 88
		rent, ...	35 00
		city and town bonds, .	11,600 75
Cash on hand Oct. 31, 1893, .	4,575 20	Cash on hand Oct. 31, 1894,	17,744 56
	$135,340 73		$135,340 73

Reconciliation of Share Account with Dues and Profits Capital.

DATE OF ISSUE.	Series.	Value per Share.	Shares in Force.	Total Value.		
Mar., 1883, .	5	$203 66	82	$16,700 12	Dues capital, as per general ledger, . . .	$208,473 00
Nov., 1883, .	6	188 04	47	8,837 88	Profits capital, as per general ledger, . .	
May, 1884, .	7	176 44	3	529 32		
Nov., 1884, .	8	165 12	15	2,476 80	general ledger, . .	40,447 88
May, 1885, .	9	154 20	25	3,855 00	Unpaid dues, . .	946 00
Nov., 1885, .	10	143 64	110	15,800 40		
May, 1886, .	11	133 40	17	2,267 80		
Nov., 1886, .	12	123 48	107	13,212 36		
May, 1887, .	13	113 84	92	10,473 28		
Nov., 1887, .	14	104 52	90	9,406 80		
May, 1888, .	15	95 44	188	17,942 72		
Nov., 1888, .	16	86 68	157	13,609 76		
May, 1889, .	17	78 20	200	15,640 00		
Nov., 1889, .	18	70 00	216	15,120 00		
May, 1890, .	19	62 04	331	20,535 24		
Nov., 1890, .	20	54 32	244	13,254 08		
May, 1891, .	21	46 80	300	14,040 00		
Nov., 1891, .	22	39 52	361	14,266 72		
May, 1892, .	23	32 44	377	12,229 88		
Nov., 1892, .	24	25 56	368	9,406 08		
May, 1893, .	25	18 88	523	9,874 24		
Nov., 1893, .	26	12 40	549	6,807 60		
May, 1894, .	27	6 10	548	3,342 80		
Dues paid in advance, . . .				239 00		
Total, ...				$249,866 88	Total, . . .	$249,866 88

Number of shares issued during the year, ... 1,179
Number of shares now in force, ... 4,950
Number of shares now borrowed upon, ... 1,784
Largest number of shares held by any one member, . . . 25
Number of shares withdrawn during the year, ... 714
Number of shares retired during the year, ... 92
Number of shares matured during the year, ... 32
Highest per centum of interest received during the year: 6.
Lowest per centum of interest received during the year: 6.
Number of members withdrawn during the year, ... 115
Present number of members, ... 571
Present number of borrowers, ... 161
Present number of non-borrowers, ... 410
Number of loans secured by first mortgage of real estate, . . 88
Number of loans on shares, ... 73
Largest loan to any one member, ... $5,000 00
Smallest loan to any one member, ... 50 00
Amount of expenses of the corporation for the year ending Oct. 31, 1894, . 1,039 88
Date of examination by commissioner: June 22.

WEST SOMERVILLE CO-OPERATIVE BANK — WEST SOMERVILLE.

Incorporated Nov. 29, 1890.   Commenced business Dec. 11, 1890.

J. WARREN BAILEY, *President.*   OLIVER H. PERRY, *Secretary.*
OLIVER H. PERRY, *Treasurer.*

Names of security committee:
L. E. MERRY,   C. L. STEVENS,
E. S. SPARROW.

Regular meetings the third Monday of each month.

BALANCE SHEET OCTOBER 31, 1894.

ASSETS.		LIABILITIES.	
Loans on real estate, . .	$85,650 00	Dues capital, . . .	$88,054 00
Loans on shares, . . .	7,193 00	Profits capital (all series), .	8,370 91
Permanent expense account, .	295 78	Interest, ...	451 41
Unpaid interest, . . .	122 55	Premiums, . . .	39 35
Unpaid premiums, . .	13 30	Fines, ...	9 37
Unpaid fines, ...	49 50	Withdrawal profits, . .	1 20
Cash in hands of treasurer, .	3,819 11	Guaranty fund, . .	94 65
		Surplus, . . .	107 35
		Forfeited share account, .	15 00
	$97,143 24		$97,143 24

Detailed Statement of Receipts and Disbursements for the Year ending Oct. 31, 1894.

RECEIPTS.		DISBURSEMENTS.	
From dues capital, . .	$36,644 00	For real estate loans, . .	$36,777 70
interest, . . .	4,648 06	share loans, . .	7,133 00
premiums, . .	410 90	dues capital (withdrawn),	9,300 00
fines, ...	112 60	dues capital (forfeited),	15 00
transfer fees, . .	75	profits capital (with-	
real estate loans repaid,	12,700 00	drawn), . . .	575 06
share loans repaid, .	1,870 00	profits capital (forfeited),	45
withdrawal profits, .	97 08	temporary expenses, .	501 05
forfeited shares, . .	15 00	interest returned, . .	22 25
surplus (from profits),	72 42	profits (to surplus, for	
		errors), . .	72 42
Cash on hand Oct. 31, 1893, .	1,645 23	Cash on hand Oct. 31, 1894,	3,819 11
	$58,216 04		$58,216 04

Reconciliation of Share Account with Dues and Profits Capital.

DATE OF ISSUE.	Series.	Value per share.	Shares in Force.	Total Value.		
Dec., 1890, .	1	52 98	580	$30,728 40	Dues capital, as per general ledger, . .	$88,054 00
Apr., 1891, .	2	47 95	357	17,118 15	Profits capital, as per	
Oct., 1891, .	3	40 63	251	10,198 13	general ledger, . .	8,370 91
Apr , 1892, .	4	33 49	536	17,950 64	Unpaid dues, . .	812 00
Oct., 1892, .	5	26 57	268	7,120 76		
Apr., 1893, .	6	19 87	370	7,351 90		
Oct., 1893, .	7	13 39	277	3,709 03		
Apr., 1894, .	8	7 10	389	2,761 90		
Oct., 1894, .	9	1 00	222	222 00		
Dues paid in advance, . . .				76 00		
Total, ...				$97,236 91	Total, . . .	$97,236 91

Number of shares issued during the year, ... 760
Number of shares now in force, ... 3,250
Number of shares now borrowed upon, ... 755
Largest number of shares held by any one member, ... 25
Number of shares withdrawn during the year, ... 531
Number of shares forfeited during the year, ... 5
Highest per centum of interest received during the year: $7\frac{5}{10}$.
Lowest per centum of interest received during the year: $6\frac{3}{10}$.
Number of members withdrawn during the year, ... 62
Present number of members, ... 364
Present number of borrowers, ... 72
Present number of non-borrowers, ... 292
Number of loans secured by first mortgage of real estate, . . . 37
Number of loans on shares, ... 47
Largest loan to any one member, ... $5,000 00
Smallest loan to any one member, ... 12 00
Amount of expenses of the corporation for the year ending Oct. 31, 1894, . 501 05
Date of examination by commissioner: March 29.

WHITMAN CO-OPERATIVE BANK — WHITMAN.

Incorporated March 6, 1889.   Commenced business March 11, 1889.

AMOS S. STETSON, *President.*   GEO. D. SOULE, *Secretary.*

GEO. D. SQULE, *Treasurer.*

Names of security committee :

ARTHUR COLEMAN,   CHARLES D. NASH,

GEO. D. SOULE.

Regular meetings the second Monday of each month.

BALANCE SHEET OCTOBER 31, 1894.

ASSETS.		LIABILITIES.	
Loans on real estate, . .	$60,650 00	Dues capital, . . .	$54,549 00
Loans on shares, . . .	1,445 00	Profits capital (all series), .	7,092 72
Permanent expense account,	123 44	Interest, ...	493 18
Temporary expense account,	44 09	Premiums, ...	39 05
Cash in hands of treasurer, .	387 50	Fines, ...	4 28
		Withdrawal profits, . .	32 79
		Guaranty fund, . . .	107 21
		Surplus, ...	331 80
	$62,650 03		$62,650 03

Detailed Statement of Receipts and Disbursements for the Year ending Oct. 31, 1894.

RECEIPTS.		DISBURSEMENTS.	
From dues capital, . .	$19,321 00	For real estate loans, . .	$18,650 00
interest, . . .	3,366 18	share loans, . . .	1,345 00
premiums, . . .	324 30	dues capital (withdrawn), .	8,623 00
fines, ...	81 56	dues capital (retired), .	1,181 00
transfer fees, . .	25	profits capital (with-	
real estate loans repaid,	7,550 00	drawn), . . .	753 69
share loans repaid, .	600 00	profits capital (retired),	195 30
withdrawal profits, .	188 56	temporary expenses, .	252 93
		permanent expenses, .	88 44
		forfeited shares, . .	20 05
		interest on retired shares,	31 86
Cash on hand Oct. 31, 1893, .	96 92	Cash on hand Oct. 31, 1894,	387 50
	$31,528 77		$31,528 77

Reconciliation of Share Account with Dues and Profits Capital.

DATE OF ISSUE.	Series.	Value per Share.	Shares in Force.	Total Value.		
Mar., 1889, .	1	$81 25	151	$12,268 75	Dues capital, as per general ledger, . .	$54,549 00
Sept., 1889, .	2	72 86	93	6,775 98		
Mar., 1890, .	3	64 76	190	12,304 40	Profits capital, as per general ledger, . .	7,092 72
Sept., 1890, .	4	56 88	100	5,688 00		
Mar., 1891, .	5	49 22	140	6,890 80	Unpaid dues, . .	347 00
Sept., 1891, .	6	41 80	70	2,926 00		
Mar., 1892, .	7	34 59	101	3,493 59		
Sept., 1892, .	8	27 62	127	3,507 74		
Mar., 1893, .	9	20 89	246	5,138 94		
Sept., 1893, .	10	14 39	68	978 52		
Mar., 1894, .	11	8 10	200	1,620 00		
Sept., 1894, .	12	2 00	148	296 00		
Dues paid in advance, . . .				100 00		
Total, ...				$61,988 72	Total, . . .	$61,988 72

Number of shares issued during the year, ... 401
Number of shares now in force, ... 1,634
Number of shares now borrowed upon, ... 379
Largest number of shares held by any one member, ... 25
Number of shares withdrawn during the year, ... 401
Number of shares retired during the year, ... 18
Highest premium received during the year, ... $0 55
Lowest premium received during the year, ... 05
Number of members withdrawn during the year, ... 79
Present number of members, ... 259
Present number of borrowers, ... 63
Present number of non-borrowers, ... 196
Number of loans secured by first mortgage of real estate, . . . 50
Number of loans on shares, ... 14
Largest loan to any one member, ... 4,400 00
Smallest loan to any one member, ... 25 00
Amount of expenses of the corporation for the year ending Oct. 31, 1894, . 292 93
Date of examination by commissioner: March 29.

WINCHENDON CO-OPERATIVE BANK — WINCHENDON.

Incorporated Sept. 9, 1891.　Commenced business Sept. 16, 1891.

FREDERICK W. RUSSELL, *President.*　　　WALDO C. COREY, *Secretary.*
SILAS A. GREENWOOD, *Treasurer.*

Names of security committee :
AMOS S. LAMB,　　　　　　　BENJ. M. WRIGHT,
JOHN SWEETSER.

Regular meetings the third Wednesday of each month.

BALANCE SHEET OCTOBER 31, 1894.

ASSETS.		LIABILITIES.	
Loans on real estate, . .	$24,750 00	Dues capital, . . .	$27,913 00
Loans on shares, . . .	2,403 00	Profits capital (all series), .	2,234 31
Permanent expense account,	105 00	Interest, ...	234 56
Temporary expense account,	4 50	Premiums, ...	12 80
Unpaid fines, ...	2 00	Transfer fees, . . .	50
Bonds of town of M i d d l e -		Withdrawal profits, . .	8 36
borough, Mass., 4 per cent ,	2,000 00	Guaranty fund, . . .	82 24
Cash in hands of treasurer, .	1,327 00	Surplus, ...	101 41
		Forfeited share account, .	4 32
	$30,591 50		$30,591 50

Detailed Statement of Receipts and Disbursements for the Year ending Oct. 31, 1894.

RECEIPTS.		DISBURSEMENTS.	
From dues capital, . .	$11,287 00	For real estate loans, . .	$12,750 00
interest, . . .	1,537 85	share loans, . . .	2,075 00
premiums, . . .	79 50	dues capital (withdrawn),	2,883 00
fines, ...	50 15	dues capital (forfeited),	22 00
transfer fees, . .	1 00	profits capital (with-	
real estate loans repaid,	3,300 00	drawn), . . .	186 67
share loans repaid, .	695 00	profits capital (forfeited),	1 51
withdrawal profits, .	20 84	temporary expenses, .	106 73
forfeiture profits, .	1 44	forfeited shares, . .	107 14
forfeited shares, . .	22 34	town and city bonds, .	3,048 21
city and town bonds, .	5,000 00		
Cash on hand Oct. 31, 1893, .	512 14	Cash on hand Oct. 31, 1894,	1,327 00
	$22,507 26		$22,507 26

Reconciliation of Share Account with Dues and Profits Capital.

DATE OF ISSUE.	Series.	Value per Share.	Shares in Force.	Total Value.		
Sept., 1891, .	1	$41 44	488	$20,222 72	Dues capital, as per general ledger, . .	$27,913 00
Mar., 1892, .	2	34 37	163	5,602 31		
Sept., 1892, .	3	27 51	62	1,705 62	Profits capital, as per general ledger, . .	2,234 31
Mar., 1893, .	4	20 85	54	1,125 90		
Sept., 1893, .	5	14 38	57	819 66	Unpaid dues, . . .	158 00
Mar., 1894, .	6	8 10	81	656 10		
Sept., 1894, .	7	2 00	77	154 00		
Dues paid in advance, . . .				19 00		
Total, ...				$30,305 31	Total, . . .	$30,305 31

Number of shares issued during the year, ... 194
Number of shares now in force, ... 982
Number of shares now borrowed upon, ... 239
Largest number of shares held by any one member, . . . 25
Number of shares withdrawn during the year, ... 137
Number of shares forfeited during the year, ... 1
Highest per centum of interest received during the year: 6.
Lowest per centum of interest received during the year: 3½.
Number of members withdrawn during the year, ... 37
Present number of members, ... 211
Present number of borrowers, ... 39
Present number of non-borrowers, ... 172
Number of loans secured by first mortgage of real estate, . . . 28
Number of loans on shares, ... 15
Largest loan to any one member, ... $3,400 00
Smallest loan to any one member, ... 25 00
Amount of expenses of the corporation for the year ending Oct. 31, 1894, . 121 73
Date of examination by commissioner: May 22.

WINCHESTER CO-OPERATIVE BANK — WINCHESTER.

Incorporated Nov. 13, 1893.   Commenced business Nov. 13, 1893.

L. C. PATTEE, *President.*   T. B. COTTER, *Secretary.*
T. B. COTTER, *Treasurer.*

Names of security committee :

N. T. APPOLONIO,   LEWIS PARKHURST,
F. J. O'HARA.

Regular meetings the first Monday of each month.

BALANCE SHEET OCTOBER 31, 1894.

ASSETS.		LIABILITIES.	
Loans on real estate, . .	$12,150 00	Dues capital, . . .	$13,414 00
Loans on shares, . . .	600 00	Profits capital (all series), .	393 38
Permanent expense account,	240 00	Guaranty fund, . . .	15 00
Unpaid interest, . . .	12 50	Surplus, ...	20 00
Unpaid premiums, . .	65	Profit and loss, . . .	5 97
Unpaid fines, ...	14 84		
Cash in hands of treasurer, .	830 36		
	$13,848 35		$13,848 35

Detailed Statement of Receipts and Disbursements for the Year ending Oct. 31, 1894.

RECEIPTS.		DISBURSEMENTS.	
From dues capital, . .	$14,200 00	For real estate loans, . .	$12,150 00
interest, . . .	420 50	share loans, . . .	700 00
premiums, . . .	38 50	dues capital (withdrawn),	786 00
fines, ...	45 65	profits capital (with-	
transfer fees, . .	2 25	drawn), . . .	11 10
share loans repaid, .	100 00	temporary expenses, .	46 16
withdrawal profits, .	4 47	permanent expenses, .	287 75
		Cash on hand Oct. 31, 1894,	830 36
	$14,811 37		$14,811 37

Reconciliation of Share Account with Dues and Profits Capital.

DATE OF ISSUE.	Series.	Value per Share.	Shares in Force.	Total Value.		
Nov., 1893, .	1	$12 38	916	$11,340 08	Dues capital, as per general ledger, . .	$13,414 00
May, 1894, .	2	6 10	453	2,763 30	Profits capital, as per general ledger, . .	393 38
Dues paid in advance, . . .				70 00	Unpaid dues, . .	. 366 00
Total, ...				$14,173 38	Total, . . .	$14,173 38

Number of shares issued during the year, ... 1,488
Number of shares now in force, ... 1,369
Number of shares now borrowed upon, ... 141
Largest number of shares held by any one member, ... 25
Number of shares withdrawn during the year, ... 119
Highest premium received during the year, ... $0 20
Lowest premium received during the year, ... 05
Number of members withdrawn during the year, ... 19
Present number of members, ... 209
Present number of borrowers, ... 14
Present number of non-borrowers, ... 195
Number of loans secured by first mortgage of real estate, . . . 7
Number of loans on shares, ... 7
Largest loan to any one member, ... 3,400 00
Smallest loan to any one member, ... 50 00
Amount of expenses of the corporation for the year ending Oct. 31, 1894, . 93 91
Date of examination by commissioner : November 26.

WOBURN CO-OPERATIVE BANK — WOBURN.

Incorporated Feb. 21, 1887.   Commenced business March 10, 1887.

JAMES SKINNER, *President.*   A. W. WHITCHER, *Secretary.*
A. W. WHITCHER, *Treasurer.*

Names of security committee:

GEORGE BUCHANAN,   THOMAS SALMON,
S. B. GODDARD,   LAWRENCE READE,
J. W. HAMMOND.

Regular meetings the second Thursday of each month.

BALANCE SHEET OCTOBER 31, 1894.

ASSETS.		LIABILITIES.	
Loans on real estate, . .	$137,850 00	Dues capital, . . .	$122,922 00
Loans on shares, . . .	6,881 68	Profits capital (all series), .	21,521 84
Real estate by foreclosure, .	1,500 00	Interest, ...	528 51
Unpaid interest, . . .	414 25	Premiums, ...	39 25
Unpaid premiums, . .	29 75	Fines, ...	3 44
Unpaid fines, ...	46 57	Withdrawal profits, . .	53 89
Cash in hands of treasurer, .	670 36	Forfeiture profits, . .	3 36
		Guaranty fund, . . .	688 38
		Surplus, ...	1,721 88
		Forfeited share account, .	10 06
	$147,392 61		$147,392 61

Detailed Statement of Receipts and Disbursements for the Year ending Oct. 31, 1894.

RECEIPTS.		DISBURSEMENTS.	
From dues capital, . .	$36,217 00	For real estate loans, . .	$34,750 00
interest, . . .	8,441 21	share loans, . . .	4,180 00
premiums, . . .	603 10	dues capital (withdrawn),	15,536 00
fines, ...	460 57	dues capital (forfeited),	104 00
transfer fees, . .	3 75	dues capital (retired), .	5,903 00
real estate loans repaid,	13,750 00	profits capital (withdrawn), . .	2,215 30
share loans repaid, .	3,302 22	profits capital (forfeited),	13 36
withdrawal profits, .	535 68	profits capital (retired),	1,313 21
forfeiture profits, . .	3 36	temporary expenses, .	600 43
forfeited shares, . .	114 00	forfeited shares, . .	140 55
		real estate by foreclosure,	1,500 00
Cash on hand Oct. 31, 1893, .	3,495 32	Cash on hand Oct. 31, 1894,	670 36
	$66,926 21		$66,926 21

Reconciliation of Share Account with Dues and Profits Capital.

DATE OF ISSUE.	Series.	Value per Share.	Shares in Force.	Total Value.		
Mar., 1887, .	1	$117 85	205	$24,159 25	Dues capital, as per general ledger, . .	$122,822 00
Oct., 1887, .	2	106 85	139	14,852 15	eral ledger, . .	
April, 1888, .	3	97 70	116	11,333 20	Profits capital, as per	
Oct., 1888, .	4	88 87	78	6,931 86	general ledger, . .	21,521 84
April, 1889, .	5	80 21	168	13,475 28	Unpaid dues, . . .	1,064 00
Oct , 1889, .	6	71 87	216	15,523 92		
April, 1890, .	7	63 75	129	8,223 75		
Oct., 1890, .	8	55 91	82	4,584 62		
April, 1891, .	9	48 24	276	13,314 24		
Oct., 1891, .	10	40 84	161	6,575 24		
April, 1892, .	11	33 65	290	9,758 50		
Oct., 1892, .	12	26 69	190	5,071 10		
April, 1893, .	13	19 97	222	4,433 34		
Oct., 1893, .	14	13 43	189	2,538 27		
April, 1894, .	15	7 11	592	4,209 12		
Oct., 1894, .	16	1 00	288	288 00		
Dues paid in advance, . .				136 00		
Total, ...				$145,407 84	Total, . . .	$145,407 84

Number of shares issued during the year, ... 951
Number of shares now in force, ... 3,341
Number of shares now borrowed upon, ... 922
Largest number of shares held by any one member, ... 25
Number of shares withdrawn during the year, ... 408
Number of shares forfeited during the year, ... 8
Number of shares retired during the year, ... 83
Highest premium received during the year, ... $0 25
Lowest premium received during the year, ... 05
Number of members withdrawn during the year, ... 49
Present number of members, ... 479
Present number of borrowers, ... 127
Present number of non-borrowers, ... 352
Number of loans secured by first mortgage of real estate, . . . 134
Number of loans on shares, ... 20
Largest loan to any one member, ... 3,500 00
Smallest loan to any one member, ... 25 00
Amount of expenses of the corporation for the year ending Oct. 31, 1894, . 600 43
Date of examination by commissioner : June 7.

WOLLASTON CO-OPERATIVE BANK — WOLLASTON.

Incorporated April 8, 1889.   Commenced business April 16, 1889.

WENDELL G. CORTHELL, *President.*   HERBERT W. PINKHAM, *Secretary.*
HERBERT W. PINKHAM, *Treasurer.*

Names of security committee :

QUINCY A. FAUNCE,   ALBERT G. OLNEY,
WILLIAM FENTON.

Regular meetings the third Tuesday of each month.

BALANCE SHEET OCTOBER 31, 1894.

ASSETS.		LIABILITIES.	
Loans on real estate, . .	$89,000 00	Dues capital, . . .	$87,768 00
Loans on shares, . . .	6,260 00	Profits capital (all series), .	11,759 94
Permanent expense account,.	60 00	Interest, ...	267 42
Unpaid fines, ...	22 22	Premiums, ...	21 45
Cash in hands of treasurer, .	5,084 32	Transfer fees, . . .	50
		Withdrawal profits, . .	26 27
		Guaranty fund, . . .	360 00
		Surplus, ...	222 96
	$100,426 54		$100,426 54

Detailed Statement of Receipts and Disbursements for the Year ending Oct. 31, 1894.

RECEIPTS.		DISBURSEMENTS.	
From dues capital, . .	$32,343 00	For real estate loans, . .	$34,850 00
interest, . . .	5,746 60	share loans, . . .	9,030 00
premiums, . . .	633 35	dues capital(withdrawn),	12,536 00
fines, ...	227 18	dues capital (retired), .	10,841 00
transfer fees, . .	3 00	profits capital (with-	
real estate loans repaid,	23,550 00	drawn), . . .	1,037 70
share loans repaid, .	11,495 00	profits capital (retired), .	1,976 30
withdrawal profits, .	258 61	temporary expenses, .	695 76
Cash on hand Oct. 31, 1893, .	1,809 86	interest on retired shares,	15 52
		Cash on hand Oct. 31, 1894,	5,084 32
	$76,066 60		$76,066 60

Reconciliation of Share Account with Dues and Profits Capital.

DATE OF ISSUE.	Series.	Value per Share.	Shares in Force.	Total Value.		
Apr., 1889, .	1	$80 22	339	$27,194 58	Dues capital, as per general ledger, . .	$87,768 00
Oct., 1889, .	2	71 83	167	11,995 61		
Apr., 1890, .	3	63 69	189	12,037 41	Profits capital, as per general ledger, . .	11,759 94
Oct., 1890, .	4	55 81	170	9,487 70		
Apr., 1891, .	5	48 15	157	7,559 55	Unpaid dues, . .	733 00
Oct., 1891, .	6	40 75	118	4,808 50		
Apr., 1892, .	7	33 58	220	7,387 60		
Oct., 1892, .	8	26 65	314	8,368 10		
Apr., 1893, .	9	19 91	229	4,559 39		
Oct., 1893, .	10	13 40	167	2,237 80		
Apr., 1894, .	11	7 10	577	4,096 70		
Oct., 1894, .	12	1 00	409	409 00		
Dues paid in advance, . . .				119 00		
Total, ...				$100,260 94	Total, . . .	$100,260 94

Number of shares issued during the year, ...	1,058
Number of shares now in force, ...	3,056
Number of shares now borrowed upon, ...	685
Largest number of shares held by any one member, ...	25
Number of shares withdrawn during the year, ...	625
Number of shares retired during the year, ...	180
Highest premium received during the year, ...	$0 30
Lowest premium received during the year, ...	05
Number of members withdrawn during the year, ...	87
Present number of members, ...	371
Present number of borrowers, ...	77
Present number of non-borrowers, ...	294
Number of loans secured by first mortgage of real estate, . . .	68
Number of loans on shares, ...	46
Largest loan to any one member, ...	4,000 00
Smallest loan to any one member, ...	10 00
Amount of expenses of the corporation for the year ending Oct. 31, 1894, .	715 76

Date of examination by commissioner : June 15.

WORCESTER CO-OPERATIVE BANK — WORCESTER.

Incorporated Oct. 19, 1877.   Commenced business Oct. 19, 1877.

STEPHEN C. EARLE, *President.*   T. J. HASTINGS, *Secretary.*
T. J. HASTINGS, *Treasurer.*

Names of security committee:
HENRY BRANNON,   H. H. BIGELOW,
M. S. BEAMAN.

Regular meetings the third Monday of each month.

BALANCE SHEET OCTOBER 31, 1894.

ASSETS.		LIABILITIES.	
Loans on real estate, . .	$431,240 00	Dues capital, . .	$390,192 00
Loans on shares, . . .	13,500 00	Profits capital (all series), .	73,298 33
Temporary expense account,	474 74	Fines, ...	88 62
Real estate by foreclosure, .	25,176 58	Transfer fees, . . .	1 00
Unpaid interest, . . .	227 44	Guaranty fund, . . .	2,850 00
Cash in hands of treasurer, .	3,448 14	Surplus, ...	7,469 29
		Forfeited share account, .	96 53
		Rent account, . . .	71 13
	$474,066 90		$474,066 90

Detailed Statement of Receipts and Disbursements for the Year ending Oct. 31, 1894.

RECEIPTS.		DISBURSEMENTS.	
From dues capital, . .	$114,415 00	For real estate loans, . .	$105,500 00
interest, . . .	29,289 85	share loans, . . .	7,740 00
fines, ...	1,101 64	dues capital (withdrawn),	68,529 00
transfer fees, . .	18 50	dues capital (forfeited),	375 00
real estate loans repaid,	113,010 00	dues capital (retired), .	43,201 00
share loans repaid, .	12,975 00	dues capital (matured),	11,033 00
withdrawal profits, .	935 99	profits capital (with-	
forfeiture profits, . .	6 55	drawn), . . .	11,446 67
forfeited shares, . .	231 26	profits capital (forfeited),	76 35
expense, . . .	178 25	profits capital (retired),	13,034 31
rents, ...	654 45	profits capital (matured),	5,197 60
real estate by fore-		temporary expenses, .	2,177 15
closure, . . .	1,200 00	forfeited shares, . .	396 66
		real estate by fore-	
		closure, . . .	5,162 88
		profit and loss, . .	110 00
Cash on hand Oct. 31, 1893, .	3,411 27	Cash on hand Oct. 31, 1894,	3,448 14
	$277,427 76		$277,427 76

Reconciliation of Share Account with Dues and Profits Capital.

DATE OF ISSUE.	Series.	Value per Share.	Shares in Force.	Total Value.		
Oct., 1883, .	7	$191 28	72	$13,772 16	Dues capital, as per general ledger, . . .	$390,192 00
April, 1884, .	8	179 30	75	13,447 50		
Oct., 1884, .	9	167 72	87	14,591 64	Profits capital, as per general ledger, . .	73,298 33
April, 1885, .	10	156 55	103	16,124 65		
Oct., 1885, .	11	145 74	115	16,760 10	Unpaid dues, . .	3,306 00
April, 1886, .	12	135 27	120	16,232 40		
Oct., 1886, .	13	125 17	118	14,770 06		
April, 1887, .	14	115 35	215	24,800 25		
Oct., 1887, .	15	105 90	223	23,615 70		
April, 1888, .	16	96 73	223	21,570 79		
Oct., 1888, .	17	87 87	352	30,930 24		
April, 1889, .	18	79 28	451	35,755 28		
Oct., 1889, .	19	71 02	400	28,408 00		
April, 1890, .	20	63 04	595	37,508 80		
Oct., 1890, .	21	55 30	474	26,212 20		
April, 1891, .	22	47 79	535	25,567 65		
Oct., 1891, .	23	40 50	714	28,917 00		
April, 1892, .	24	33 42	687	22,959 54		
Oct., 1892, .	25	26 55	752	19,965 60		
April, 1893, .	26	19 88	773	15,367 24		
Oct., 1893, .	27	13 40	800	10,720 00		
April, 1894, .	28	7 11	1,123	7,984 53		
Oct., 1894, .	29	1 00	514	514 00		
Dues paid in advance, . . .				301 00		
Total, ...				**$466,796 33**	**Total, . . .**	**$466,796 33**

Number of shares issued during the year, ...	2,117
Number of shares now in force, ...	9,521
Number of shares now borrowed upon, ...	2,615
Largest number of shares held by any one member, . . .	25
Number of shares withdrawn during the year, . . .	2,005
Number of shares forfeited during the year, ...	14
Number of shares retired during the year, ...	442
Number of shares matured during the year, ...	80
Highest per centum of interest received during the year: 8⅖.	
Lowest per centum of interest received during the year: 6.	
Number of members withdrawn during the year, ...	269
Present number of members, ...	1,080
Present number of borrowers, ...	246
Present number of non-borrowers, ...	834
Number of loans secured by first mortgage of real estate, . .	269
Number of loans on shares, ...	83
Largest loan to any one member, ...	$5,000 00
Smallest loan to any one member, ...	50 00
Amount of expenses of the corporation for the year ending Oct. 31, 1894, .	1,998 90
Date of examination by commissioner: May 7.	

WORKINGMEN'S CO-OPERATIVE BANK — BOSTON.

Incorporated June 9, 1880.   Commenced business June 11, 1880.

ROBERT TREAT PAINE, *President.*   FRANK E. BURBANK, *Secretary.*
FRANCIS B. SEARS, *Treasurer.*

Names of security committee:

GEORGE W. POPE,   JAMES D. MCLELLAN,
HENRY A. ROOT.

Regular meetings the second Friday of each month.

BALANCE SHEET OCTOBER 31, 1894.

ASSETS.		LIABILITIES.	
Loans on real estate, . .	$558,600 00	Dues capital, . . .	$522,799 00
Loans on shares, . . .	17,200 00	Profits capital (all series), .	92,974 96
Temporary expense account,	481 61	Interest, ...	2,154 63
Real estate by foreclosure, .	11,794 13	Premiums, ...	67 55
Real estate sold and awaiting		Fines, ...	38 12
completion of papers, .	20,247 40	Transfer fees, . . .	50
Cash in hands of secretary, .	677 28	Withdrawal profits, . .	276 88
Cash in hands of treasurer, .	17,294 12	Rent, ...	29 20
		Guaranty fund, . . .	3,728 00
		Surplus, ...	3,957 57
		Forfeited share account, .	132 89
		Security committee, .	105 00
		Personal accounts, . .	30 24
	$626,294 54		$626,294 54

*Detailed Statement of Receipts and Disbursements for the Year ending
Oct. 31, 1894.*

RECEIPTS.		DISBURSEMENTS.	
From dues capital, . .	$179,354 00	For real estate loans, .	$191,925 00
interest, . . .	35,464 88	share loans, . . .	15,550 00
premiums, . . .	2,252 67	dues capital (withdrawn),	86,301 00
fines, . . .	2,001 83	dues capital (forfeited),	2,904 00
transfer fees, . .	7 25	dues capital (retired), .	44,490 00
real estate loans repaid,	164,875 00	dues capital (matured),	6,419 00
share loans repaid, .	10,500 00	profits capital (with-	
withdrawal profits, .	2,532 81	drawn), . . .	10,783 21
forfeiture profits, .	35 04	profits capital (forfeited),	430 79
forfeited shares, .	164 65	profits capital (retired),	13,242 80
real estate, . . .	15,696 57	profits capital (matured),	3,133 14
retired shares, . .	58,230 06	temporary expenses, .	3,121 32
insurance, . . .	3,669 50	matured shares, . .	2,831 92
rent, ...	267 72	forfeited shares, . .	421 18
matured shares, . .	2,831 92	interest, ...	580 48
security committee, .	17 50	fines, ...	14 48
cash over, . . .	8 74	real estate, . . .	31.590 13
real estate loss, . .	642 30	surplus, . . .	642 30
profits, ...	1 00	rent, ...	46 85
		cash short, . . .	6 00
		retired shares, . .	58,230 06
		insurance, taxes, etc., .	4,159 65
		security committee, .	300 00
		withdrawal profits, .	5 00
Cash on hand Oct. 31, 1893, .	16,546 27	Cash on hand Oct. 31, 1894,	17,971 40
	$495,099 71		$495,099 71

Reconciliation of Share Account with Dues and Profits Capital.

Date of Issue.	Series.	Value per Share.	Shares in Force.	Total Value.		
Dec., 1883, .	8	$191 62	15	$2,889 30	Dues capital, as per general ledger, . .	$522,799 00
June, 1884, .	9	180 31	23	4,147 13	Profits capital, as per	
Dec., 1884, .	10	168 40	93	15,661 20	general ledger, . .	92,974 96
June, 1885, .	11	156 89	106	16,630 34	Unpaid dues, . .	6,636 00
Dec., 1885, .	12	145 77	161	23,468 97		
June, 1886, .	13	135 04	221	29,843 84		
Dec., 1886, .	14	124 63	175	21,810 25		
June, 1887, .	15	114 62	167	19,141 54		
Dec., 1887, .	16	104 93	253	26,547 29		
June, 1888, .	17	95 56	393	37,555 08		
Dec., 1888, .	18	86 53	607	52,523 71		
June, 1889, .	19	77 76	513	39,890 88		
Dec., 1889, .	20	69 32	659	45,681 88		
June, 1890, .	21	61 19	602	36,836 38		
Dec., 1890, .	22	53 28	750	39,960 00		
June, 1891, .	23	45 68	763	34,853 84		
Dec., 1891, .	24	38 32	1,000	38,320 00		
June, 1892, .	25	31 20	885	27,612 00		
Sept., 1892, .	26	27 74	528	14,646 72		
Dec., 1892, .	27	24 32	918	22,325 76		
Mar., 1893, .	28	20 96	981	20,561 76		
June, 1893, .	29	17 66	817	14,428 22		
Sept., 1893, .	30	14 42	575	8,291 50		
Dec., 1893, .	31	11 24	812	9,126 88		
Mar., 1894, .	32	8 11	1,056	8,564 16		
June, 1894, .	33	5 03	1,511	7,600 33		
Sept., 1894, .	34	2 00	1,074	2,148 00		
Dues paid in advance, . . .				1,343 00		
Total, ...				$622,409 96	Total, . . .	$622,409 96

Number of shares issued during the year, ...	5,226
Number of shares now in force, ...	15,658
Number of shares now borrowed upon, ...	3,497
Largest number of shares held by any one member, ...	25
Number of shares withdrawn during the year, ...	3,951
Number of shares forfeited during the year, ...	198
Number of shares retired during the year, ...	527
Number of shares matured during the year, ...	48

Highest per centum of interest received during the year: 6½.
Lowest per centum of interest received during the year: 6.

Number of members withdrawn during the year, ...	461
Present number of members, ...	1,822
Present number of borrowers, ...	352
Present number of non-borrowers, ...	1,470
Number of loans secured by first mortgage of real estate, . .	346
Number of loans on shares, ...	76
Largest loan to any one member, ...	$5,000 00
Smallest loan to any one member, ...	50 00
Amount of expenses of the corporation for the year ending Oct. 31, 1894, .	3,121 32

Date of examination by commissioner: March 27.

CONSOLIDATED BALANCE SHEET,

OCTOBER 31, 1894.

ASSETS.		LIABILITIES.	
Loans on real estate, . .	$16,590,389 14	Dues capital, . .	$15,644,529 69
Loans on shares, . . .	784,731 74	Profits capital (all series), . . .	2,535,982 66
Permanent expense account,	12,188 33	Interest, . . .	122,194 48
Temporary expense account,	10,169 86	Premiums, . . .	7,518 89
Real estate by foreclosure, .	139,136 92	Fines, ...	4,678 58
Unpaid dues, . . .	21,055 12	Transfer fees, . .	43 50
Unpaid interest, . . .	73,395 26	Surplus, . . .	111,507 58
Unpaid premiums, . .	5,488 76	Guaranty fund, . .	88,128 90
Unpaid fines, . . .	7,499 24	Forfeited share account,	13,856 13
Notes and bonds of cities and towns, . . .	62,391 06	Withdrawal profits, .	6,452 68
Mortgages, ...	43,649 59	Forfeiture profits, .	163 39
Furniture and fixtures, .	1,000 00	Advance payments, .	3,928 92
Sundry assets, . . .	4,309 51	Matured share account,	35,817 71
Cash, ...	829,266 60	Retired share account,	3,572 87
		Due on mortgage loans,	3,956 25
		Sundry liabilities, .	2,338 90
	$18,584,671 13		$18,584,671 13

Number of shares issued during the year, ...	117,210
Number of shares now in force, ...	434,433
Number of shares now borrowed upon, ...	113,273
Number of shares withdrawn during the year, ...	94,243
Number of shares forfeited during the year, ...	1,952
Number of shares retired during the year, ...	12,213
Number of shares matured during the year, ...	1,869
Number of members withdrawn during the year, . . .	12,441
Present number of members, ...	57,369
Present number of borrowers, ...	14,144
Present number of non-borrowers, ...	43,225
Number of loans secured by first mortgage of real estate, . .	12,334
Number of loans on shares, ...	4,150
Amount of expenses of the corporation for the year ending Oct. 31, 1894,	$93,881 01
Amount of profits credited to shares during the year, . . .	1,044,594 21

STATEMENTS

OF

COLLATERAL LOAN AND MORTGAGE LOAN

AND

INVESTMENT COMPANIES.

COLLATERAL LOAN COMPANY — BOSTON.

Incorporated April 5, 1859.

FRANCIS D. COBB, *President.*   LUTHER S. MOORE, *Cashier.*

Directors:

FRANCIS D. COBB,   LAWRENCE TUCKER,
JOHN P. LYMAN,   JOHN O. SHAW, Jr.,
LUTHER S. MOORE.
LAWRENCE TUCKER, *Acting Director for State.*
ROBERT F. CLARK, *Director for the City of Boston.*

BALANCE SHEET OCTOBER 31, 1894.

ASSETS.		LIABILITIES.	
Loans outstanding,	$249,780 71	Capital stock,	$150,000 00
Cash on hand,	2,865 31	Reserve fund,	75,000 00
Expense,	13,056 51	Notes payable,	5,000 00
General interest,	940 03	Auction reserve,	644 99
State tax,	2,664 00	Interest,	39,763 45
Rent,	4,888 87	Profit and loss,	2,786 99
Insurance fund investment, City of Boston, Mass., and State of Massachusetts bonds,	10,000 00	Insurance fund,	11,000 00
	$284,195 43		$284,195 43

Date of examination: December, 1894.

WORKINGMEN'S LOAN ASSOCIATION — BOSTON.

Incorporated 1888.

ROBERT TREAT PAINE, *President.*   FRANCIS B. SEARS, *Vice-President.*
ROBERT TREAT PAINE, 2d, *Treasurer.*   ARTHUR LYMAN, *Clerk.*

Directors:

EDMUND BILLINGS,	ARTHUR S. JOHNSON,	ROBERT TREAT PAINE, Jr.,
HERBERT LYMAN,	JOSEPH LEE,	ROBERT TREAT PAINE, 2d,
HENRY B. CABOT,	ARTHUR LYMAN,	FRANCIS B. SEARS,
WM. ENDICOTT, 3d,	JOHN F. MOORS,	SAMUEL CARR, Jr.
CHAS. W. HUBBARD,	CHAS. C. JACKSON,	
CHAS. L. YOUNG,	ROBERT TREAT PAINE,	

BALANCE SHEET OCTOBER 31, 1894.

ASSETS.		LIABILITIES.	
Loans, ...	$121,896 16	Capital stock, . . .	$90,400 00
Cash on hand, . . .	1,674 99	Notes payable, . . .	25,000 00
Expenses, ...	655 18	Profit and loss, . . .	350 33
		Unclaimed balance, . .	73 55
		State tax, ...	602 06
		Interest, ...	1,252 40
		Undivided profits, . .	3,696 96
		Risk fund, ...	1,089 75
		Bad debt fund, . . .	1,761 28
	$124,226 33		$124,226 33

Date of examination: August 1.

GLOBE INVESTMENT COMPANY — BOSTON.

Allison Z. Mason, *President.*   J. Lowell Moore, *Treasurer.*

BALANCE SHEET OCTOBER 31, 1894.

Assets.		Liabilities.	
Loans secured by first liens on real estate,	$445,702 99	Capital stock paid in,	$362,500 00
Loans secured by second liens on real estate,	85,808 22	Guaranty fund,	24,764 71
Tax sale certificates,	27,337 13	Undivided profits,	42,490 85
Stocks and bonds,	33,026 25	Bills payable,	28,900 00
Real estate acquired by foreclosure,	159,951 32	Debenture bonds outstanding,	416,941 36
Expenses on account of foreclosure,	19,262 41	Interest paid in advance by borrowers,	1,892 08
Furniture and fixtures,	3,974 10	Due on coupons not presented,	9,468 46
Current expenses,	35,543 81	Loans paid, but not remitted for,	7,197 50
Remittances for interest matured within 60 days,	17,699 15	Deposits awaiting investment,	81,054 05
Other past due interest remitted for, but not paid to us,	126,487 70	Due to banks and bankers,	113,874 52
Past due loans remitted for, but not paid to us,	36,224 00	Due to sundry persons,	5,432 71
Due from branch offices and agents,	21,091 23	Accrued interest on debentures, coupons of which are not yet due,	7,364 79
Due from sundry persons,	43,099 82		
Cash on hand and in banks,	9,808 04		
Notes secured by collateral,	723 06		
Chattel note account,	400 00		
Accrued interest,	35,741 80		
	$1,101,881 03		$1,101,181 03

Date of examination: November, 1894.

Description of Stocks and Bonds.

	Par Value.	Market Value.	Amount Invested.
Colorado Springs Rapid Transit Railway Co. bonds,	$15,000 00	$15,000 00	$13,875 00
Fitchburg R.R. 1st mortgage 6s,	2,000 00	2,100 00	2,200 00
Fitchburg R.R. 1st mortgage 5s,	3,000 00	3,135 00	3,105 00
City of Newton, Mass., 4s,	3,000 00	3,180 00	3,180 00
City of Minneapolis, Minn., 4s,	6,000 00	6,030 00	5,820 00
City of Cleveland, O., 6s,	2,000 00	2,140 00	2,350 00
Eastern R.R. 6s,	2,000 00	2,430 00	2,496 25
	$33,000 00	$34,015 00	$33,026 25

How much of its capital stock is owned by officers of the Company ? 223 shares.

How much, if any, of the stock owned by its officers is pledged to the company as collateral ? None.

State the sections of country in which loans are made, giving the principal counties : Eastern half of Kansas ; North-western Missouri ; the following counties in Nebraska : Antelope, Madison, Wheeler, Custer; eight counties in Minnesota, of which Douglas is the centre, all known as the " Park Region ; " irrigated portions of Colorado.

Total amount loaned to date,		$5,593,576 79
Total amount of loans paid,		2,210,054 64
Number and amount of loans extended the past two years,	121	98,385 00
Total amount of loans unpaid and outstanding, { Guaranteed,		2,204,227 66
{ Unguaranteed,		1,179,294 49
Total amount in process of foreclosure,		315,946 60
Total amount of debentures certified,		419,151 36
Less amount on hand and with agents,		2,210 00
Total liability for debenture bonds,		416,941 36

NATIONAL MORTGAGE AND DEBENTURE COMPANY — BOSTON.

W. X. FULLER, *President.*   CHARLES A. ROGERS, *Treasurer.*

BALANCE SHEET OCTOBER 31, 1894.

ASSETS.		LIABILITIES.	
Loans secured by first liens on real estate, ...	$620,870 90	Capital stock paid in, .	$258,900 00
Matured interest due on same,	21,243 39	Guaranty fund, . . .	3,300 00
Commission notes secured by second liens on real estate, .	34,783 62	Debenture bonds, outstanding, . . .	488,988 00
Tax sale certificates, .	466 75	Coupons on same not presented, ...	423 10
Real estate acquired by foreclosure, ...	65,472 49	Certificates of deposit bearing interest (money borrowed), ...	500 00
Other real estate, . .	1,579 32	Bills payable, . . .	70,925 00
Furniture, fixtures and supplies, ...	3,883 49	Due sundry persons, .	7,432 21
Current expenses, . .	6,738 78		
Legal expenses in foreclosure,*	3,138 73		
Past due interest remitted for but not paid to us, . .	28,011 50		
Due from branch offices and agents, ...	1,883 53		
Bills receivable, . .	554 31		
Cash, ...	735 58		
Due from sundry persons, .	1,266 92		
Profit and loss account, . .	39,839 00		
	$830,468 31		$830,468 31

* To be reduced by collections from clients.

Date of examination: November 1.

How much of its capital stock is owned by officers of the company? $15,900.

How much, if any, of the stock owned by its officers is pledged to the company as collateral? None.

State the sections of country in which loans are made, giving principal counties: COLORADO, — Arapahoe, Boulder, Carbon, Delta, Garfield, Grand, Grover, La Plata, Laramie, Morgan, Rio Blanco, Weld, Yuma; DAKOTA, — Beadle, Brookings, Brown, Clark, Codington, Davison, Edmunds, Hamblin, Lake, Lincoln, Marshall, McPherson, Spink; KANSAS, — Allen, Anderson, Barton, Bourbon, Butler, Chautauqua, Cherokee, Clark, Clay, Coffee, Crowley, Crawford, Dickinson, Douglas, Edwards, Elk, Ellsworth, Ellis, Ford, Garfield, Graham, Gray, Harvey, Harper, Hodgeman, Jackson, Jefferson, Kingman, Kiowa, Lincoln, Lyon, Marion, Meade, Mitchell, Morris, Neosha, Osborne, Ottawa, Pawnee, Pottawatomie, Pratt, Reno, Rice, Rooks, Rush, Russell, Saline, Shawnee, Stafford, Wilson, Woodson; FLORIDA, — Putnam; MICHIGAN, — Delta, Mackinaw, Schoolcraft; MINNESOTA, — Murray, Pipestone; MISSOURI, — Holt; NEBRASKA, — Butler, Dodge, Hayes, Holt; WYOMING, — Laramie.

Total amount of loans to date, approximating, ... $3,500,000 00

Number and amount of loans extended the past two years: Cannot answer.

Total amount of loans unpaid and { Guaranteed, ... None.
outstanding, ... } Unguaranteed, . . . Cannot answer.

Total amount in process of foreclosure: Cannot answer.

Total amount of debentures certified, ... $501,988 00

Less amount on hand and with agents, ... 13,000 00

Total liability for debenture bonds, ... 488,988 00

APPENDIX.

INDEX.

SECTION 1. Twenty-five or more persons who associate themselves together by an agreement in writing with the intention of forming a corporation for the purpose of accumulating the savings of its members paid into such corporation in fixed periodical instalments and lending to its members the funds so accumulated shall, by and with the consent of the board of commissioners of savings banks, become a corporation upon complying with the provisions of the three following sections. *Corporations for accumulation of savings of members and lending funds to members. 1877, 224, § 1. 1890, 243.*

SECT. 2. The agreement shall set forth the fact that the subscribers thereto associated themselves with the intention of forming a corporation; the name by which *Agreement, what to set forth. 1877, 224, § 2.*

the corporation shall be known; the purpose for which it is formed; the town or city, which shall be within this Commonwealth, in which it is located; and the limit of capital to be accumulated.

Name.
1877, 224, § 3.
1883, 98.

SECT. 3. The name shall be one not previously in use by any existing corporation established under the laws of this Commonwealth, and shall be changed only by act of the General Court. The words " co-operative bank" shall form a part of the name.

Public Statutes,
117. Title
amended.
1883, 98.

The title of said chapter one hundred and seventeen of the Public Statutes is hereby amended by striking out the words " Saving Fund and Loan Associations," and inserting in place thereof the word " Banks."

Co-operative
banks.
1883, 98.

The names of all co-operative saving fund and loan associations heretofore organized are hereby changed by striking out in each the words " saving fund and loan association," and inserting in place thereof the word " bank," and they shall hereafter be known as " co-operative banks."

Corporation,
how organized.
1877, 224, § 4.

SECT. 4. The provisions of sections eighteen, twenty, and twenty-one of chapter one hundred and six shall apply to such corporations, except that, in the certificate signed by the secretary of the Commonwealth, the limit of capital to be accumulated, as fixed in the agreement of association, shall be inserted, instead of the amount of the capital, that the certificate required by said section twenty-one to be filed and recorded may be signed and sworn to by the presiding and financial officers, and a majority at least of the officers possessing the powers of directors by whatever name they may be called, and that the fees to be paid for filing and recording the certificates required by said section twenty-one, including the issuing of the certificate of organization, shall be five dollars.

Limit of capital.
1887, 216, § 1.

SECT. 5. The capital to be accumulated shall not exceed one million dollars, and shall be divided into shares of the ultimate value of two hundred dollars each. The limitation of capital to be accumulated in any co-operative bank now organized or hereafter formed under the provisions of chapter one hundred and seventeen of the Public Statutes shall be held to apply to capital actually paid in, and no such bank shall be restrained from issuing shares so long as the capital actually paid in on shares is not in excess of one million dollars. The shares may be issued in quarterly, half-yearly, or yearly series, in such amounts and at such times as the members may determine. No person shall hold more than twenty-five shares in the capital of any one such corporation. No shares of a prior series shall be issued after the issue of a new series. *Plans of issuing stock, etc. 1877, 224, § 5.*

SECT. 6. The number, title, duties and compensation of the officers of the corporation, their terms of office, the time of their election, as well as the qualifications of electors, and time of each periodical meeting of the officers and members, shall be determined by the by-laws; but no member shall be entitled to more than one vote at any election. All officers shall continue in office until their successors are duly elected, and no corporation shall expire from neglect on its part to elect officers at the time prescribed by the by-laws. *By-laws. Officers to hold office until successors are elected. 1877, 224, §§ 6, 16.*

In any co-operative bank now or hereafter formed under the provisions of chapter one hundred and seventeen of the Public Statutes, the offices of secretary and treasurer may be held by one and the same person. *One person may be both secretary and treasurer. 1885, 121, § 1.*

SECT. 7. The officers shall hold stated monthly meetings. At or before each of these meetings every member shall pay to the corporation, as a contribution to its capital, one dollar as dues upon each share held by him until the share reaches the ultimate value of two hundred dollars, or is withdrawn, cancelled, or forfeited. Payment of dues on each series shall commence from its issue. *Monthly meetings. Dues. 1877, 224, §§ 5, 7, 9. 1881, 271, § 1, cl. 3.*

SECT. 8. A member may withdraw his unpledged shares at any time by giving thirty days' notice of his *Withdrawal of shares. 1887, 216, §§ 2, 3.*

intention so to do, written in a book held and provided by the corporation for that purpose. Upon such withdrawal the shareholder's account shall be settled as follows : — From the amount then standing to the credit of the shares to be withdrawn there shall be deducted all fines, a proportionate part of any unadjusted loss, together with such proportion of the profits previously credited to the shares as the by-laws may provide, and such shareholders shall be paid the balance : *provided*, that at no time shall more than one-half of the funds in the treasury be applicable to the demands of withdrawing members without the consent of the directors. The directors may, at their discretion, under rules made by them, retire the unpledged shares of any series at any time after four years from the date of their issue, by enforcing the withdrawal of the same; but whenever there shall remain in any series, at the expiration of five years after the date of its issue, an excess above one hundred unpledged shares, then it shall be the duty of the directors to retire annually twenty-five per centum of such excess existing at said expiration of five years after the date of its issue, so that not more than one hundred unpledged shares shall remain in such series at the expiration of nine years from the date of its issue, and thereafter the directors may in their discretion retire such other unpledged shares as they consider the best interests of the bank to require : *provided*, that whenever under the provisions of this section the withdrawal of shares is to be enforced the shares to be retired shall be determined by lot, and the holders thereof shall be paid the full value of their shares, less all fines and a proportionate part of any unadjusted loss ; *provided also*, that shares pledged for share loans shall be treated as unpledged shares.

Shares may be issued in the name of a minor, and if so issued may, at the discretion of the directors, be withdrawn, in manner as provided in section two of this act [chap. 216, Acts of 1887], by such minor, the parent or guardian of such minor, and in either case payments made on such withdrawals of shares shall be valid. When a share or shares are held by any one in trust for another, the name and residence of the person for whom such share or shares are held shall be disclosed; and the account shall be kept in the name of such holder as trustee for such person; and, if no other notice of the existence and terms of such trust has been given in writing to the corporation, in the event of the death of the trustee, such shares may be withdrawn by the person for whom such deposit was made or by his legal representatives.

SECT. 9. When each unpledged share of a given series reaches the value of two hundred dollars, all payments of dues thereon shall cease, and the holder thereof shall be paid out of the funds of the corporation two hundred dollars thereof, with interest at the rate of six per cent. a year from the time of such maturity to the time of payment: *provided*, that at no time shall more than one-half of the funds in the treasury be applicable to the payment of such matured shares without the consent of the directors; *provided further*, that when any series of shares, either pledged or unpledged, reaches maturity between the dates of adjustment of profits, or whenever shares are retired between such dates, the holders of such shares shall in addition to the value thereof, be entitled to interest at the rate of six per cent. per annum for all full months from the date of the preceding adjustment, and that before paying matured shares all arrears and fines shall be deducted. *[margin: Shares, when matured. 1881, 271, § 1, cl. 3. 1887, 216, § 5.] [margin: Amendment. 1882, 251.]*

SECT. 10. The moneys accumulated, after due allowance made for all necessary and proper expenses and for the withdrawal of shares, shall, at each stated monthly meeting, be offered to the members according to the premiums bid by them for priority of right to a loan. Each member whose bid is accepted shall be entitled upon giv- *[margin: Moneys to be lent by monthly sales; how invested, if unsold. 1877, 224, § 7. 1881, 271, § 1, cl. 4. 1890, 78.]*

ing proper security to receive a loan of two hundred dollars for each share held by him, or such fractional part of two hundred dollars as the by-laws may allow. If a balance of money remains unsold after a monthly sale, the directors may invest the same in any of the securities named in the second clause of section twenty of chapter one hundred and sixteen, or may loan the same upon the shares of the corporation, on the approval of the directors or investing committee thereof, at the highest rate paid at the last preceding monthly sale of such moneys.

SECT. 11. Premiums for loans shall consist of a percentage charged on the amount lent in addition to interest, and shall be deemed to be a consideration paid by the borrower for the present use and possession of the future or ultimate value of his shares, and shall, together with interest and fines, be received by the corporation as a profit on the capital invested in the loan, and shall be distributed to the various shares and series of said capital as hereinafter provided.

SECT. 12. A borrowing member, for each share borrowed upon, shall, in addition to his dues and monthly premium, pay monthly interest on his loan at the rate of six per cent. per annum until his shares reach the ultimate value of two hundred dollars each, or the loan has been repaid; and when said ultimate value is reached, said shares and loan shall be declared cancelled and satisfied, and the balance, if any, due upon the shares shall be paid to the member.

Any corporation organized under said chapter one hundred and seventeen may provide in its by-laws that the bid for loans at its stated monthly meeting shall, instead of a premium, be a rate of annual interest upon the sum desired, payable in monthly instalments. Such bids shall include the whole interest to be paid, and may be at any rate not less than five per centum per annum.

SECT. 13. For every loan made a note shall be given, Security. 1894, 342. accompanied by a transfer and pledge of the shares of the borrower, and secured by a mortgage of real estate situated in this Commonwealth, unencumbered by any mortgage or lien other than such as may be held by the bank making the loan. The shares so pledged shall be held by the corporation as collateral security for the performance of the conditions of said note and mortgage. Said note and mortgage shall recite the number of shares pledged and the amount of money advanced thereon, and shall be conditioned for the payment at the stated meetings of the corporation of the monthly dues on said shares, and the interest and premium upon the loan, together with all fines on payments in arrears, until said shares reach the ultimate value of two hundred dollars each, or said loan is otherwise cancelled and discharged: *provided*, that the shares without other security may in the discretion of the directors be pledged as security for loans, to an amount not exceeding their value as adjusted at the last adjustment and valuation of shares before the time of the loan.

If the borrower neglects to offer security satisfactory to the directors within the time prescribed by the by-laws, his right to the loan shall be forfeited, and he shall be charged with one month's interest and one month's premium at the rate bid by him, together with all expenses, if any, incurred; and the money appropriated for such loan may be re-loaned at the next or any subsequent meeting.

SECT. 14. A borrower may repay a loan at any time, Payment. 1877, 224, § 11. 1887, 216, § 4. upon application to the corporation, whereupon, on settlement of his account, he shall be charged with the full amount of the original loan, together with all monthly instalments of interest, premium, and fines in arrears, and shall be given credit for the withdrawing value of his shares pledged and transferred as security; and the balance shall be received by the corporation in full satisfaction and discharge of said loan: *provided*, that all settlements made at periods intervening between stated meetings of the directors shall be made as of the date of

the stated meetings next succeeding such settlement; and
provided, that a borrower desiring to retain his shares and
membership may at his option repay his loan without
claiming credit for said shares, whereupon said shares
shall be re-transferred to him, and shall be free from any
claim by reason of said cancelled loan. Partial payment
of loans on real estate made by any co-operative bank
may be received in sums of fifty dollars or any multiple
thereof; and for each two hundred dollars so repaid one
share of stock shall be released from pledge.

Fines, forfeiture of shares.
1877, 224, § 13. SECT. 15. Members who make default in the payment
of their monthly dues, interest and premiums, shall be
charged a fine not exceeding two per cent. a month on
each dollar in arrears. No fines shall be charged after the
expiration of six months from the first lapse in any such
payment, nor upon a fine in arrears. The shares of a
member who continues in arrears more than six months
shall, at the option of the directors, if the member fails
to pay the arrears within thirty days after notice, be declared forfeited, and the withdrawing value of the shares
at the time of the first default shall be ascertained, and,
after deducting all fines and other legal charges, the balance remaining shall be transferred to an account to be
designated the "Forfeited Share Account," to the credit
of the defaulting member. Said member, if not a borrower, shall be entitled, upon thirty days' notice, to
receive the balance so transferred without interest from
the time of the transfer, in the order of his turn, out of
the funds appropriated to the payment of withdrawals.
All shares so forfeited or transferred shall cease to partici-
pate in any profits of the corporation accruing after the
last adjustment and valuation of shares before said first
default.

Recovery of loan.
1882, 251.
1885, 121, § 4. SECT. 16. If a borrowing member is in arrears for
dues, interest, premium or fines for more than six months,
the directors may, at their discretion, declare the shares
forfeited, after one month's notice, if the arrears continue

unpaid. The account of such borrowing member shall then be debited with the arrears of interest, premium and fines to date of forfeiture, and the shares shall be credited upon the loan at their withdrawing value. The balance of the account may, and after six months shall, be enforced against the security, and be recovered as secured debts are recovered at law.

SECT. 17. The general accounts of every such corporation shall be kept by double entry. All moneys received by the corporation from each member shall be receipted for by persons designated by the directors, in a pass-book provided by the corporation for the use of, and to be held by, the member; and said pass-book shall be plainly marked with the name and residence of the holder thereof, the number of shares held by him, and the number or designation of the series or issue to which said shares respectively belong, and the date of the issue of such series. All moneys so received shall be originally entered by the proper officer in a book to be called the "cash-book," to be provided by the corporation for the purpose, and the entries therein shall be so made as to show the name of the payer, the number of shares, the number or designation of the series or issues of the particular share or shares so entered, together with the amount of dues, interest, premiums and fines paid thereon, as the case may be. Each payment shall be classified and entered into a column devoted to its kind. Said cash-book shall be closed after the termination of each stated meeting, and shall be an exhibit of the receipts of all moneys paid at said meeting. All payments made by the corporation for any purpose whatsoever shall be by order, check or draft upon the treasurer, signed by the president and secretary, and endorsed by the persons in whose favor the same are drawn. The name of the payee, the amount paid, and the purpose, object or thing for which the payment is made, together with its date, shall be entered on the margin of said order, check or draft.

The treasurer shall dispose of and secure the safe keeping
of all moneys, securities, and property of the corporation,
in the manner designated by the by-laws, and the treasurer and secretary shall give such security for the faithful
performance of their respective duties as the by-laws may
direct.

Distribution of
profits and
losses.
1881, 271, § 1,
cl. 2. SECT. 18. The profits and losses may be distributed
annually, semi-annually or quarterly, to the shares then
existing, but shall be distributed at least once in each
year, and whenever a new series of shares is to be issued.
Profits and losses shall be distributed to the various shares
existing at the times of such distribution, in proportion
to their value at that time, and shall be computed upon
the basis of a single share fully paid to the date of distribution. Losses shall be apportioned immediately after
their occurrence.

Guarantee fund
to be reserved
from profits.
1885, 121. At each periodical distribution of profits the directors
shall reserve as a guaranty fund a sum not less than one
nor more than five per cent. of the net profits accruing
since the next preceding adjustment, until such fund
amounts to five per cent. of the dues capital, which fund
shall thereafter be maintained and held; and said fund
shall be at all times available to meet losses in the business
of the corporation from depreciation of its securities or
otherwise.

Corporation
may buy and
sell real estate.
1877, 224, § 17. SECT. 19. Any such corporation may purchase at any
sale, public or private, any real estate upon which it may
have a mortgage, judgment, lien or other incumbrance, or
in which it may have an interest; and may sell, convey,
lease or mortgage, at pleasure, the real estate so purchased
to any person or persons whatsoever. All real estate so
acquired shall be sold within five years from the acquisition of the title thereto.

Powers of sav-
ings bank
commissioners.
1879, 129, §§ 1, 2. SECT. 20. The commissioners of savings banks shall
perform, in reference to every such corporation, the same
duties, and shall have the same powers, as are required of
or given to them in reference to savings banks, and shall

annually make report to the general court of such facts
and statements respecting such associations, and in such
forms as they deem that the public interest requires.
Every officer of such corporation shall answer truly all
inquiries made, and shall make all returns required by the
commissioners.

AN ACT RELATING TO CO-OPERATIVE BANKS.
(Section 2 of Chapter 159, Acts of 1889.)

Every co-operative bank shall annually within twenty
days after the last business day of October make a return to
the commissioners of savings banks in such form as may
be prescribed by them, showing accurately the condition
thereof at close of business on said day, which return
shall be signed and sworn to by the secretary and treasurer
of such corporation. The president and five or more of
the directors shall certify and make oath that the report is
correct according to their best knowledge and belief.

AN ACT RELATING TO LOANS BY CO-OPERATIVE BANKS.
(Section 2 of Chapter 342, Acts of 1894.)

When a member of a co-operative bank purchases
money at a lower rate than that paid by him on an existing loan, secured by a mortgage, for the purpose by him
declared of reducing the premium or rate of interest upon
said loan, no new mortgage shall be required, but an
agreement in writing for the reduction of said premium or
rate of interest, signed by said borrowing member and the
secretary of the bank, with the written approval of the
president, shall be valid, and shall in no respect impair or
affect the existing mortgage contract; and thereafter said
borrowing member shall make the monthly payments on
said loan in accordance with the terms of said agreement,
and the sum of money previously so purchased by him
may be resold by the bank at the same meeting. The
borrower shall be required to give notice to the secretary
before the sale, if he intends to re-buy his money.
Nothing in this section shall be construed to exempt the
re-borrower from paying the interest and premium for the
current month on the loan made by him for the substitu-
tion of which the new loan is made.

AN ACT IN RELATION TO THE BUSINESS OF CO-OPERATIVE
BANKING.

Be it enacted, etc., as follows :

SECTION 1. Except as is hereinafter provided, no person, association or corporation shall carry on the business
of accumulating the savings of its members and loaning
to them such accumulations in the manner of a co-operative
bank within this Commonwealth, unless incorporated under
the laws thereof for such purpose.

SECTION 2. The board of commissioners of savings
banks may authorize any such association or corporation
duly established under the laws of another state to carry
on such business in the Commonwealth, but said association or corporation shall not transact such business in this
Commonwealth unless it shall first deposit with the treasurer of the Commonwealth the sum of twenty-five thousand
dollars and thereafter a sum equal to fifteen per cent. of
the deposits made in such association or corporation by
citizens of the Commonwealth, the amount of percentage of
deposits so required to be determined from time to time by
said board of commissioners of savings banks; or in lieu
thereof the whole or any part of said sum may consist of
any of the securities named in the first, second and third
clauses of section twenty of chapter one hundred and sixteen of the Public Statutes and acts amendatory thereof, at
their par value, and the said deposit shall be held in trust
by said treasurer for the protection and indemnity of the
residents of the Commonwealth with whom such associa-

tions or corporations respectively have done or may transact business. Said moneys or property shall be paid out or disposed of only on the order of some court of competent jurisdiction made on due notice to the attorney-general of the Commonwealth, and upon such notice to the creditors and shareholders of such association or corporation as the court shall prescribe. For the purpose of ascertaining the business and financial condition of any such association or corporation doing or desiring to do such business, said board may make examinations of such associations or corporations at such times and at such places as said board may desire, the expense of such examinations being paid by the association or corporation examined, and may also require returns to be made to them in such form and at such times as they may elect. Whenever, upon examination or otherwise, it is the opinion of said board that any such association or corporation is transacting business in such manner as to be hazardous to the public, or its condition is such as to render further proceedings by it hazardous to the public, said board shall revoke or suspend the authority given to said association or corporation, but this section shall not prevent such a bank or institution, incorporated under the laws of another state, from loaning money upon mortgages of real estate located within the Commonwealth.

SECTION 3. Every such person, association or corporation transacting business in the Commonwealth at the time of the passage of this act shall, within sixty days after such passage, conform to the requirements of this act.

SECTION 4. Whoever violates any provision of the preceding sections shall be punished by a fine not exceeding one thousand dollars; and any provision thereof may

on petition be enforced by injunction issued by a justice of
the supreme judicial court or of the superior court.

SECTION 5. This act shall take effect upon its passage.
[*Approved May 21, 1890.*

[CHAP. 403, ACTS OF 1891.]

AN ACT TO AUTHORIZE THE COMMISSIONERS OF SAVINGS
BANKS TO PREVENT FOREIGN CO-OPERATIVE BANKING
CORPORATIONS FROM TRANSACTING BUSINESS IN THIS
COMMONWEALTH.

Be it enacted, etc., as follows :

Whenever, upon examination or otherwise, it is the
opinion of the board of commissioners of savings banks
that any association or corporation established under the
laws of another state, for the purpose of carrying on the
business of accumulating the savings of its members and
loaning to them such accumulations in the manner of a
co-operative bank, and authorized to do business in this
Commonwealth, is transacting such business in a manner
hazardous to the public, or its condition is such as to render further proceedings by it hazardous to the public, said
board shall revoke or suspend the authority given to such
association or corporation if it has been authorized to do
business in the Commonwealth as aforesaid, and if not so
authorized said board shall notify it to cease the transaction
of such business ; and in either case such association or
corporation shall thereafter have no authority to transact
such business within the Commonwealth. But nothing
herein contained shall prevent such association or corporation from loaning money upon mortgages of real estate
located within the Commonwealth. [*Approved June 11,
1891.*

STATUTES

RELATING TO

MORTGAGE LOAN AND INVESTMENT COMPANIES.

AN ACT

IN RELATION TO

MORTGAGE LOAN AND INVESTMENT COMPANIES.

(Chapter 387, Acts of 1888.)

SECTION 1. Every corporation now or hereafter established under the laws of this Commonwealth for the
special purpose of negotiating or making loans of money
secured by deed of trust or mortgage of real estate situated outside of this Commonwealth, may exercise and
enjoy all the powers, and shall be governed by the provisions and be subject to the duties, restrictions and
liabilities prescribed in this act and any acts which may
hereafter be passed in amendment or lieu thereof. All
such corporations heretofore chartered shall continue to
exercise and enjoy their powers and privileges according
to their respective charters, and shall be subject to all the
liabilities imposed by the same, except so far as said
powers, privileges and liabilities are modified and con-
trolled by the provisions of this act.

SECT. 2. Every such corporation may make loans of
money secured by deed of trust or mortgage of real estate
situated in any state, other than this Commonwealth, or
territory of the United States to an amount not exceeding
fifty per cent. of the appraised value of said property;
but no loan shall be made on any property subject to a
prior mortgage, encumbrance or lien. Every such corporation may also hold, sell and assign the bonds, notes,
mortgages and securities taken for such loans; may guarantee the payment of the interest and principal of any
bonds, notes or other evidences of debt secured as aforesaid, and may guarantee the title to the property securing
such evidences of debt for the time such debt remains
unpaid : *provided,* that nothing contained in this act shall

be construed as authorizing such corporations to engage in the business of title insurance.

SECT. 3. Every such corporation may purchase, hold, guarantee, sell and assign notes or bonds, and the mortgages or deeds of trust securing the same, or other papers securing any loan made by any individual, firm, corporation or association, provided such loan shall have been made in accordance with the conditions under which such corporations can make loans, as prescribed in section two of this act.

SECT. 4. Every such corporation may receive money from any individual, firm, corporation or association, for investment in the securities which such corporations are by this act authorized to sell or issue, and may allow interest on such money from the time of its receipt to the time of its investment as aforesaid, at such rate as may be agreed upon; may receive, care for, manage and sell stocks, bonds and evidences of debt, the avails of which are intended for investment as aforesaid. No such corporation shall receive money on deposit, except as hereinbefore provided, or engage in any form of banking or trust business other than as permitted by the terms of this act.

SECT. 5. Every such corporation may act as agent for the purpose of foreclosing mortgages and collecting claims arising by reason of any evidence of debt deposited with it under the provisions of section four of this act; may purchase real estate at any public auction sale thereof made by virtue of the power contained in any deed of trust or mortgage owned, held or guaranteed by it, or at a private sale thereof made for the purpose of cancelling the debt secured by any such deed of trust or mortgage; may hold, sell, transfer and convey said property: *provided*, all real estate purchased or acquired under the provisions of this section shall be sold within five years after such purchase or acquisition.

SECT. 6. Every such corporation may issue debentures or bonds, to secure the payment of which, such corporation shall from time to time assign, transfer and set over to trustees, none of whom shall be officers of the corporation, or to a trust company established under the laws of this Commonwealth, deeds of trust or mortgages of real estate on which loans have been made in accordance with the provisions of this act, to be held by such trustees or company in trust for the benefit of the holders of said debentures or bonds, whereupon such trustees or company shall indorse their or its certificate of such fact upon debentures or bonds not exceeding in amount the face value of securities so transferred to them or it.

SECT. 7. The total amount of mortgages guaranteed and of debentures or bonds issued by any such corporation shall at no time be in excess of ten times the amount of its capital stock actually paid in and its surplus.

SECT. 8. All bonds, notes and other evidences of debt taken by such corporation for money loaned shall be payable to such corporation at its principal place of business within this Commonwealth, and shall pass by delivery, by transfer on the books of such corporation at its principal place of business within this Commonwealth, or by certificate of its transfer agent at such other place as it may appoint. No transfer except on the books of the corporation or by certificate of its transfer agent, shall be valid unless the last transfer shall have been to bearer. A complete record of such transfer by said transfer agents shall be forwarded to and kept at the principal place of business of such corporation within this Commonwealth.

SECT. 9. Every such corporation may hold real estate within this Commonwealth suitable for the transaction of its business, to an amount not exceeding twenty-five per cent. of its capital actually paid in.

SECT. 10. No such corporation shall be the purchaser or holder of any of the shares of its own capital stock, unless such purchase shall be necessary to prevent loss upon a debt previously contracted in good faith ; and stock so purchased shall, within six months from the time of its purchase, be sold or disposed of at public or private sale.

Sect. 11.   The shareholders of every such corporation shall be held individually liable in the same manner and to the same extent, and not otherwise, as stockholders of manufacturing corporations are or may be held liable under the laws of this Commonwealth.   The provisions contained in sections sixty-two to seventy-one inclusive of chapter one hundred and six of the Public Statutes shall apply to and regulate the enforcement of this iiability.

Sect. 12.   Every such corporation shall set apart as a guaranty fund a sum not less than five per cent. of its paid in capital, and shall thereafter annually add thereto a sum not less than ten per cent. of its net earnings, until such fund, with the accumulated interest thereon, shall be equal to not less than twenty-five per cent. of its paid in capital.   Said fund shall be invested in United States bonds ; English consols ; first mortgage bonds of any railroad corporation which has paid a dividend on its stock for at least three years next preceding the date of said investment ; in the legally authorized bonds for municipal purposes of any city of the United States of not less than thirty thousand inhabitants whose whole indebtedness shall not exceed five per cent. of its last assessed valuation ; or in any securities in which savings banks of this Commonwealth are allowed to invest.

Sect. 13.   The books of every such corporation shall at all reasonable times be open for inspection to the stockholders and to all holders of bonds and debentures issued by such corporation, or of notes and other evidences of debt guaranteed by such corporation.

Sect. 14.   The commissioners of savings banks shall have access to the vaults, books and papers of every such corporation ; and it shall be their duty to inspect, examine and inquire into its affairs and take proceedings in regard to them at such times as they shall deem necessary, in the same manner and to the same extent as if such corporation was a savings bank, subject to all the laws which are now or hereafter may be in force relating to such institutions in this regard : *provided, however*, said commissioners may cause any examination to be made by an expert under their direction but at the expense of the corporation. Every such corporation shall annually, within ten days after the last business day of October, make a return to said commissioners, which return shall be in the form of a trial balance of its books, and shall specify the different kinds of its liabilities and the different kinds of its assets, stating the amount of each kind in accordance with a blank form to be furnished by said commissioners, and such annual returns shall be published in a newspaper of the city or town where such corporation is located, at the expense of such corporation, at such times and in such manner as may be directed by said commissioners. Said commissioners shall annually make report to the general court of such facts and statements respecting such corporations, and in such forms as they deem that the public interest requires.

INDICES.

GENERAL INDEX.

[Alphabetically by Location.]

CO-OPERATIVE BANKS.

COLLATERAL LOAN COMPANIES.

MORTGAGE LOAN AND INVESTMENT COMPANIES.

INDEX TO THE ANNUAL REPORTS.

[Alphabetically by Corporate Name.]

CO-OPERATIVE BANKS.

www.ingramcontent.com/pod-product-compliance
Lightning Source LLC
Chambersburg PA
CBHW031410270326
41929CB00010BA/1394